DATE DUE

The Ennobling Power of Love
in the Medieval German Lyric

University of North Carolina
Studies in the Germanic Languages
and Literatures

Initiated by RICHARD JENTE (1949–1952), *established by* F. E. COENEN (1952–1968),
continued by SIEGFRIED MEWS (1968–1980)

RICHARD H. LAWSON, Editor

Publication Committee: Department of Germanic Languages

90 KARL EUGENE WEBB. *Rainer Maria Rilke and "Jugendstil": Affinities, Influences, Adaptations.* 1978. Pp. x, 137.

91 LELAND R. PHELPS AND A. TILO ALT, EDS. *Creative Encounter. Festschrift for Herman Salinger.* 1978. Pp. xxii, 181.

92 PETER BAULAND. *Gerhart Hauptmann's "Before Daybreak."* Translation and Introduction. 1978. Pp. xxiv, 87.

93 MEREDITH LEE. *Studies in Goethe's Lyric Cycles.* 1978. Pp. xii, 191.

94 JOHN M. ELLIS. *Heinrich von Kleist. Studies in the Character and Meaning of His Writings.* 1979. Pp. xx, 194.

95 GORDON BIRRELL. *The Boundless Present. Space and Time in the Literary Fairy Tales of Novalis and Tieck.* 1979. Pp. x, 163.

96 G. RONALD MURPHY. *Brecht and the Bible. A Study of Religious Nihilism and Human Weakness in Brecht's Drama of Mortality and the City.* 1980. Pp. xi, 107.

97 ERHARD FRIEDRICHSMEYER. *Die satirische Kurzprosa Heinrich Bölls.* 1981. Pp. xiv, 223.

98 MARILYN JOHNS BLACKWELL, ED. *Structures of Influence: A Comparative Approach to August Strindberg.* 1981. Pp. xiv, 309.

99 JOHN M. SPALEK AND ROBERT F. BELL, EDS. *Exile: The Writer's Experience.* 1982. Pp. xxiv, 370.

100 ROBERT P. NEWTON. *Your Diamond Dreams Cut Open My Arteries. Poems by Else Lasker-Schüler.* Translated and with an Introduction. 1982. Pp. x, 317.

101 WILLIAM SMALL. *Rilke - Kommentar zu den "Aufzeichnungen des Malte Laurids Brigge."* 1983. Pp. x, 175.

102 CHRISTA WOLF CROSS. *Magister Ludens: Der Erzähler in Heinrich Wittenweilers "Ring."* 1984. Pp. xii, 112.

103 JAMES C. O'FLAHERTY, TIMOTHY F. SELLNER, AND ROBERT M. HELM, EDS. *Studies in Nietzsche and the Judaeo-Christian Tradition.* 1985. Pp. xii, 393.

104 GISELA N. BERNS. *Greek Antiquity in Schiller's "Wallenstein."* 1985. Pp. xi, 154.

105 JOHN W. VAN CLEVE. *The Merchant in German Literature of the Enlightenment.* 1986. Pp. xv, 173.

106 STEPHEN J. KAPLOWITT. *The Ennobling Power of Love in the Medieval German Lyric.* 1986. Pp. vii, 212.

For other volumes in the "Studies" see pages 213–14

Number One Hundred and Six
University of
North Carolina
Studies in the
Germanic Languages
and Literatures

The Ennobling Power of Love
in the Medieval German Lyric

Stephen J. Kaplowitt

The University of North Carolina Press
Chapel Hill and London 1986

© 1986 The University of North Carolina Press
All rights reserved
Manufactured in the United States of America

Library of Congress Cataloging in Publication Data

Kaplowitt, Stephen J.
  The ennobling power of love in the Medieval German
lyric.

  (University of North Carolina studies in the
Germanic languages and literatures; no. 106)
  Bibliography: p.
  Includes index.
  1. German poetry—Middle High German, 1050–1500—
History and criticism. 2. Minnesingers. 3. Love in
literature. I. Title. II. Series.
PT217.K36 1986   831'.04'09354   83-21804
ISBN 0-8078-8106-6

Contents

The Ennobling Power of Love
in the Medieval German Lyric

1. Introduction

In almost any handbook on medieval German literature, the section on *Minnesang* conveys the impression that the theme of the ennobling power of love, or the educative force exerted by love, plays an overwhelming role in the love poetry of the period. This is also true of most of the special treatises on the medieval German lyric. For example, Helmut de Boor's widely read and influential history of the literature of the *Blütezeit* makes it appear as if the moral improvement of the knight were the primary goal of the knight's wooing of the lady.[1] W. T. H. Jackson speaks of the "ennobling power of love which is such an important feature of the vernacular love lyric."[2] Friedrich Ranke maintains that being allowed to serve a noble lady enriches a knight's soul and "erhöht seinen inneren Wert," and that "der Gedanke an die Herrin gibt ihm die Kraft zum unermüdlichen Streben nach Selbstveredelung."[3] Hans Eggers says the knight's service is "ein Erziehungsprozeß (*zuht*), den er auf sich nimmt, indem er in den Minnedienst eintritt, und die Minneherrin übernimmt die Rolle der edlen Erzieherin zu höfischer Tugend."[4] Gustav Ehrismann asserts that love has "sittlich erzieherische Kraft, sie ist Quelle aller Tugenden, fons et origo omnium bonorum."[5] Hennig Brinkmann claims that the man looks up to the woman because she is "was er werden möchte," and the man understands "daß er sich überwinden und verwandeln muß, wenn er, der wild Wachsende, die schöne und reine Gestalt gewinnen soll, die er in der Frau bewundert";[6] and M. O'C. Walshe states: "The theory arose that the real reward of the knight's devoted service was educative. If the lady really was . . . a paragon of all the virtues, then her influence on him must be to the good, and he would be ennobled by serving her."[7] Similar generalizations can be found in most of the other more or less standard presentations of *Minnesang*.[8]

When one proceeds from these generalizations about the poetry to a reading of the texts themselves, however, then one begins to wonder if perhaps too much emphasis has been placed on this feature of the *Minnesang*.[9] The apparent discrepancy between what most scholars have had to say on the subject and what meets the eye of the reader of the poems contained in *Des Minnesangs Frühling* is,[10] to say the least, somewhat disconcerting and certainly seems to call for clarification. But despite the prevailing generalizations, no one has ever attempted to assess the importance of the motif of the ennobling or educative power of love based on an actual review of its occurrence in the medieval German lyric. Thus, it will be the purpose of this study to scrutinize the entire body of lyric love poetry from the beginning through the songs of Walther von der Vogelweide in order to establish the extent of the role played by this idea and its variants.

As traditionally presented, the ideas of the ennobling or educative power of love include the following features:

1. The knight-poet, following the example of the virtuous lady, attempts to improve himself, to become a better person in her service; in the process he becomes ennobled and hence increases his inner worth.
2. The purpose of the knight's self-betterment in the service of his lady is to become worthy of her love.
3. The knight's self-improvement—instead of being the means to an end, namely, the reward of the lady's love—is an end in itself, of value in itself, and its own reward.
4. The lady encourages the knight in her service to strive to improve himself or to conform to a high standard of behavior.
5. Love is the source of all virtues, of all good things.

Every poem, including those often relegated to the status of *unecht* by previous scholars,[11] will be examined for evidence of the presence of these features. Only then will it be possible to determine whether the "standard" presentations are justifiable or whether, perhaps, the significance of the concept of the ennobling power of love has been greatly exaggerated.

2. Der von Kürenberg

All but one of the thirteen poems of Der von Kürenberg are completely untouched by the idea of ennobling love and present no easy opportunities for its introduction. One does not yet find in these songs the knight in the service of the lady, love as the hoped for reward of such service, and the lament of the knight because his wooing has been in vain. On the contrary, in most of the songs one encounters not the distant lady who is uninterested in the attentions of the knight, but rather a woman in love. Where there are lamentations, they come from the loving woman, and, in most of the songs where the man appears as the wooer, he does not act as the humble servant of his lady but instead with the boldness and at times even haughtiness of a man who is confident of his irresistibility. In 9,21 the man almost propositions the woman with the words "Wîp vile schoene,   nu var du sam mir" (9,21–22) and says he is ready to share both joy and sorrow with her, whereas in 10,17 he boasts of his ability to woo a woman successfully: "Wîp und vederspil   diu werdent   lîhte zam: / swer si ze rehte lucket,   sô suochent si den man" (10,17–20). Conversely, in response to being courted by an aggressive female who expresses her determination to possess him in the first stanza (8,1) of a *Wechsel*, the knight reveals his independence of spirit in the second stanza with the following words:

Nu brinc mir her vil balde   mîn ros, mîn îsengwant,
wan ich muoz einer frouwen   rûmen diu lant.
diu wil mich des betwingen   daz ich ir holt sî.
si muoz der mîner minne   iemer darbende sîn.   (9,29–36)

In such an atmosphere it is hardly surprising that one does not encounter the slightest trace of the idea of the ennobling power of love.

The man's boldness is not evident in two of the poems in which a knight is the only speaker. In 10,1, where he seems assured of the lady's affection, he merely gives her advice on how to keep their relationship secret (by looking at another man when he is present), whereas in 10,9 he sends his messenger to a maiden—whose response to his courtship is still unknown—out of fear that his going to her in person could do her harm. But neither song indicates any awareness of the idea that the man can earn the woman's love by becoming a better person in the course of his courtship.

5

The eight poems in which a loving woman speaks reveal a wide range of subjects and sentiments. In 7,1 the woman praises the virtue of constancy and admonishes her lover (through a messenger) to be faithful, whereas in 7,10 she says she would let the world know how miserable she was if she ever lost her lover. The separation of lovers is the topic of two of these songs—7,19, where the lady complains about the *merker* who have taken her knight away from her, and 9,13, where the woman curses the *lügenaere* who are responsible for her losing her knight and expresses the wish that someone might reunite her with her lover. Similar to the sorrow of separation in these two poems is the lady's painful realization in 8,25 that she will never be able to obtain what she desires—something she assures her audience is not gold or silver, but rather something very human. In 8,17 the woman says that when she is alone, clad in her chemise, and thinks of her noble knight, she blushes and becomes very sad. And, finally, the two songs that a woman shares with a male speaker show the lady to be forceful, if not aggressive. In the brief conversation of 8,9 the lady as much as curses her lover for his timidity when he tells her that he did not dare to wake her even though he was standing at her bedside, whereas in the woman's stanza of the *Wechsel* 8,1 (+9, 29) the speaker says that the only way a certain knight she has heard singing will get away from her is if he leaves her territory. In none of these poems, however, does one note any consciousness on the part of the woman that it is incumbent upon her to have an uplifting effect on her beloved, nor is there any suggestion that the knight gained the lady's favor by having become worthy of her love through self-improvement.[1]

The only song of the Kürenberger that might have anything to do with the notion of the ennobling power of love is his much-discussed *Falkenlied*, 8,33. In the first stanza a woman states that a falcon she had trained for more than a year flew off to other lands. In the second strophe she says that, later catching sight of the falcon in flight, she was able to observe that its jesses were made of silk and its feathers were decorated with gold. The song concludes with the lady's wish that God might bring together lovers who are separated. In the case of this *Falkenlied* it could be argued that the image of the woman training and taming a falcon, which can easily be taken here as a symbol of a beloved knight, reveals an awareness of the educative influence of the woman in a love relationship.[2] Although this may be so, nothing in the poem suggests that the falcon-knight is improved morally or ennobled in any inner sense. The falcon is tamed, to be sure, but this domestication is not necessarily symbolic of any kind of improvement in his character. All the lady says is that she got him to be the way she wanted him (or so she thought): "Dô ich in gezamete   als ich in wolte hân" (8,35–36). What the end result of that training was, or was intended to be, is neither stated nor implied. The falcon's taming could just as well be interpreted as nothing more than the lady's attempt to keep a tight rein on her beloved.[3] In view of the ambiguities with reference to the notion of taming and training, it hardly seems likely that this poem is a clear-cut example of the ennobling or educative power of love.[4]

3. Dietmar von Aist

In thirteen of the twenty-five poems included in *MF* under the name of Dietmar von Aist there is not the slightest trace of the idea of the ennobling power of love, nor are there any situations that would have lent themselves to its introduction. The predominating theme in ten of these songs is the pain of separation, the reasons for which may or may not be clearly delineated. In all but one the lady is presented as a loving woman longing for her beloved. In 32,1 she says she would know how to combat her sadness if it were not for her *huote*, which prevents her from meeting with her beloved, whereas in 32,5, a brief conversation between lovers as they part, the exact reason for their separation is not revealed. Similarly, in 32,13, a *Wechsel* in which both the man and the woman convey to a messenger their anguish about being apart, it is not clear why the knight has had to leave. Another *Wechsel*, 35,16—again without specifying why the lovers are apart—also portrays the unhappiness resulting from the separation of two people who long for each other. What is clear here, however, is that neither party is correctly informed of the other's feelings, for each seems to imply that the other's lack of interest is responsible for their sorrow.

Ignorance of the cause of her beloved's absence is also expressed in 34,11 by a woman who says it seems a thousand years since she has been in her lover's arms. But whatever the reason, she is certain it is not her fault. In the *Tagelied*, 39,18, on the other hand, there is no mystery about what makes the lovers unhappy, because it is the dawn that puts an end to a night of love and causes the lady to weep over her sweetheart's departure. The reason for the lady's woe is likewise clear in another two of these songs—she has run into competition that is distracting her beloved. In 37,4 the woman complains that the man she has freely chosen for herself is being lured away by envious women, whereas in 37,18 the lady admonishes her beloved, who used to think she was lovely, to renounce his interest in other women. The lady in 33,7, though she does not speak directly of her own situation, does hint perhaps at her predicament when she condemns anyone who would abandon a woman because she is not able to please everyone all the time. Finally, in 32,9—the one poem where the lady apparently has rejected the man's advances—the speaker asks, as he lies awake at night unable to sleep because of his yearning, why God has inflicted this torment on him, which will lead him to his grave. In none of these ten poems dealing with the sorrow of separation does any of the loving women indicate that her lover won her affection by becoming worthy through self-improvement. Likewise, the men who speak in five of the songs reveal no awareness that they were expected to become more noble or refined.[1]

Three of this group of thirteen poems treat themes other than the pain of not being together. In one brief poem, 34,3, the song of a bird awakens a man's fond memories of a lady whose love he presumably has enjoyed. A woman in the second song, 35,32, says that, although she is perfectly willing to show her gratitude to those who increase her knowledge, she intends to remain a stranger to men. Apparently, however, this is not because she is of an unloving nature, but rather because she fears the suffering she might have to endure if she became too deeply involved and then were rebuffed by her beloved. In the last of these three songs, 33,15, the speaker expresses his delight at the end of winter and the coming of spring. Although the question of love is not specifically mentioned, it perhaps can be assumed that the consolation his heart anticipates has something to do with his hopes of experiencing love. Nowhere in these three poems does one find the motif of the ennobling or educative force of love. Neither the men who sing either of fond memories of love or of the anticipated consolation that spring will bring, nor the woman who is afraid of love, in any way demonstrate their familiarity with the view that the man can become deserving of love by dint of self-betterment.

Eight of the poems under Dietmar's name contain situations that would have lent themselves easily to the introduction of the idea of ennobling love. In six of these the knight is portrayed either explicitly or implicitly as in his lady's service. Whereas the man in 36,34 addresses his lady as "mînes lîbes frouwe" (36,34) and asks to be allowed to be with her and to be taken into her *genâde*, the speaker in H.S.249,V.S.317 complains that his heart has betrayed him by leading him to a woman who is *tugendrîch* but who loves him less than he does her. Indeed, his heart, determined to subject itself to the lady no matter how unkind she is to the knight, has abandoned him, acting like a daughter who has deceived her dear mother. In the *Wechsel*-like 37,30 the knight states that, despite the fact that the summer is over, his heart is still in the power of the woman he has served. The second stanza shows the lady very much in love with the knight, whereas in the third a messenger, speaking of the knight's impatient anticipation, appeals to the lady to satisfy her lover before his joy turns to sorrow. In the single stanza of 38,24 the speaker's chances of success are by no means as clear. He prays that God may give his beloved the good sense to embrace him and love him. That she has not been responding to his entreaties becomes obvious in the last line, where he refers to her as one "diu sich dâ sündet ane mir,   und ich ir vil gedienet hân" (38,30–31). Even more pessimistic is the *Wechsel*, 40,19. Here the man claims that his beloved lady, who is "âne wandel" (40,19), has robbed him of his senses and brought him to death's door, though she should have mercy on him and remember that he has always been her vassal. He also says he could prove that she is not so well guarded—and that would be a blow to her—for she should remember that she did spend a night with him. To this the lady replies that he has no reason to anticipate future joy, for what he has just said about her has caused her pain and will result in his losing her favor. His malicious quarrelsomeness does not trouble her, she concludes, for their union was not consummated. In 34,19 the speaker also complains that his love will be the end of him if it remains unrequited. Nothing seems to help his cause with the lady whose servant he is and whose character is "valshes frî" (34,34), though she has robbed him of his heart, which no woman had ever done before.

In none of the six songs just reviewed is the idea of service connected in any way with the notion of the ennobling power of love. There is never even a suggestion that the man has become worthy of the lady's love in the course of his service. What is implicit here is only the basic concept that there should be a reward for service rendered, and not that the man's vassalage has made him a better person. Indeed, in 40,19 one could even claim that the knight's service has done anything but refine his character, inasmuch as he threatens the lady and maligns her in a most uncourtly manner.

Three of the six poems in which the idea of service plays a role (H.S.249, 34,19, and 40,19) also contain the motif of praise of the lady's goodness or good qualities. This theme is also found in the last two songs of the group of eight presently under discussion, 36,5 and 36,23. Although the woman in the *Wechsel*, 36,5, is reluctant to cause her beloved pain by staying away from him, as people have advised her to do, the man implies that he will never cease to praise her, for whenever he sees her, his distress disappears. In 36,23 the speaker lavishly extols his beloved's beauty and her *tugende* at the same time that he expresses his exuberant joy over having embraced her.

Like the appearance of the theme of service, the occurrence of the motif of praise of the lady's good qualities would have presented an easy opportunity to introduce the idea of the ennobling power of love. But this opportunity is not seized by the poet in any of the five songs in question. The lady's good qualities are alluded to neither in the songs of unrequited love (H.S.249, 34,19, and 40,19) as a source of inspiration for the man to emulate in the hope of becoming worthy of her love, nor in the poems of mutual love (36,5 and 36,23) as having exerted a beneficial influence on the man, which helped him to gain the lady's favor.

Two poems under the name of Dietmar von Aist at least hint at the idea of ennobling love or contain passages where one might be tempted to think in such terms. One poem, 39,30, combines the theme of the pain of separation with that of the joy of love fulfilled in a *Wechsel*-like situation. Whereas the knight hopes that the long nights of winter will compensate him for the sorrow summer has brought him, the woman, after expressing her annoyance that her beloved has stayed away so long, speaks of the pleasure she and her lover have indulged in during the long winter nights. She also says of him: "er ist als in mîn herze wil" (40,10). Her saying that her beloved is just as her heart would have him could—in the right context—be interpreted to mean that he has conformed to a certain standard of behavior expected by the lady in order to please her and thus gain her affection. There is, however, no clue in the rest of the poem about the knight's character or behavior. Because the words she speaks only mean "he is as my heart would have him" and not "he *behaves* as my heart would have him," it seems more likely that her statement indicates merely that she likes him the way he is, without implying any effort on his part to act in a manner that might help him merit her love.

The other poem hinting at the idea of ennobling love, 33,31, is not a love song, but rather a gnomic stanza giving advice on courtly behavior. Because it does at least touch upon the topic of the relations between the sexes, however, it must also be examined briefly here. The speaker says that one should always hold dear "die biderben und die guoten" (33,31) and that whoever boasts too much—presumably about his success with women[2]—does not know how to practice moderation. In addition, he states, a courtly man should not praise all women indiscriminately, for whoever does so is not his own master.

It has been suggested that in this poem the author is presenting himself to his lady as the kind of person whose behavior he is recommending and is thus hinting to her that she should love him for this reason.[3] Although it is not impossible that this is the case, surely nothing in the poem itself points in this direction. There is no cause to assume that the poet is addressing his words to a particular lady, and every reason to believe that he is making generalizations without having his own particular predicament in mind. He does, to be sure, indicate his concern with the upgrading of the conduct of his courtly audience. But because he does not make any specific connection between the notion of self-improvement and any benefit it might have in helping a man to win a lady's favor, he clearly does not intend to link the two. More likely than not he was not familiar with any consistent ideal of ennobling love, for, if such an ideal had been traditional, he could hardly have failed to refer to it here.

Clear examples of the idea of ennobling love can be found in only two of the poems attributed to Dietmar von Aist. In the *Wechsel*, 39,11, the notion of ennobling love is linked to the theme of knightly service, which occurs in each of its three stanzas. In the first the man wonders how his heart will ever become joyful, because the lady to whom he has rendered so much service does not seem to take pity on his woes. The second strophe, in which the lady speaks, reveals that his pleading has not been in vain, for she does love him and she indicates that this knight, about whose good qualities she has heard much, has earned her love through his service. In the last stanza, where the knight declares happily that his goal has been achieved, that a noble lady, to whom he has subjected himself, has taken him in her power, one encounters the idea of the educative force of love:

> der bin ich worden undertân,
> als daz schif dem stiurman,
> swanne der wâc sîn ünde   sô gar gelâzen hât.
> sô hôh ôwî!
> si benimt mir mange wilde tât.   (38,34–39,1)

In other words, the knight's having subjected himself to the lady has had a taming influence on him—he has given up certain wild forms of behavior for her sake.[4]

The second poem under Dietmar's name containing clear evidence of one of the attitudes under investigation is the single stanza of 32,23. Here the knight speaks of the benefit he has reaped from his having loved his lady for so long:

> du hâst getiuret mir den muot.
> swaz ich dîn bezzer worden sî   ze heile müeze ez mir ergân.
> machestu daz ende guot,   sô hâst duz allez wol getân. (33,26–30)

It is clear that love has had an ennobling effect on the man.[5] It is also obvious, however, that the man's betterment is not to be viewed as an end in itself, but rather as something that has earned him the right to some compensation. To the extent he has become better for his lady's sake, he expects—or at least hopes—that she will reward him with her love. To him this appears to be the only fitting conclusion to his courtship.[6]

4. Anonymous Songs

One of the eight poems in *MF* under the heading "Namenlose Lieder"—the apparently fragmentary 4,13—deals solely with the joy experienced by "die guoten,   die dâ hôhe sint gemuot" (4,13) at the approach of summer, without any clear connection with the theme of love, and hence need not be discussed further here. Of the remaining seven, three (3,1, 3,17, and 4,1) offer no evidence of the ennobling power of love. All three share the theme of the woman in love. The speaker in 3,1, which actually might have been written by a woman,[1] expresses her love with the formula "Dû bist mîn, ich bin dîn" (3,1) and the sentiment that her beloved must stay locked in her heart because the key has been lost. Two of the songs present women who complain about the absence of their lovers. In 3,17 no reason is given for the man's failure to appear. The woman merely says there is nothing as good as a radiant rose and the love of her man, but, if her dear friend does not come to her, she will derive no joy from summer. The lady in 4,1, however, makes it clear why her beloved stays away—his affections have been alienated by the deception of "unstaeten wîbe" (4,5) who have robbed him of his senses, and she can only attribute his inability to realize that she loves him more than anyone else to his youth and inexperience. In none of these three songs is there a trace of the idea of ennobling love. Neither the girl in 3,1 with her beloved locked in her heart nor the two ladies in 3,17 and 4,1 who are unhappy because their sweethearts have not put in an appearance give any indication that their lovers originally had become worthy of their favor by means of self-betterment.

The four remaining songs present situations where one at least might be inclined to think in terms of the concept of the ennobling power of love. Two of these (6,14 and 6,5) reveal loving women who are eager to enjoy the embraces of their lovers. The speaker in 6,14 happily tells how his beloved has given him unmistakable signs of her affection. Even though circumstances have prevented them from having a more intimate rendezvous, her intentions become clear when he quotes her as saying "schiere soltu mich enphân / unde troesten mînen lîp" (6,28–29), a desire he is perfectly willing to fulfill. In 6,5 a woman exclaims with joyful anticipation that a knight who has served her according to her wishes must be rewarded before the season changes. No matter what people may think, she is determined to let him have his way with her. In both these poems the temptation to suspect the presence of the notion of ennobling love is connected with the knight's willingness to do his lady's bidding. In 6,5, for example, the lady clearly states that her knight has earned her love by fulfilling her desires, and in 6,14 the man expresses his eagerness to please the lady by saying: "swie du wilt sô wil ich sîn" (6,30). But such temptation must be resisted in both cases, because there is no justification for concluding either that the knight's service to the lady in 6,5 had anything to do with self-improvement on his part, or that the man in 6,14 has anything in mind other than complying with his beloved's request to be happy and to console her.

In the third of the songs, 3,7, where it is at least possible to think in terms of ennobling love, it is not absolutely clear that the poem is dealing with the relationship between the sexes, for it is debatable whether the speaker is male or female and whether the person mentioned in line 3,10 is the king of "Engellant," as the original manuscript reads, or the queen thereof, as a later hand has corrected it.[2] According to the only interpretation of concern here, a male speaker says that, if the whole world were his, he would give it all up if the Queen of England lay in his arms. The willingness to renounce worldly goods for the sake of attaining a lady's love might conceivably be considered within the realm of the concept of the ennobling power of love. There is, however, no reason to believe that this idea plays any role in the brief situation under discussion here, inasmuch as no clues are given about anyone's possible reaction to, or interpretation of, the man's readiness to sacrifice worldly riches.

The speaker in the last of the anonymous songs to be examined, 3,12, praises "tougen minne" (3,12) as something that produces "hôhen muot" (3,13) and recommends that one apply oneself to it. But anyone who does not practice it "mit triwen" (3,15), he concludes, should be reproached. Under the appropriate circumstances, a concern with the importance of *triuwe* or *staete* in a love relationship could very well be connected with the idea of ennobling love. If, for example, the lady expects or demands constancy or faithfulness from the man and he in turn feels constrained to meet this requirement if he wishes to reap love's reward, then it can be said that the man is striving to improve his conduct in at least this one respect in order to become deserving of the lady's favor and that therefore love—or the lady—is exerting an educative effect on the man. In this poem, however, none of the above-mentioned factors appears to be present. Nothing is either said or implied about the lady's expecting *triuwe*, nor is it stated that *triuwe* is even necessary to win love. Indeed, the presupposition is clearly that *minne* can be attained without *triuwe,* and it is precisely this state of affairs that the speaker finds reprehensible. Unlike the situation in several poems with somewhat similar themes to be examined later, there is no reference here to the theory of the educative function of love and the role of the woman in influencing the man's behavior by her expectations.[3]

5. The Burggraf von Regensburg

All three poems preserved under the name of the Burggraf von Regensburg reveal a woman in love. Two of them, 16,8 and 16,15, which show the lady determined to foster the relationship despite the obstacles put in her way by society, offer no evidence of the idea of ennobling love. In the single stanza of 16,8 the lady simply asserts that, try as "they" may, they will not be able to take her beloved away from her. The woman's antagonists appear to have been more successful in the *Wechsel*, 16,15, in which the man complains that the *merkaere* have prevented his beloved from bringing him joy, and the lady, remembering the bliss of lying in his arms, states that she cannot keep away from this knight whom she has been admonished to avoid. Neither poem indicates in any way that the lady's love was won by the knight's having become worthy.

In the third poem, 16,1, however, where the lady speaks of her devotion to her knight and says it does her heart good to embrace him, one might have cause to at least suspect the presence of the idea of the ennobling power of love when she declares, presumably with her lover in mind: "der sich mit mangen tugenden guot / gemachet al der werlde liep,   der mac wol hôhe tragen den muot" (16,5–7). Although the poet does not specify here that there is a cause-and-effect relationship between the knight's character and the lady's affection for him, there is a temptation to make a connection between the fact that she has given herself to this man and her obviously admiring reference to his good qualities. But even if it could be assumed that she felt his virtues made him deserving of her love, the situation would still only come close to, but not be a genuine example of, the educative force of love. What is missing here is some indication that the lady has exerted pressure on the knight to conform to a certain standard of behavior, that he has been ennobled through his love, that his virtues have increased, that he has in the course of his courtship striven to become better in order to merit his lady's love.

6. The Burggraf von Rietenburg

One of the six poems of the Burggraf von Rietenburg, 19,7, need not be of concern here, inasmuch as the speaker merely expresses his sadness at the passing of summer, without making either a direct or an indirect connection with the theme of love. Of the five love songs to be discussed, three contain no trace of the idea of ennobling love, although they present easy opportunities to introduce it in relation to the mention of knightly service. In the *Wechsel*, 18,1, the lady defiantly expresses her determination to circumvent all efforts to alienate her from her beloved, and the knight, fearing no threats by their enemies, is elated because he has earned her favor through his service. The knight in 18,17 offers a lady his service in the hope of some reward, even though the summer is over, whereas the man in 19,27 complains that his lady has asked him to leave her and says that death would be less painful than her not giving him any recognition for the service he has rendered. Despite the emphasis on service in these three poems, there is no hint that the knight could be ennobled in the lady's service and hence become worthy of her love.

Another of the love songs, 18,25, makes it look—in the text printed in *MF*—as if one of the attitudes under consideration in this study is about to make an appearance. The speaker states that he has heard "wie minne ein saelic arbeit waere / und unversuochten nie erkôs" (18,27–28). If *minne* is viewed as *arebeit* and has never favored anyone who has not been put to the test, it would seem that the speaker were dealing with the idea of proving himself worthy of love. Unfortunately, however, this sense of the quoted lines is derived solely from the reconstruction suggested by von Kraus, which has little or no basis in the essentially unintelligible manuscript versions. Thus it is not possible to view this passage as an example of the idea of ennobling love. Even if the verses quoted were the words of the poet, it would still be a dubious case, because he would not have drawn the right conclusion from his statement when he continues with: "des möhte ich werden sorgen lôs, / ob si erbarmen wil mîn swaere" (19,1–2). This would make it clear that it is not a question of the knight's becoming worthy by self-improvement, but rather of the lady's taking pity on his suffering. The view that one becomes better through suffering would still not have been expressed in this poem, even if the emended verses were correct.

That the Burggraf von Rietenburg was acquainted with this idea, however, becomes apparent in 19,17, where the theme of *versuochen* is developed along the lines missed in 18,25. Here the speaker says that he will gladly accept his lady's desire to put him to the test, for then he would become like gold that is refined in the fire: "bezzer wirt ez umbe daz, / lûter, schoener unde clâr" (19,22–23). Thus it is clear that the knight views his period of courtship as an opportunity for him to become better and, presumably, worthier of the lady's favor than he was before.

7. Meinloh von Sevelingen

Five of the dozen one-stanza poems attributed to Meinloh von Sevelingen neither offer any evidence of the idea of ennobling love nor contain situations that would have lent themselves especially to its introduction. Two of these, 13,14 and 13,27, present different views of the loving woman. The lady in 13,14 is determined to prevail over the machinations of the *merkaere* who have tried to cause a rift between her and her lover by their malicious gossip. She proudly declares that she is his *friundinne*, even though she has not slept with him, and nothing they can do will make her give him up. In 13,27 the lady directs her attention to other women who are jealous of her because of her relationship with a "kindeschen man" (13,28). She not only defends herself by saying that she has done nothing to them except make sure that her lover finds her the most attractive of all, but she also magnanimously declares that she will not be nasty to any woman who has lost his favor if she happens to notice her in her misery. Neither of these songs intimates in any way that the man the lady adores gained her favor by means of self-improvement.[1]

Another of the songs without a trace of the educative effect of love is 14,1, where the knight's courtship is presented by a messenger who asks the lady if she does not remember that a knight has offered her his service. He urges her to raise the knight's fallen spirits, for he will never be happy again until he is lying in her arms. The two other songs that do not touch on the question under investigation offer generalizations concerning the attainment of success in winning the love of a fair lady. Whereas in 12,14 the speaker recommends a speedy courtship, contending that a drawn-out affair is more likely to run into interference, in 14,14 secrecy and concealment are emphasized as the qualities most likely to lead to the desired goal.

Although another three songs of Meinloh von Sevelingen present clear opportunities to introduce the idea of ennobling love, they, too, contain no trace of its presence. All three are songs of courtship and have praise of the lady as a major theme. In 12,17 the speaker says that only a certain lady can alleviate his sadness. He has never seen a woman conduct herself better, he contends, and "an ir ist anders wandels niht" (12,36). The knight in 13,1 is just as convinced of his lady's good qualities: "sist saelic zallen êren,   der besten tugende pfligt ir lîp" (13,9–10). Every day he serves her, he says, she pleases him more and more, and if he died of love for her and then came back to life, he would begin wooing her all over again. In 15,1 the lady is also pictured as the epitome of perfection; because she is so beautiful and so good, the knight is determined to do whatever she commands. Despite the emphasis in these songs on the lady's perfection, however, there is not the slightest suggestion that her goodness should serve as a model for the knight's self-improvement. The mention of the man's readiness to fulfill the lady's every wish in 15,1 would likewise have been an excellent occasion for introducing the idea of the educative force of love. By specifying certain things that the lady demanded of the knight to improve his character, the poet could have made clear how the knight could become worthy of the lady's love. But because he did not take advantage of this opportunity, one cannot speak here in terms of the ennobling power of love.[2]

Four of Meinloh's poems either contain elements that might lead one to think of the idea of ennobling love or present hints of or analogues to it. In 14,26 a lady rejoices at the news that her lover has returned to the country. As she states her intention of sleeping with this young knight who knows how to serve women so well, she remarks about him as follows: "mich heizent sîne tugende   daz ich vil staeter minne pflege" (14,32–33). This certainly seems to point to a causal connection between his good qualities and her feeling for him. It must be remembered, however, that this situation only borders on the notion of the educative power of love, for there is no suggestion that the lady exerted pressure on the knight or that he has been ennobled or has improved in the course of his service and hence become worthy of what he was not before.[3]

The second song, 11,14, is a *Botenlied* in which the messenger, after informing the lady that she has driven all thoughts of other women —or of anything else, for that matter—out of his master's mind, begins to tell her of a change in the knight for which she is responsible: "du hâst im nâch bekêret   beidiu sin unde leben" (11,22–23). Although this transformation could be—and has been—interpreted as an example of the ennobling power of love,[4] the messenger's next words make it seem much more likely that, rather than becoming better through his love for her, the knight merely has experienced a change from joy to sadness: "er hât dur dînen willen / eine ganze fröide   gar umbe ein trûren gegeben" (11,24–26).

In 11,1 the speaker tells how he first heard his lady extolled from afar and became eager to make her acquaintance. Now that he has met her he knows that she is indeed "der besten eine" (11,9). He also makes a generalization about her that could be seen to touch upon the problem of ennoblement: "er ist vil wol getiuret,   den du wilt, frouwe, haben liep" (11,7–8). This could be interpreted to mean that anyone the lady chooses to love will be a better person for it. If so, it would reflect a variation of the idea of the ennobling power of love. In the context of the poem, however, the word *getiuret* seems more likely to mean made valuable in the sense of esteemed. What the poet is probably saying, then, is that anyone the lady loves will be highly honored by it, and not that the knight's character will have been improved. But whichever interpretation one chooses to follow, there is no reason to believe that the knight has earned love by becoming better and hence worthy. If anything, the opposite is true. If there is improvement, it is the result of the lady's having granted her love, not a condition of its bestowal.[5] It should be noted that the above discussion of 11,1 is based on the version of lines 7–8 in manuscript B. If one uses the reading of manuscript C—"er ist vil wol getiuret,   den du frowe wilt haben in pfliht"—the situation changes. Now the man is not *getiuret* because the lady loves him, but only because she has taken him into her service. This reading offers a more traditional example of the uplifting power of love, namely, the notion that the man's service to the lady will have a beneficial effect on him.

The last song in this grouping, 12,1, is one of those that offer prescriptions for success in love. Like 14,14 discussed above in a different category, this poem also recommends secrecy and concealment. In the concluding lines the poet comes very close to the idea of ennobling love when he says:

swer biderber dienet wîben,   die gebent alsus getânen solt.
ich waene, unkiuschez herze
  wirt mit ganzen triuwen   werden wîben niemer holt. (12,9–13)

According to this statement, the quality of the reward will correspond to that of the service. Thus an *unkiuschez herze* cannot count on winning the love of noble, worthy ladies. Although the poet does not speak directly of self-improvement for the purpose of becoming worthy of a lady's love, he certainly leaves the way open for taking such a step and reaching such a conclusion—namely, if one does not have a *kiuschez herze*, one could strive to achieve such a state in order to merit the reward of love.

8. Kaiser Heinrich

The three poems attributed to Kaiser Heinrich contain various expressions of the effects of love and hence would have lent themselves easily to the introduction of the idea of ennobling love. In no case, however, is there any clear evidence of its presence. The lady in the *Wechsel*, 4,17, says she is "wol gemuot" (4,29) because her relationship with a knight has taken a happy turn, a fact of which other women are jealous.[1] The man, on the other hand, asserts that the lady has freed him of all sorrow "mit ir tugende" (4,21), and when she is lying with him, he feels even more than powerful. This elation, this feeling of well-being, which is clearly the result of love's fulfillment, is not to be confused with ennoblement in the sense of improvement or betterment of character. Rather, it is yet another variation of the concept of *hôher muot*—that feeling de Boor so aptly characterized as a "freudige Hochstimmung"[2]—which one finds expressed again and again as a desired state of being, the achievement of which seems impossible without love.[3]

In 5,16 the speaker emphasizes the sorrows and tribulations of separation from his beloved. Here, too, however, one has the opportunity to see the effect love has upon him. Only when he is with his beloved does he really feel himself to be the powerful ruler that he is. When he is separated from her, the only possession he is aware of is his pain. Indeed, the reward he expects from his lady is such that he would rather renounce his crown than give her up. Love, then, gives him his reason for being; it makes his life worthwhile; it gives meaning to what he is and what he has. But one does not hear a word about its ennobling or educative force in the sense of this investigation.

The first stanza of 4,35 shows the lady filled with sadness as she bids farewell to the knight who must ride off. If he does not come again soon, she says, she will die. In the second strophe the speaker —it is not clear whether it is still the woman or the man responding to her[4]—also talks about the feelings engendered by fulfillment:

> Wol dir, geselle guote,   deich ie bî dir gelac.
> du wonest mir in dem muote   die naht und ouch den tac.
> du zierest mîne sinne   und bist mir dar zuo holt:

nu merke et wiech daz meine:
als edelez gesteine,   swâ man daz leit in daz golt.   (5,7–15)

But no matter who is talking, the idea expressed is that the beloved one is always in the speaker's thoughts and adorns them like precious stones that are set in gold. One might be tempted to see in these verses an example of the ennobling power of love if one interpreted "du zierest mîne sinne" to mean the same as Dietmar von Aist's "du hâst getiuret mir den muot" (33,26), as Sayce does when she says this is likely to refer to "the refining influence of the lady on the man."[5] One can do this, however, only if one takes *sinne* to mean something more than "thoughts." Although this reading is possible, it seems more likely in the context that the speaker is merely elaborating on the statement "du wonest mir in dem muote die naht und ouch den tac" by saying that, because the beloved one is constantly present in the other's mind, that presence enhances the person's thoughts by making them more pleasant or beautiful than they were.[6] There is nothing here to indicate a refining influence in the sense of moral betterment.[7] At any rate, because of the obvious difficulties involved in interpreting its ambiguities, this stanza certainly does not present a clear-cut case of the ennobling power of love.

9. Friedrich von Hausen

Most of the seventeen love poems of Friedrich von Hausen are laments of unrequited love in which the effects of love upon the knight are predominantly pain, sorrow, and misery. The theme of suffering has almost endless variations: love wounds the knight's heart so that he is in constant pain (49,13 and 52,37), and only she who has inflicted this hurt can heal him; love robs him of his senses (52,37) or confuses his perceptions so that he is completely unaware of his surroundings (45,37); or separation from his beloved makes his suffering seem even greater (51,33 and 45,1). Considering the idea of the ennobling or educative power of love, one might well ask whether the poet sees any purpose in all this suffering. After all, if this motif is supposed to play an important role in the *Minnesang*, this would be the most obvious situation in which it could have manifested itself. In other words, is there any indication that the knight becomes better for his having endured the woes he constantly laments, and does such self-improvement better his chances of receiving his lady's favor?

Seven of the poems neither reveal a trace of the idea of ennobling love nor offer any easy opportunities for its introduction. Five of these concentrate on a particular aspect of the man's troubles and leave no room for thoughts of the problem under investigation. In 48,23 the speaker sees his beloved in a dream, but when he awakens, the realization that she is nowhere to be seen distresses him and he curses his eyes for having been the cause of such pain. In two songs, 50,19 and 48,32, those who keep watch over the lady are primarily responsible for the man's misery. The suitor in 50,19 does find some consolation in the fact that those who would malign him are also kept away from his lady by the same guardians who deny him access to her.[1] But in 48,32—a *Wechsel*—the man who is disconsolate as a result of his inability to communicate with his lady curses those who are eager to destroy the relationship, whereas the woman—the only loving one in Friedrich von Hausen's songs—expresses her determination not to renounce the man who has rendered her service. In 45,1 the knight's suffering is accentuated by his absence. Now that he is far away from her, the woes he endured in her presence seem like nothing compared with his present pain; if he is fortunate enough to return home, he says, no one will ever see him sad again.

And in 45,19 the woman's outright hostility makes it impossible to think in terms of ennobling love. Here the speaker says his lady does not believe that he loves her and has acted toward him with distrust and defiance, which he claims is hardly an appropriate way for a lady to behave toward a man who loves her more than anyone in the world.

The last two songs in this category are crusade poems that deal with a conflict between the knight's duty to his lady and his obligation to God and that show love having anything but edifying results. In 45,37 there is a concise summary of the effect that love has had on him—that debilitating effect that has been observed before:

> ich quam sîn dicke in solhe nôt,
> daz ich den liuten guoten morgen bôt
> engegen der naht.
> ich was sô verre an si verdâht
> daz ich mich underwîlent niht versan,
> und swer mich gruozte daz ichs niht vernam.   (46,3–8)

Confronted with the appeal to participate in a crusade, however, the knight concludes that service to his beloved must be subordinated to service to God. Although he does not renounce her, he does point out somewhat bitterly that the master he will now serve will, unlike his lady, not leave him unrewarded. What is interesting from the point of view of this discussion is the way he interprets some of the effects love has had on him:

> ich hâte liep daz mir vil nâhe gie:
> dazn liez mich nie
> an wîsheit kêren mînen muot.
> daz was diu minne, diu noch mangen tuot
> daz selbe klagen.[2]   (46,21–25)

Far from having ennobled the knight, love has kept him away from the course of wisdom—here, presumably, from his obligations to God.

Essentially the same view is found in 47,9, except that here the knight appears to be having difficulty carrying out his resolution to serve God first and then noble ladies. The conflict is now presented in the form of a bitter struggle between his *herze* and his *lîp*, the latter desiring to fight against the heathens and the former determined to remain with his lady. The idea that love prevents the knight from doing what he feels obliged to do with respect to the crusade is expressed as follows:

ich solte sîn ze rehte ein lebendic man,
ob ez den tumben willen sîn verbaere.
nu sihe ich wol daz im ist gar unmaere
wie ez mir an dem ende süle ergân.   (47,21–24)

This poem thus presents a strong indictment of love as a force that is the opposite of ennobling, for the knight even goes so far as to accuse his heart of being completely indifferent to what happens to him "in the end," that is, to the question of his eternal salvation.

In seven poems of Friedrich von Hausen one encounters passages that seem ideally suited to the introduction of the theme of the ennobling power of love. Yet the poet consistently fails to take advantage of such situations. In 49,13, after complaining about his wounded heart and the fact that consolation can come only from his lady, who should reward him for having given her his heart, he concludes that the reason he must suffer is that his heart has set itself too high a goal. He ends the song by saying that, if Love is ultimately unkind to him, then no one should have faith in Love again.

A similar note is struck in 51,33, where the speaker, on a journey that has caused a separation between him and his lady, laments:

Het ich sô hôher minne
nie mich underwunden,
mîn möhte werden rât.   (52,7–9)

In neither poem, however, is it even implied that by striving to become better the knight could reach the level of his beloved and hence become worthy of her love. On the contrary, in 51,33 the situation seems hopeless: if he continues to serve her, despite the pain she causes him, he does so first because he cannot help himself, and second because he still clings to the belief that eventually faithful service, which he has rendered her more than any other man, must be rewarded.

Three more poems where the theme of ennobling love might have been introduced are 49,37, 43,28, and 51,13. In 49,37 the speaker states he is willing to bear pain if it will help him win the love of his lady whose beauty and character he extols, whom he has loved since he was a child, and whom he is determined to continue to serve. But neither expressed nor implied is the idea that his suffering will make him a better person and that therefore the attainment of his goal will be the result of self-improvement, which will have made him deserving of her love. All that is implicit here, as so often elsewhere, is that devoted service will find its reward.

The idea of the knight's willingness to endure pain is also found in 43,28. This time the topic comes up in a discussion of *huote*. After stating that neither his service nor the intensity of his love seems able to help him win his lady's affection, he confesses that his beloved, not those who keep watch over her, is the cause of his misery. Indeed, nothing would please him more than to be able to complain that her *huote* was keeping them apart. He recognizes that one cannot have "grôze fröide âne kumber" (44,1), and it is precisely this woe accompanying the joy of love that he longs to experience. Just as in 49,37, however, there is no indication that the purpose of his suffering is to make him a better person so that he will merit her love.

In 51,13 the speaker also emphasizes the degree of his suffering, as well as his willingness to bear it, even though he feels he has already endured enough to deserve his reward. Indeed, if he had borne for God's sake what he has had to put up with from his lady, he says, God would have granted him eternal salvation. Again one sees a perfect opportunity to relate suffering with the idea of becoming worthy through self-improvement, but the poet does not take advantage of it.

Friedrich von Hausen also fails to make a similar connection in 52,37, a poem that more than any other is dominated by the theme of the pain caused by love:

> Waz mac daz sîn daz diu werlt heizet minne,
> unde ez mir tuot alsô wê zaller stunde
> unde ez mir nimt alsô vil mîner sinne?   (53,15–17)

Love inflicts pain; it robs the knight of his senses; it will destroy him if his lady does not respond to his pleas. If he continues to serve her, it is because he believes she is the best woman he has ever met:

> deich in der werlt bezzer wîp iender funde,
> seht dêst mîn wân.   dâ für sô wil ichz hân,
> und dienen nochdan   mit triuwen der guoten,
> diu mich dâ bliuwet vil sêre âne ruoten.   (53,10–14)

This would have been the place to state a belief in the principle of self-betterment through imitation of the lady's virtues—to strive to become as good as she, who is the very best, and hence to become deserving of her affection. But of a possible ennobling or edifying effect of love one hears not a word. To the contrary, the effect of love is thoroughly debilitating. The poem ends with the knight's cursing of Lady Love for having destroyed his joy and having saddled him with so much pain and misery.

The last of the poems with unseized opportunities, 44,13, also contains the idea that the beloved lady is a model of perfection. After stating that the sweet words he has heard the best people say about her cause him to think only of her, the speaker claims that she should let him derive some benefit from the fact that he has never loved anyone else as much. In the second stanza he says that God has endowed his lady with more good qualities and beauty than any other woman and that, though this might cause him to suffer at times, it also often makes his heart leap up. And if she would pity him because of the deep wound she has inflicted on him,[3] there might be some hope for him after all. But in the concluding strophe this optimism gives way to an expression of fear that his lady, despite the good things God has bestowed on her, may be hard-hearted enough to be able to bear with indifference the wailing and lamenting to which his unhappiness has driven him. In this song, too, the poet does not take advantage of the opportunity to link the lady's virtues with the idea that they should act as a model for the man to imitate, even though he specifically mentions the effects of the woman's perfection on the knight. Here the man's expectations are in no way based on the principle of his becoming worthy through self-improvement, but rather on the fact that he loves his lady more than anyone else and believes she should feel sorry for him because he is so miserable.

More or less clear examples of certain aspects of ennobling love are found in three of the poems of Friedrich von Hausen. In two of these songs—42,1 and 43,1—the theme under investigation is closely related to the ideas of *staete* and the lady's goodness.[4] The speaker begins 42,1 by claiming he has good reason to be unhappy because his lady said that, even if he were Aeneas, she would never be his Dido. Although she avoids him, he says, she has robbed him of his heart, which no other women ever did. He then affirms in the second stanza that sadness and woe, which were previously unknown to him, are now his lot, and he claims that he never expected to suffer from any women the distress he now knows because of one. In the last strophe he states that his heart must be her shrine as long as he lives, whereas previously all women were unjostled there (i.e., there was always plenty of room for them in his heart).[5] He concludes by hoping that, no matter how easily she might console herself, it will now become apparent whether true steadfastness is of any use, for this virtue, which he says has come to him from her *güete*, he intends to practice toward her always.

An aspect of ennobling love makes an appearance in this poem when the speaker says that his *staete* has come to him from his lady's *güete*. It is, to be sure, not clear exactly what he means by this.[6] It could signify that her goodness in general has been the inspiration for one of his virtues, but it might also merely mean that he looks upon her *güete* as the reason he can expect a reward for his loyal devotion, that is, someone as good as she is could not fail to recompense him for his steadfastness. But even if it is possible to say only that there is some kind of cause-effect relationship between her *güete* and his *staete*, there is still no doubt that this poem is dealing with a variation of the notion of the educative effect of love. It is evident that the lady does insist on the virtue of *staete*, that the speaker has *become* steadfast in her service under the influence of her *güete*, and that he believes this improvement in his behavior merits a reward.

In this connection Bekker suggests a possible interpretation of the poem that makes plausible another type of causal relationship between *güete* and *staete*. According to his reading, the contrast seen by most commentators between the speaker's present devotion to only one lady and his past interest in *elliu wip* is shunted aside, and the knight is viewed as being "not only devoted to the lady," but also as having "become a devotee of (all) womankind (in general)."[7] As far as the crucial lines in the third strophe are concerned, the speaker's statement that all women must be unjostled in his heart is taken to mean that there is ample room there for them: "because of the lady's effect on the speaker, the capacity of his heart is such that it can harbor all her sisters."[8] The result for the poem's last line is that the lady's *güete* is seen "to consist in her being effective on the speaker in such a way as to compel him to open his heart to all women—a courtly compliment indeed."[9] This reading of 42,1 offers an example of that variation of ennobling love wherein the lady's good qualities have a beneficial effect on the knight by influencing him to improve his behavior. But no matter which line of interpretation one prefers, some consciousness of the idea of the ennobling power of love is evident in this song.

In the first stanza of 43,1 the speaker says that his absence from his lady pains him deeply, but he hopes the fact that he has always been her servant will benefit him. He cannot give her up; he has had to be true to her since he began (the relationship), he declares, "wan sie daz beste gerne tuot" (43,9). In the concluding strophes he says that people can tell by looking at him that he is separated from the woman he chose above all others and whose beauty was created to cause him sorrow. If he didn't care so much about her, it would not be so painful to be separated from her. But being unable to forget her, he hopes that she will not forget him, either, for the last time he saw her he took leave of all joy.

In this song, too, it is at least implied that the speaker's steadfastness represents an improvement in his behavior. And evidently the fact that the lady gladly does what is best compels him to practice *staete*. But, again, the relationship between her goodness and his steadfastness is not clear. It is possible that the speaker regards the lady's virtues as a model to be imitated. On the other hand, he merely may be counting on her goodness to reward him for his loyalty. Despite this lack of clarity, however, the song still contains almost the same evidence of an awareness of the notion of ennobling love as 42,1, namely, the knight has become steadfast in the lady's service. This virtue in him has been caused by her goodness, and he expects that this improvement in his conduct will help him to attain his goal.

The third example of ennobling love is found in a crusade poem, 48,3, which contains a kind of commentary on the knight's personal situation as represented in the two crusade songs discussed above in the first category—45,37 and 47,9. Having already departed for the Holy Land, the speaker states that if Love could have kept a man at home, he would have stayed behind. From the discussion of the other two crusade poems, it is clear that Love tried very hard to keep him at home, but that his better judgment triumphed over Love. Nevertheless, he commends those he left behind to God's care and concludes the poem with words that are both advice and a warning to fair ladies. Whereas in the aforementioned songs love did not have an ennobling effect as far as the crusade was concerned, now that the knight has escaped from the snares of love, which prevented him from being a *lebendic man*, he tells good ladies how they should behave:

> Ich gunde es guoten frouwen niet
> daz iemer mêre quaeme der tac
> dazs ir deheinen heten liep
> der gotes verte alsô erschrac.   (48,13–15,18)

A truly good and noble lady would not love a man who refused to participate in the crusade. How could a lady accept the service of such a man? It would be a blow to her honor, he concludes. Here it is quite clear that love is supposed to have a morally elevating effect, that the lady should exert an educative influence on the knight. That these sentiments are expressed in the form of advice and a warning, however—"dar zuo send ich in disiu liet, / und warnes als ich beste mac" (48,19–20)—only underscores the poet's disappointment, as revealed in the other two crusade poems, in the role played by the ladies. Instead of inspiring the knight to noble deeds, Love has conspired to keep him from them. That the poet feels it is necessary to instruct the fair sex in this way emphasizes the fact that he has little faith in the ennobling power of love and the educative role of the lady.

In addition to the seventeen songs just considered, there is one poem (54,1) listed in *MF* as unauthentic under the name of Friedrich von Hausen. Here a lady debates with herself whether or not she should yield to the entreaties of a man who desires her love. At first it appears that, in spite of her affection for him, she will not consent to his desires, for to do so could lead to dishonor and sorrow. In the end, however, she decides to give in to his urgings regardless of the consequences. Because in rationalizing her decision she touches upon the problems under investigation, her words should be examined closely. She asks:

> Solte er des geniezen niht
> daz er in hôher wirde wol bewîsen mach
> daz man im des besten giht
> und alle sîne zît im guoter dinge jach
> unde ouch daz sîn süezer munt des ruomes nie geplach
> dâ von betrüebet iender wurde ein saelic wîp?   (54,37–55,2)

In other words, should not her beloved be rewarded with her love for being what he is, a man who is capable of proving that all the good things people say about him are true and who has behaved impeccably toward the fair sex? Interestingly enough, it is not specifically for any service that he is to be rewarded, but for his moral and social qualities. At first glance this might seem to be a good example of the principle that a knight becomes worthy of a noble lady's love through self-improvement. If the case is considered more carefully, however, it becomes clear that the poem never indicates that the knight has striven to become better and hence worthy of love. From the evidence at hand, one can say only that she appears to love him for what he is and not for what he has become. Thus it is difficult to view this as a genuine example of ennobling love, although it must be admitted that the lady's willingness to yield to the man because of his good character is but one step away from the notion that the man can become deserving of love by means of self-betterment.[10]

10. Rudolf von Fenis

Of the seven poems of Rudolf von Fenis—all songs of complaint by a knight whose service to his lady appears to be in vain—two reveal neither the slightest trace of the notion of the ennobling power of love nor an appropriate moment when it might have been introduced. The knight in 83,11 blames himself for his misery because, even though there are women whose love he could easily win, he desires one who does not care for him. If he had only known what he was getting into, he says, he would have turned away before becoming so deeply involved. Now he fears his foolish hope will bring him only more suffering. In 83,25 the speaker says he does not lament the passing of summer, inasmuch as he has been unsuccessful in his attempts to win a lady's favor; if he is more fortunate in winter, then it will be that season that he praises. Indeed, without the consolation of the woman who has overwhelmed "daz herze und den lîp" (84,1), he maintains, summer can bring him no joy.

Five of the songs of Rudolf von Fenis present themes that would have lent themselves easily to the introduction of the idea of ennobling love. In 81,30, after saying that his singing has not been able to lessen his cares and that he would be a fool to give up the woman from whom he hopes to receive great joy, the speaker talks about his lady's *güete*. Because, as noted previously, this quality can be the knight's inspiration for self-improvement, this passage will be examined more carefully to see what effect the lady's *güete* has upon him.

When he is far from his lady and filled with woe, he thinks all will be better again if only he can see his beloved. He discovers, however, that proximity does not bring relief:

> So ich bî ir bin, mîn sorge ist deste mêre,
> als der sich nâhe biutet zuo der gluot:
> der brennet sich von rehte harte sêre:
> ir grôziu güete mir daz selbe tuot.
> so ich bî ir bin, daz toetet mir den muot.
> und stirbe ab rehte, swenne ich von ir kêre,
> wan mich daz sehen dunket alsô guot.   (82,12–18)

Far from being a source of inspiration, the lady's *güete* has had the opposite effect. The speaker repeats the idea with the image of the moth that is attracted to the light:

> Ir schoenen lîp hân ich dâ vür erkennet,
> er tuot mir als der fiurstelîn daz lieht;
> diu fliuget dran, unz si sich gar verbrennet:
> ir grôziu güete mich alsô verriet.   (82,19–22)

Again one is made aware not of any elevating power of love, but rather only of its destructive force.

In the other four songs the theme of service might have presented an opportunity to introduce the notion of ennobling love. Because the concept of service is much more clearly pronounced by Rudolf von Fenis than by any other poet thus far considered, it might be appropriate to ask whether his works demonstrate any awareness of the theory that the purpose of the knight's service is his self-betterment and that his improvement makes him worthy of love.

The idea of service appears only in the last of the three stanzas of 80,1. After expressing his despair over the apparent hopelessness of his situation through various images, such as that of the man who after climbing halfway up a tree can neither go up farther nor come down, the speaker pleads with his lady to let him continue to serve her and not to drive him away, for merely being allowed to serve her at least partially relieves his distress. There is, however, no connection here between the concept of service and the idea of the ennobling power of love.

In the three stanzas of 82,26 the idea of service is expressed only at the beginning of the middle stanza. After a nature introduction the speaker, using the terminology of feudalism, states: "Lîp unde sinne die gap ich für eigen / ir ûf genâde: der hât si gewalt" (82,34–35). This basic premise of the feudal relationship, however, is not conducive to the introduction of the idea of self-improvement and its implication of becoming worthy. On the contrary, the idea conveyed here is that the knight, of lower station and humbly given over into her hand, is not worthy of her; if he is to be rewarded, it is not because he has improved in her service, but rather because his lady exercises *genâde*.

The theme of service dominates 80,25. Love has commanded the knight to serve a lady who does not love him, and he must bear the burden of unrequited love without complaint. To be sure, he realizes that, from a feudal point of view, he would have a perfect right to terminate his service, but his constancy will not permit him to do so. He will serve her forever, he says, even though he knows that he will never be rewarded. He also realizes that it would be more reasonable to serve elsewhere, where he had hopes of being recompensed, but he cannot help himself. Even if she does not want his service, he will continue to serve her and, through her, all good women; if he must suffer for it, he will not show it, for his distress is his greatest joy.

It is quite clear that one will look here in vain for any relationship between service and the ennobling power of love. Service is viewed as being pointless, against all reason, for no reward will result from it. The knight appears compelled by love to behave in a way he knows is unreasonable, and one hears not a word about any possible beneficial effect upon him. On the contrary, the destructive or debilitating power of love is emphasized. In addition, the knight's steadfastness cannot be connected with the idea of the educative function of love, inasmuch as there is no indication that the lady demands this quality of him or that such an expectation on her part has induced him to improve his behavior. It also is evident that the knight does not believe that practicing this virtue will help him attain his goal.

The motif of love as service in the feudal sense is also central to 84,10. In contrast to 80,25, however, the knight appears more hopeful that loyal service will lead to an appropriate reward. The speaker's optimism is based here, as it was in 82,26, on the premise underlying the relationship between lord and vassal:

> bî gwalte sol genâde sîn.
> ûf den trôst ich ie noch singe.
> genâde diu sol überkomen
> grôzen gwalt durch miltekeit:
> genâde zimt wol bî rîcheit.
> ir tugende sint sô vollekomen
> daz durch reht mir ir gwalt sol fromen. (84,12–18)

As pointed out in connection with 82,26, there seems to be no place in this concept for the idea of the ennobling power of love. The view that the knight can become worthy of the lady's love through self-improvement, inspired by her, would hardly seem to fit in with the image of the all-powerful feudal mistress who should reward the vassal because it is appropriate for generosity to go hand in hand with power and wealth.

Despite the missed opportunity to introduce the idea of ennobling love in connection with the concept of service, however, a passage in the last stanza of 84,10 at least hints at the notion of the educative force of love. The speaker extols certain virtues that he believes will produce the desired results:

> trûren sich mit freuden gildet
> dem der wol gebîten kan,
> daz er mit zühten mac vertragen
> sîn leit und nâch genâden klagen:
> der wirt vil lîhte ein saelic man. (84,31–35)

He clearly feels that patient waiting, bearing pain with decorum, and lamenting with moderation will lead to success. This raises several questions. Does this imply an improvement on the part of the knight? Is the lady making him wait so long so that he will be improved by this testing? Can it be assumed that the knight is without these qualities and has to acquire them in order to become worthy of the reward? As far as can be seen, there is no justification in the poem itself, or in any of the songs of Rudolf von Fenis, for an affirmative answer to any of these questions. To say that the man must have certain qualities, or behave in a certain way, if he expects to be rewarded in love, does not necessarily imply that he lacked these virtues and had to acquire them. Because nothing is said specifically about improvement, this does not seem to be a genuine example of the idea that the man can become deserving of love in this way. Nonetheless, the poet's belief that behaving in a certain exemplary manner will lead to positive results does come close to the notion of the educative force of love. What is missing here, then, is the idea that the man has improved and that the lady's expectations have caused him to do so.

There is also one incomplete poem, 84,37, included as *unecht* under the name of Rudolf von Fenis. It is a knight's lament of the great pain he is suffering because of his love for a lady whose loftiness causes him to despair of ever winning her love. In two stanzas of this poem ideas are expressed that at first glance might be thought to hint at the concept of the ennobling power of love. The poem opens with the knight's statement that he had hoped to remain happy by staying free of emotional involvement with a woman. He realizes, however, that this hope was foolish, for "wer gewan ie sanfte guot?" (85,6). But the idea that if something is worth having, it is also worth striving for, is not connected specifically with the notion of any improvement as a result of the struggle. In the second stanza the knight retracts some of his complaints in the form of the following query: "wê, war umbe spriche ich daz? / tuot ez wê, ez tuot ouch baz" (85,29–30). In other words, even though his love causes him great pain, it also does (or will do) some good. Again, however, there is no indication that the good has anything to do with the ennobling effect of love and every reason to assume that it refers to the joy he ultimately anticipates. Thus it is not possible to consider this an example of the educative effect of love.

11. Bernger von Horheim

The six poems by Bernger von Horheim deal almost exclusively with the pain of unrequited love and range in mood from despair over the hopelessness of the knight's situation to hope that eventually his lady will reward him with her love. In all of the songs one finds passages that would have lent themselves more or less appropriately to the introduction of the motif of the ennobling power of love. Even in the little *Reimspiel*, 115,27, where the speaker—in addition to talking about the distress caused by the lady who has so overwhelmed him—mentions his lady's *güete*, one might expect some reference to her goodness as a source of inspiration for him. But instead of indicating that her good qualities have an edifying effect on him, he merely expresses his desire to exert an influence on her. In other words, what he looks for in her *güete* is not an example for himself, but rather a source of kindness that will induce her to grant his wishes.

In 112,1, after stating that he loves his lady even more than Tristan loved Isolde and that she remains indifferent to him despite his protestations of woe, the knight expresses his determination to remain faithful to her. He then asks God to show him what else he can do to please her. He concludes by saying he will continue to sing and lament his sad condition even though those more fortunate than he might scorn him. When the knight turns to God for advice, it is obvious that he is at a loss as to what he can do to meet with his lady's approval other than to make sure that his heart remains steadfast. Although his eagerness to cultivate steadfastness might be connected with the idea of the educative power of love because he evidently believes this will please his lady, his lack of imagination regarding anything else he could do to win her favor makes it seem improbable that even this determination to be constant is related to the idea of self-improvement. It is more likely that he would be willing to do anything to please her, whether or not it had some connection with the notion of self-betterment.

Bernger's so-called *Lügenlied*, 113,1 gives no indication of an awareness of the possible ennobling power of love, although the opportunity is presented on several occasions where the speaker leads his audience to believe his lady has rewarded him—before revealing that in each case he has not been telling the truth. Yet when he says that he seems to be floating in air, that he is bursting with the joy of love, or that his sorrow has been transformed into bliss, he never says or implies that his self-improvement was a condition for winning her favor. The only thing that is said about the reason why his lady finally decided to make him happy is: "sît daz mîn vrouwe ist sô rîche unde guot" (113,19).

In 113,33 the knight speaks of the sorrow his love has brought him and complains that his love, whose beginning was so sweet, appears to be headed for a painful conclusion because his service thus far has been unrewarded. Despite his disappointment, he is determined to persist, believing as he does that devoted service ultimately will be recognized. In words similar to those of Rudolf von Fenis he characterizes the relationship between the lady and the knight. He states that he will not turn to other women for consolation, nor has he ever done so since the time that he gave her "beidiu herze unde lîp / ûf ir genâde" (114,15–16). Thus one sees here, too, the same feudal concept that does not easily admit the notion of the ennobling power of love. If the knight is to be rewarded, it will not be because he has become deserving by means of self-betterment, but rather because his lady has deigned to be gracious. All he can do is wait until she thinks it is time, as he says at the end of the poem. However, nothing is said about what might make the lady think it was time, namely, that he had become worthy through self-improvement.

The motif of separation in 114,21 could also have been presented in the context of ennobling love. The knight's duty to his "real" feudal master has called him off to war. He speaks of the pain of separation and assures his lady that she will always be in his heart, even though he can no longer be near her. Unlike the crusade poems of Friedrich von Hausen, however, these verses do not reveal a true conflict between Love and Duty. Here, the knight's obligation to his feudal lord unquestionably comes first. Nevertheless, Bernger could have taken the opportunity to call upon the ennobling power of love, as did Friedrich von Hausen in 48,13. In other words, he could have emphasized that a lady would not accept the love service of a man who failed in his military obligations. But he says not a word to this effect.

Finally, in 115,2, a lament in which a knight claims his pain is too great for him to keep on singing and asks the ladies to think of him after he has died of love, one finds the following lines:

Zer werlte ist wîp   ein fröide grôz:
bî den so muoz man hie genesen.

doch es mîn lîp   noch nie genôz,
mîn herze deist in bî gewesen:
ich hete ie zuo der werlte muot.   (115,19–23)

At this point, where the poet so clearly demonstrates his knowledge
of the importance of the lady's role in courtly society as a source of
fröide, one might also expect some sign of his awareness of the "doc-
trine" of the ennobling or elevating power of love. Instead of a belief
in the educative or uplifting force of love, however, one encounters
only another indication of the destructive effect of love when, at the
end of the poem, the speaker hints that his sorrow will be the death
of him. Despite the fact that he has not benefited from his devotion
to women, he declares he is unwilling to say anything but good
things about them. And if he dies—presumably of love—he asks the
ladies to remember him.

12. Heinrich von Rugge

Three of the ten *Lieder* by Heinrich von Rugge in *MF* (102,14, 102,27, and 108,14) have nothing to do with either love or women and hence need not be considered in this investigation. Of the remaining seven, four contain neither the slightest trace of the idea of ennobling love nor any situations that would have lent themselves to its introduction. In 107,35 the speaker merely says that he must take his leave, but that he will be miserable as long as he cannot see the woman whose greeting would please him more than if he were to be made emperor. In 101,15 the knight laments the fact that his lady, apparently unmoved by his distress, has not rewarded his devoted service. He is a prisoner of love, which has robbed him of his senses. He knows his situation is hopeless, but he has so succumbed to his passion that he can no longer do what he feels he ought to do:

> daz tuot diu minne: diu nimt mir die sinne,
> wande ich mich kêre   an ir lêre   ze vil,
> diu mich der nôt niht erlâzen enwil,
> sît ich niht mâze begunde   nochn kunde.   (101,19–22)

Once again the destructive, or at least the debilitating force of love is emphasized. Instead of contributing to his betterment, love has paralyzed his ability to control himself.

The other two songs in this group speak of love requited. In 102,1 the speaker laments that he has lost his lady's favor, though she had once said that he was dearer to her than life itself; in 108,6 the man rejoices in the coming of summer, for, he says, "ein wîp mich des getroestet hât / daz ich der zît geniezen sol" (108,11–12). Neither poem, however, gives any indication that the ennobling power of love played a role in gaining the lady's love. To be sure, the latter poem ends with the words: "nu bin ich hôhes muotes: daz ist wol" (108,13), but there is no evidence that self-improvement is involved with this elevation of the spirit, which here quite clearly is the result of love's fulfillment.

Three songs of Heinrich von Rugge contain passages that would have presented easy opportunities for the introduction of the idea of ennobling love. In 101,7, a short hymn of praise to a lady, the speaker, after stating that he would rather have his lady live "nâch

êren" (101,8) than have power over the whole world, expresses his
admiration for her character with the following words:

> in kunde an ir erkennen nie
> enkein daz dinc dazs ie begie
> daz wandelbaere möhte sîn.   (101,11–13)

Here might have been the place to introduce some remarks about the
influence of her perfection on him, for example, that her behavior
inspired him to become like her. Instead of words to this effect, how-
ever, one meets only the statement that "ir güete gêt mir an daz
herze mîn" (101,14).

The other two poems in this category are not love songs, but po-
ems containing ethical observations at least partially of concern to
this study. In 107,27 the speaker tells his audience that what is impor-
tant is a woman's inner qualities, not her beauty. But he fails to say
anything about a good woman's qualities being a guide for the self-
improvement of the admiring male. The other poem, 108,22, is a
general lament over the sad state of society, including the decline of
love service. The speaker agrees with those who claim that joy is
disappearing from courtly society; nevertheless, he concludes his
poem on a somewhat optimistic note. Among ladies, he says, the
downhill trend is not as pronounced as some would have him
believe:

> wan ist ir einiu niht rehte gemuot,
> dâ bî vind ich schiere   wol drî oder viere
> die zallen zîten sint höfsch unde guot.   (109,5–8)

Just as in the case of 107,27, however, nothing is said specifically
about the educative function of the noble lady in relation to the
knight.

The only example of the theme of ennobling love in the poems of
Heinrich von Rugge is found in his *Leich*, which is essentially an
extended crusade appeal. Although most of the poem deals with
strictly religious questions and hence does not fall within the scope
of this investigation, two short sections, X and X^b, present the
knight's conflict between duty to God and service to noble ladies.
The poet's views on the matter are quite similar to those of Friedrich
von Hausen in 48,13. A conversation between two women reveals
what they think of a knight who would prefer to stay at home and
"die zît wol vertrîben   vil schône mit wîben" (98,31–32). Such a
man is "nieht bastes wert" (98,34), says one of them; she continues:
"Waz schol er danne ze friuntschefte mir? / vil gerne i'n verbir"

(98,35–36). Clearly it is implied that such a shirker is not worthy of the lady's affection. Here the idea of the ennobling or educative power of love is manifested in an active demand of the lady: in order to merit the lady's love, the knight must fulfill his obligation to serve God as a crusader. Thus the attitude of the lady is supposed to have an educative effect on the knight.

In addition to the authentic poems just discussed, the fourteen songs designated as *unecht* in *MF* under the name of Heinrich von Rugge must also be examined. Three of these offer no opportunity to think in terms of ennobling love. The speaker in the one stanza of 109,36 tells in general terms of his relationship to society and of his determination to sing the praises of good women no matter how unhappy his own lot might be. Because he does not say or imply anything that touches upon the topic of this study, the poem need not be examined further. In 109,9 the speaker complains that his joy in summer has been turned to woe by his unrequited love. All his sorrow would come to an end, he says, if only he could spend two days and a night with his lady. He concludes by saying he would not care how others mistreated him as long as she showed him her favor. The third song, 106,15, presents a woman as a suitor who apparently has been rebuffed by the man of her choice. In this poem, however, the world of *Hohe Minne* is turned upside down, for the lady speaks of *her* steadfastness and of the fact that *she* should be rewarded for *her* service. Obviously, there is no place here for the traditional idea of the ennobling force of love.

Three of the songs categorized as *unecht* under the name of Heinrich von Rugge present situations that would have lent themselves to the introduction of the theme of ennobling love. All of these missed opportunities are connected with the idea of the lady's goodness. In 103,35, after saying in the first stanza that he is a fool for loving a woman who does not want him, the speaker extols her virtues in the second strophe, concluding that she is so perfect that no man is suitable for her. Thus her perfection, instead of acting as an inspiration, has the opposite effect. Despite his lavish praise, however, he does find one fault with her in the final stanza when he states it is not appropriate for anyone to accept service without offering a reward. It is clear that he places his hopes of success on the feudal principle rather than on the notion of becoming worthy.

This same reliance on the feudal concept can be found in 104,24. After generalizing about the evils of boasting, the speaker states that the hope of receiving his lady's *genâde* is the only thing that will be able to sustain his joy. This time, however, his praise of her goodness is directly connected with his belief in the justice of the expected compensation:

> Diu albegarwe waere guot,
> diu soldes mich geniezen lân
> daz si sô vil der tugende tuot.
> ich bin ir worden undertân.
> genâde, frouwe, saelic wîp,
> und troeste sêre mînen lîp.   (105,6–11)

Thus her goodness should let him benefit from the fact that he has become her vassal. Nowhere is there an indication that he must earn her love by self-improvement, or that her virtues should inspire him to become like her. To be sure, it could be argued that the speaker's discussion in the first strophe of the bad habit of boasting and his determination to refrain from such conduct indicate a desire on his part to conform to a high standard of behavior and hence might be considered as evidence of the idea of the ennobling power of love. Unfortunately, however, because his concern with boasting does not relate in any way to the rest of the poem and nothing points to any connection between his wish to keep free of this vice and his hope of attaining the lady's favor, it is not possible to view this as an example of the educative effect of love.

In 105,15 the knight complains that he is separated from his beloved lady, apparently because duty demands that he be with *friunden*. Although not explicitly stated here, it is perfectly possible that the fulfillment of a feudal obligation keeps him away from his lady. In such a situation one might very well expect to find the notion of the morally uplifting power of love in the form of the lady encouraging the knight to do his duty. On the contrary, however, the poet's portrayal of the lady reveals that this is not the case:

> si zürnet sêre, waene ich wol,
> diu guote diech da sende lie,
> und hât von mînen schulden leit.   (105,17–19)

Clearly the goodness of this woman that is so highly praised—"ezn lebt niht wîbes alse guot" (105,23)—has no salutary effect in this regard. The view that a good woman does not bestow her love on a man who fails to live up to his responsibilities is completely lacking here.

Four of the unauthentic songs under Heinrich von Rugge's name present situations that either tempt one to think in terms of, or come fairly close to the idea of, ennobling love. In the first strophe of the *Wechsel*, 107,7, a knight who claims he is ready to do whatever a certain lady commands says that she should make him happy by letting him hear "liebiu maere" (107,16). In the second stanza the lady makes it clear that he has nothing to worry about, for she tells a messenger to inform the knight how very much she wants to see him and hear of his joy. Although the knight's statement that he is prepared to do whatever his lady desires might conjure up the notion of the educative power of love, nothing that either the man or the woman says here indicates that the fulfillment of her wishes is connected with a possible self-improvement on his part.

The lament, 106,24, introduces the question of *staete* and with it touches upon the notion of the educative function of love. The speaker, after a brief *Natureingang*, claims that even if he had a choice of any woman on earth, *unstaete* would never lead him to select anyone but his beloved. She has found him to be *staete*, he asserts, and by rights she should reward him with her love. But he says his hope of success is being destroyed by the machinations of "valscher liute" (107,1), leaving his heart sorely oppressed. Yet even this misery could be overcome, he concludes, if his beloved would only do his bidding. Although the knight does not state specifically that his loyalty entitles him to a reward, he certainly implies that this is the case. There is, to be sure, no indication that his steadfastness actually represents an improvement in his character. Yet the emphasis on the man's belief that he should be rewarded for acting in an exemplary way does come close to an awareness of the ennobling force of love.

In 99,29, a variation of the *Wechsel*-form, the man not only hopes that his lady will consider him worthy of a reward, but also states that he has desired it "ân alle valsche missetât" (100,6). Unfortunately for him he has until now reaped only sorrow for his devotion and good behavior, and he complains that he has been unjustly treated. A possible explanation of her attitude does occur to him, however: "doch denke ich si versuoche mich / ob ich iht staete künne sîn" (100,19–20). He responds to this sentiment as follows: "solt ich ez bî dem eide sagen, / sô was ez ie der wille mîn" (100,21–22). The final stanza of the poem, in which the lady speaks, does not throw any light on the situation because she does not directly address the problems he has been discussing. Instead, she talks in the most general terms about the sorrow that seems to be inevitably connected with love. At most one can conclude that her coolness to the knight is based on her fear of the misery that is sure to result from becoming involved with him. At any rate, there is not the slightest suggestion in her words that she is testing the knight to see whether he is worthy of her love.

The idea of the lady putting the knight to the test was discussed earlier in connection with a poem by the Burggraf von Rietenburg.[1] Such a concept could very well be related to that of the educative power of love, that is, if the point of it, or the result of it, was improvement of the man's character to make him deserving of the lady's love. In the poem under consideration, however, this does not appear to be the case, for there is no indication of a betterment in the general character traits mentioned. The knight has wooed the lady "ân alle valsche missetât" and has always been true to her; thus he feels he has always been worthy of her love. Again, it is a question of *being*, rather than *becoming*, deserving. Nonetheless, the knight's recognition of the need to conform to a high standard of behavior in order to win the lady's favor clearly approaches the idea of the educative effect of love.

In the single strophe of 100,34 the poet plays with the noun *minne* and the verb *minnen*, employing these forms a total of twenty times in the eleven lines of the poem. Although this *tour de force* need not otherwise be of concern in this investigation, its opening lines do indicate an aspect of the problem of the ennobling power of love that has been observed several times in the course of this discussion:

> Minne minnet staeten man.
> ob er ûf minne minnen wil,
> sô sol im minnen lôn geschehen.   (100,34–36)

In other words, if a man is steadfast in his relationship to his lady, he can expect to receive the reward of love. Thus one can see here another example of the view that comes close to the idea of ennobling love, namely, that exemplary behavior on the part of the man will lead to the desired goal.

More or less clear examples of the idea of the ennobling power of love are found in four of the poems listed as *unecht* under Heinrich von Rugge's name. In 103,3 the knight, who claims he has given up all other women for the sake of his lady, concludes his rapturous praises of his beloved, which here are not qualified in any way by complaints, with the following words:

> si tiuret vil der sinne mîn.
> ich bin noch staete als ich ie pflac
> und will daz iemer gerne sîn.   (103,24–26)

Why no lamentations are found in the three stanzas in which the knight speaks becomes obvious from the loving words of his lady in the last strophe. There is no doubt about the reciprocal nature of the relationship:

daz ist uns beiden guot gewin,
daz er mir wol gedienen kan
und ich sîn friunt dar umbe bin.   (103,32–34)

Although the lady does not refer specifically to the idea of an educative effect of love, the knight's renunciation of other women would appear to point in this direction.[2] In addition, his statement that "si tiuret vil der sinne mîn" can certainly be interpreted as indicating an improvement in his inner being and hence be viewed as an example of the ennobling power of love.

In the *Wechsel*, 110,8, the lady herself is clearly aware of her role in putting pressure on the knight to conform to a certain standard of behavior. If he wants her "ze friunde" (110,12), she says in her strophe, then he must do what is best "mit allen sînen sinnen" (110,13), and he should make sure that news of any inconstancy on his part never reaches her ears. In the next stanza the knight rejoices at the prospect of achieving his goal, for he is determined to fulfill the conditions she has set and is ready to accept the consequences if he does not. Even though it cannot be shown that the knight's character has definitely improved, the lady's insistence on upright behavior and constancy as a prerequisite for attaining her love certainly must be viewed as an example of the ennobling power of love.[3]

In another *Wechsel*-type poem, 110,26, a knight is seeking advice on how to keep the love of his lady whose perfection he so lavishly praises. Although no such counsel is actually given in the poem, the words of the woman in the fragmentary last stanza seem to point toward the notion that exemplary behavior will assure the knight of favorable treatment. For with respect to the question of whether she should contribute to his joy, the lady says: "des er betwinget   mich mit sîner güete. / an mir er niemer missevert" (111,8–9). Thus the lady definitely seems to be aware of a certain obligation on her part to reward the knight for having shown himself worthy of her. Hence one can also speak here, as in the case of the previously discussed poem, of at least one aspect of the ennobling power of love. In addition, one other statement in the poem could be viewed as an instance of a role played by the same power. In the course of extolling the virtues of the lady, the knight says: "ir güete mich gehoehet hât" (110,32). Precisely what *gehoehet* means in this context is not clear. It might be used simply to convey the idea of "raised his spirits" or "made him feel good," in which case the term "ennoblement" in the sense it has been used in this investigation would not apply. On the other hand, it could be interpreted as indicating a moral raising or uplifting, because, according to the "theory" of ennoblement, the woman's goodness is supposed to have an exemplary effect on the knight, and there is no doubt that in this sentence *güete* is the subject of *gehoehet*. Therefore, the statement could very well mean: "Her goodness has been responsible for my moral betterment."

At first reading the first two stanzas of 105,24 do not appear to have any direct bearing on the problem of love. Here the poet sings the praises of anyone "der sô gewendet sînen muot / daz er daz beste gerne tuot" (105,28–29), and then seems to consider himself such a person when he says: "Ich hân der werlte ir reht getân / ie nâch der mâze als ez mir stuont" (105,33–34). If, then, things should not go well with him, it will not be his fault, for he has tried his very best. In the last stanza, however, he implicitly relates his previous generalizations to the question of love by speaking of it as the greatest joy the world has to offer. The implication is clear: if he expects that making an effort to achieve exemplary behavior will help him attain happiness, and if the greatest happiness is to be found in love, there must be a connection between such behavior and the hope of success in matters of the heart. Under these circumstances it is clear that the idea of the ennobling power of love is (at least indirectly) reflected.

13. Hartwic von Rute

Two of the four poems preserved under the name of Hartwic von Rute contain neither a hint of the idea of ennobling love nor any easy opportunities for its introduction. In 117,1 love has the exact opposite of an edifying effect; namely, it causes that state of paralysis encountered so often before. The knight is so much a prisoner of love that his will has been rendered useless. He is bound at all times, he says, "als ein man   der niht enkan / gebâren nâch dem willen sîn" (117,3–5). All his efforts are concentrated on getting close enough to his beloved to be able to declare to her his most intimate desires. Under these circumstances, it is difficult to imagine that the educative effect of love is in any way connected with the achievement of the knight's goal.

The happiness the knight will experience if his lady permits him to continue to court her is expressed in 117,14. His heart will leap with joy and he will be inspired to sing "ein hôhez niuwez liet" (117,25). Although he is elated at the prospect that his lady will accept his service, there is no indication that elevation in the sense of ennoblement is involved.

A situation in the third poem, 117,26, might lead one to think in terms of ennobling love, although the overall effect love has on the knight is anything but educative. The sight of his beloved arouses in him the desire to rush toward her and take her in his arms. What restrains him from embracing her is not the presence of others, but rather the fear that he would lose whatever favor he now enjoys. It might be argued that this restraint represents an educative effect of his love service, that is, by developing self-control he becomes more pleasing to the lady and worthier of her love. Although such an interpretation is possible, nothing in the poem itself justifies such a conclusion. Under the circumstances, it seems more plausible to assume that the knight's restraint is motivated simply by the immediate fear of incurring the lady's wrath, rather than by his realization of the need to practice self-control as part of a program of self-improvement that would make him deserving of the lady's affection.

The last of the four poems by Hartwic von Rute, 116,1, contains both a clear example of the ennobling power of love and an unseized opportunity to introduce a variation of such a notion. The speaker says that only a certain lovely lady can end his misery. The strength of his love is so great that even in the face of death, when he has heard others confess their sins, he has considered his greatest woe the fact that his beloved has not shown him *genâde*. The first stanza of this song contains a passage indicating an awareness of the notion of the educative·power of love:

si solte mich durch got geniezen lân
daz ich ie bin gewesen in grôzer huote
dazs iemer kunne valsch an mir verstân.   (116,5–7)

This appears to be a deliberate attempt on the part of the knight to exhibit exemplary behavior while serving his lady, and it is clear that he believes his efforts should be rewarded. It is also implied that his behavior represents an improvement, because he has taken great pains to see that his deportment meets with her approval. Thus, in this instance one can speak of an attempt at self-improvement, presumably for the purpose of becoming worthy of the lady's favor.

The fragmentary last stanza of the poem opens up an area that could have touched upon another aspect of the problem under investigation. Here the poet says that he realizes no one can serve both the emperor and the ladies. Even though the conclusion of the song is missing, it is clear from the speaker's statement that, just as was the case in Bernger von Horheim's 114,21,[1] the ennobling power of love is not called upon to mediate the conflict between the knight's duties to his feudal lord and his beloved lady. This might have been an occasion to express the idea that the knight could become worthy of the lady's love by fulfilling his obligations as a knight, just as the crusader could merit the lady's favor by participating in a crusade. But the poet fails to take advantage of this opportunity.

14. Bligger von Steinach

Of the three poems attributed to Bligger von Steinach, one, 119,13, consists wholly of ethical observations unrelated to *minne* and need not be considered here. In the second poem, 118,1, which deals with problems of love only in its first stanza, the poet fails to make use of an occasion to introduce the idea of ennobling love in connection with the theme of faithfulness. He laments his "alte swaere" (118,1) and declares he knows his lady is tormenting him so much to discourage him from serving her. But he will not give up: "nein, ich enmac noch enlât mich mîn triuwe" (118,6). He is determined to persist in the hope of winning her favor. Nothing is said, however, about how he intends to gain her love. And as far as the lady is concerned, it is clear from her attempt to discourage him that she is not playing an active educative role in her relationship to the knight. Thus his *triuwe* does not result from his lady's insistence or represent an improvement in his character that will make him worthy of her love.

The opportunity missed in 118,1 is seized in the third poem, 118,19, which contains a clear if somewhat limited example of ennobling love. Here the poet bewails the long, joyless years of service for which he has received no reward. He will persist in his devotion, however, for he does not know how else to alleviate the pain in his heart. If he did know of some other means, he says, he certainly would do whatever was necessary. He seems to feel, however, that his renunciation of all other women is sufficient reason for being rewarded:

hulf ez mich iht, sô waere daz mîn wân,
swer alliu wîp durch eine gar verbaere,
daz man in des geniezen solte lân.   (119,3–5)

To the extent that the requirement of constancy places a demand on the knight to demonstrate a kind of exemplary behavior, and to the extent that his conduct has improved by giving up all other women, one can view the poet's awareness of this situation as an aspect of the educative function of love. The knight's inability to envision any other way of reaching his goal, however, shows the narrowness of his view, for he does not seem to be conscious of any broader scope of the idea of self-improvement as a means of gaining the lady's favor.

51

15. Ulrich von Gutenberg

Ulrich von Gutenberg is represented in *MF* by two poems, a six-stanza song, 77,36, and an extensive *Minneleich*, 69,1–77,35. The song, beginning with a nature introduction and exhibiting most of the typical features of the laments of unrequited love found in the lyrics of the period, contains one passage that might tempt one to think in terms of ennobling love and another that presents a clear example of it. In the first of these the speaker says of himself:

> ich was wilde, swie vil ich gesanc:
> ir schoeniu ougen daz wâren die ruote
> dâ mite si mich von êrste betwanc. (78,21–23)

Undoubtedly the knight is saying that this lady has, in effect, tamed him. Whether one can speak here in terms of an educative influence of the lady on the knight, however, is not clear. Certainly the idea of taming something that is wild implies a bending of the will of the tamed creature to that of the master. But there is nothing in the text to indicate that what the mistress demanded of him—if she demanded anything at all—was supposed to have a morally uplifting effect on him. It is perfectly possible that the above passage merely means that the knight, formerly free and wild, is now entirely in her power.[1]

The second passage in question points unambiguously toward a consciousness of the notion of the educative function of love. Here the knight expresses his hope that *triuwe* will result in greater compensation than *unstaete*, and he reminds the ladies of their obligation to keep in mind that, "swâ man weste einen valschaften man, / den solten alliu wîp gerne vermîden" (78,30–31). In addition, he will consider his lady's failure to give him his due as "sünde und grôz missetât" (79,5). Obviously the poet is aware of the theory that a knight who strives toward exemplary behavior is deserving of his lady's love. What is also clear, however, is that the lady in this case appears to have forgotten her part of the bargain. In view of the completely inactive role of the lady in this second passage, it now seems less likely that the idea of taming discussed above can be considered as an example of an educative influence of the lady on the knight.

Although Ulrich von Gutenberg's *Leich* runs through almost the entire range of sentiments found in the world of *Hohe Minne*, most of the approximately 350 verses of the poem contain no trace of the idea of the ennobling power of love. Instead, one is much more conscious of the knight's feeling of hopelessness. He refers to himself as a captive who is completely in the power of his lady (72,37–38, 70,27–29, 71,25, and 71,31–32) and so robbed of his senses (72,2 and 76,14–18) that he can no longer function effectively (76,11).

Certain situations in the *Leich* revolving around the notion of the lady's goodness, however, do present easy opportunities for the introduction of the idea of ennobling love. But the poet does not use the occasion to portray the woman's good qualities as a model for the man. On the contrary, most of the knight's pleas for a reward are based not on the premise that he has earned it by having become more like her (and hence better), but rather on an appeal to the lady's kindness and sense of mercy. Thus, for example, he says it is not fitting for the victor to kill the vanquished or for a lord not to show mercy to a bondsman (70,19–71,1). Again and again he points out that the lady's treatment of him is not in accord with her virtues. She should have mercy on him, he says, "daz zimt wol dîner güete" (72,22), and it would be a black mark against her "güete und ir mangiu tugent" (74,1) if she were to let him waste away his youth under this burden. He even urges her to keep in mind that it is not consonant with her goodness that she deprives him of "gwerb und fuoge" (76,11).

Finally, the *Leich* does contain a few passages indicating an awareness of the idea of the ennobling effect of love. In section III the poet says he believes his heart will someday receive compensation when his lady becomes truly conscious of the pain he suffers and of the fact that he has acted "mit zühten schône" (70,25) and "ân widerwanc" (70,26). Although a connection between his hoped-for reward and the way he has behaved in the face of suffering and distress is not explicitly stated, such a relationship of cause and effect does seem to be implied. The assumption appears to be that unflinching and decorous behavior in adversity proves that the knight is or has become worthy of the lady. A similar situation can be found in section IV, where the poet bids his lady, who first won his heart "mit schoenen siten / in zühten" (73,23–24), to remember—and act accordingly by rewarding him—that he will never abandon his service and that he will continue to bear his pain "mit zühten schône" (73,37). Here, in contrast to the references to the woman's good qualities mentioned above, the poet makes it easy to regard the lady as a model for the knight to imitate by using almost the same words to describe her deportment and that of the knight.

16. Heinrich von Veldeke

The importance of the ennobling power of love in some of the songs of Heinrich von Veldeke has been greatly exaggerated.[1] Even though the theories concerning the role of this motif in certain of Veldeke's poems have been refuted elsewhere,[2] it will still be necessary for the purposes of this study to examine the entire body of his lyric production to establish the extent of the influence of this theme.

Of the twenty-seven songs under the name of Heinrich von Veldeke dealing with the theme of love,[3] sixteen contain neither a trace of the idea of ennobling love nor any situations that might have lent themselves to its introduction. Two of these emphasize the remoteness between the knight and the lady. In the first stanza of 58,11 the man curses those who disapprove of his relationship to a lady, but wishes his supporters well. He then praises her beauty and begs her for *genâde*, indicating the great distance between them with the words: "der sunnen an ich dich / sô schîne mich der mâne" (58,21–22). In the second strophe he says he could rejoice in the coming of spring if he were not weighed down with so many cares. The image of the sun and the moon is used similarly in the single short stanza of 64,34 to convey the lack of closeness between the knight and the lady. After stating that those who have never been overwhelmed by love the way he has been cannot truly understand his predicament, the speaker says he has directed his love to a place where it shines less than the moon in the presence of the sun. The hopelessness of his situation is thus conveyed by the notion of his love making as much impression on his beloved as the moon does when the sun is shining. In neither poem is there any hint that the lady's love could be gained by means of self-improvement. Whereas in the former the man's hope of attaining his goal is based on the assumption that the lofty mistress will have pity on the lowly vassal in distress, in the latter, where the lady takes no notice of the knight's existence, one can hardly imagine the man thinking in terms of the ennobling power of love.

In the third poem of this group of sixteen—the single stanza of 58,35—the speaker uses a literary allusion to help express the strength of his love. He says his beloved should show him thanks because he loves her even more than Tristan loved Isolde, and he concludes with the plea that his lady should be his and let him be hers. In contrast to the situation in 58,11, here the man's hope does not have as its foundation the distance inherent in the feudal relationship, but rather the assumption of at least the possibility of a mutual affection. Nonetheless, there is no trace of the notion that self-betterment will make him worthy. Instead, it is with the idea of the overwhelming power of his love that he wants to persuade her to be his.

Three of the songs in the group under discussion emphasize the destructive nature of love, expressing the idea that the knight's love will lead him to his grave. After an extended *Natureingang* in the first two stanzas of 62,25, in which the speaker reveals not only his pleasure in the song of the birds as they pair off for mating, but also his own desire to be happy in the springtime, he finally comes to talk about his own love in the concluding strophe. Here he begins by wishing he could gain his lady's favor. He fears he will be destroyed if she does not deign to accept some form of atonement from him so that he can hope for her *genâde*. But his expiation (for loving her so much) should not be death, he says, for God has never commanded anyone to die willingly. The knight's reluctance to die of love is also expressed in 66,24. After stating that beautiful words combined with sweet music can comfort someone who is troubled, he confesses that he sings with sadness because his beloved has left him too long unsolaced. It would be better, he says, for her to console him than for him to die on account of her. She has the power of life or death over him, but if he dies, it will not be willingly. In the single stanza of 66,9 he pleads with Love, who has vanquished him, to induce his beloved to increase his good fortune. For if his fate is to be like the swan's, which sings before it dies, Love's loss will indeed be too great. All three of these poems, with their emphasis on the negative, destructive effects of a love that seems hopelessly unrequited, and with the knight's fear that death will be his reward, leave no room for any appearance of the idea of the ennobling power of love.

Five of the songs in this category deal either explicitly or implicitly with the theme of requited love. Success in love is treated in a somewhat humorous and lighthearted vein in the three stanzas of 63,28. In the first stanza the speaker says that his beloved is so good and beautiful that he would place the imperial crown on her head if he were the emperor. He then prays that she will reward him when he sees her again, for he knows what he will do if she is still the way she was when he left her. In the second strophe he confesses that she has treated him well and brought him great joy. Because he saw that she knew how to deceive those who are supposed to watch over her just as the rabbit can outwit the greyhound, he does not worry about the future. Finally, he says he would rather be with her and rich than far away and poor. The theme of separation of the lovers in 63,28 also appears in the single stanza of 64,17. Here the speaker says the song of the birds makes him joyful. It turns out, however, that it is really his beloved who makes it possible for him to be without cares even though he is far away from home. Although it is not stated explicitly that the lady has responded favorably to the knight's affection, the fact that his love can keep him happy even in adversity certainly points in the direction of love fulfilled.

Like 64,17, the next two poems to be discussed, 64,26 and 65,28, also begin with nature introductions. Although in 65,28 a bond of mutual love linking the knight and the lady is not actually mentioned, the warm and optimistic tone of the song does make the assumption of such affection plausible. Here the knight just says that the singing of the birds indicates the coming of summer and therefore it is appropriate for him to turn to where his heart has always been subject to love. In 64,26 winter has arrived, but despite the drabness of the season the knight says that the hopes he had of winning love are going to be fulfilled. He is sure his courtship will have a happy end; he will find that love is good and he will take possession of it. In 66,16 the knight says that, if love could conquer Solomon, the wisest king who ever lived, it should be no surprise that he, too, has been overpowered by love. A happy conclusion to the affair is revealed by the final verse: "den solt hebbe ich van here te lône" (66,23).

Neither in the poems discussed above where the knight has clearly received the reward of love, nor in the songs where a successful culmination to the knight's courtship is anticipated, is there any indication that the woman has granted (or will grant) her love because the man has become worthy through self-improvement. And as there is also never any mention of what induced the lady to fulfill her lover's desires, the opportunity to introduce the notion of ennobling love in connection with love's fulfillment never arises.

The last five of the sixteen songs presently under consideration could be classified as short aphoristic poems dealing more or less closely with the general topic of love and society. Three of these express the poet's contempt for the *bôsen*, the *wrûgere*, and the *nîdegen* who are all the enemies of love. May God save us from *bôsen*, the speaker wishes in 60,29. But even though these miserable creatures are everywhere, he feels one should not be too concerned about them after all, for they are like people who look for pears on beech trees. In 61,9 the poet says he is glad the *nîdegen* hate him, for their venom will only eat at their own hearts and destroy them that much sooner. Despite their animosity he is determined to remain among the joyful. The last of these three songs, 65,21, points out the foolishness of those who put too close a watch on women. Such a person bears the switch with which he beats upon himself. The other two aphoristic poems, 67,25 and 62,11, are more loosely connected with the general theme of love and society. Whereas in 67,25 the poet says that only those who love or have loved are joyful, and not the *dumbe* whose hearts have never been touched by love, in 62,11 the speaker says he is depressed to hear that women hate gray hair. He has nothing but disdain for those who prefer their lovers *dump* rather than *wîs*, who would rather have new tin than old gold. None of these songs either touches in any way on the question of the educative function of love or offers any opportunity to think in such terms.

Four of Heinrich von Veldeke's songs contain situations that would have lent themselves more or less easily to the introduction of the motif of ennobling love. Three of these are short aphoristic poems whose common theme is the decline of true love. In 61,1 the poet complains that frivolity and evil ways, which are the enemies of love, have become widespread and there appears to be little hope of change for the better. Similarly, in 61,9 the speaker says *rehte minne* is no longer cultivated. Instead, *bôse seden* are taught, and the contrast is lamentable. In addition, he says men speak ill of the ladies, which is not a very smart thing to do inasmuch as men's happiness depends on them. Finally, in 65,13 the poet says that the world is sad and dreary and getting worse because those who used to serve love are turning away from it. In these three lyrics, which contrast the way things used to be with the present state of affairs regarding true love, one certainly might expect some mention of decay with reference to the idea of the ennobling power of love. But there is not even a hint of an awareness of this problem.

The last of the poems in the group of four under discussion, 67,3, is a lament in which the speaker admits he has lived in misery for seven years rather than say anything that might displease his lady. She, on the other hand, has heard what he has had to say and still desires that he continue his lamentations. Thus he concludes that love is the same as it used to be. Here the extreme length of the knight's courtship might have presented an occasion for the introduction of the idea of ennobling love. But the opportunity is not seized, for there is no indication that the purpose of the knight's long service is self-improvement in order to become worthy of the lady's love. The knight's fear of offending his beloved overrides all other considerations.

Five poems of Heinrich von Veldeke either tempt one to think in terms of ennobling love or present situations that come very close to the idea of the educative function of love. In one of these, 59,23, a song of requited love, the treatment of the notion of long and arduous service—in contrast to that in 67,3 discussed above—might seem to point in the direction of the problem under investigation. The speaker says that whoever has "rechte minne / sunder rouwe ende âne wanc" (59,30–31) has every reason to thank God. He confesses that he is happy on account of a lady who has caused him to turn from sorrow. He feels like a great lord because he has embraced his beloved who has given him *rechte minne*. At the end of the song he says that those who envy him his good fortune do not concern him. They cannot prevent him from feeling joy as long as she who let him endure pain so long for the sake of *rechte minne* wants to see him. It is clear that here the knight's success has come only after a long period of suffering, and that the lady apparently has deliberately made him bear "lange pîne" (60,12). Although it is perfectly possible to link the necessity of enduring hardship in the pursuit of love with the notion of self-improvement for the sake of becoming worthy of love, these concepts are not necessarily associated. There could be, for example, any number of reasons unrelated to the idea of ennobling love why the lady made the knight suffer. She might have thought it improper to show her affection too soon; she could have wanted to see whether her knight was serious enough about her to be willing to bear torment for her; or she might have believed that only through an extended period of service would her knight have earned the reward of love. Because the song fails to give a specific reason why the man had to wait so long for love's fulfillment, it is not possible to cite this poem as an example of the educative effect of love.

Another song, 67,33, also treats the theme of lengthy service, although not in as much detail as 59,23. The speaker begins with the statement that whoever can serve and wait well will ultimately be successful. He then applies this saying to himself by asserting he has served his beloved unwaveringly since he first saw her. And when his lady rewards him, he says, they will know how to dupe those who keep watch over them. In the second stanza the knight says it would not be right for him to be unhappy, because all his sorrow is coming to an end. Love enfolds his heart, he says, a love in which no *dumpheit* plays a role, but rather joy that banishes care. As was the case in 59,23, nothing specific is mentioned or implied here to link length of service with the notion of the educative function of love. The mention of the lack of *dumpheit* in his love, however, might tempt one to think in terms of ennobling love, inasmuch as a progression away from *dumpheit* in the course of the man's courtship would point to the idea that self-improvement has merited him the lady's affection. But there is nothing in the poem to indicate such a development.[4] It is perfectly possible to believe that no *dumpheit* was ever involved in the man's behavior during his service to the lady.

In the third song in this group, 63,20, the speaker prays that God may persuade his lady to accept his songs graciously, for he would very much like to avoid saying anything that would offend her and result in his having to keep away from her. The oaths of love and loyalty bind him fast, he says, and for this reason he fears his beloved just as a child fears the switch. The simile closing the poem might incline one to think of the educative function of love. The notion of the man imagining the lady standing over him with a whip could be interpreted as her demanding of him a certain standard of behavior in order to be worthy of her favor. Such a view hardly seems justifiable here, however, for the poem offers no indication that the lady has actively encouraged him to behave in a certain way. All that can be said is that he lives in fear that something he says might make her turn away from him.

The last two poems in the set under discussion—56,1 and 57,10—make up what can be called an extended *Wechsel* involving a knight and his lady. In 56,1 the man says he is sad despite the coming of spring, for the joy a certain lady once gave him has now turned to sorrow as a result of his *dumpheit*. He has lost his lady's favor, indeed, incurred her wrath, because he was so inflamed by her beauty that he forgot himself and asked her to embrace him. He ascribes the loss of her good graces to his "al te hôge gerende minne" (56,19), which brought him "al ût den sinne" (56,20), and he views his loss of control as a lack of *wîsheit* because he is well aware of the unhappy consequences of his action. In addition, he attributes his asking for an embrace to his "dumbe wân" (57,3), and his desire for her he describes as having been immoderate ("ûter mâten," 57,4). Clearly, then, he feels he has not lived up to the lady's standard of behavior and, as a result, she has withdrawn her favor.

The woman's version of the incident is presented in 57,10. She states that she had granted a man "vele gûdes" (57,20) because he had previously served her well. This state of affairs changed drastically, however, when he misbehaved by asking her to embrace him. She had been favorably inclined toward him because she had thought he was *hovesch*. Now that he has demanded an "al te rîken solt" (58,1), an "al te lôse minne" (58,3), she does not care if he has to suffer for it, and she lets him know that he does not understand the rules of the game.

The situation presented in this set of poems at least comes close to the idea of the educative power of love, inasmuch as it is based on the premise that the lady's favor depends on the man's conforming to a certain standard of behavior. Yet the turn of events depicted is the reverse of the principle of the edifying effect of love. Instead of the lady's love being attained by self-betterment, a deterioration in behavior has led to a withdrawal of her approval. This state of affairs might have set the stage for a proper appearance of the concept of the ennobling power of love. If the knight were now to try to improve his deportment, he perhaps could hope to regain her good graces. But nothing in the poems clearly indicates that the lady is willing to give him a second chance.

Another place to look for evidence of the educative result of love would be in whatever could be assumed about the relationship prior to the knight's faux pas. In other words, is there any indication that the lady granted the knight what little favor she did because he had become worthy of it through self-improvement? Here, too, nothing points to such an assumption. It is clear only that the lady was favorably inclined toward him because she thought he was *hovesch*. Nothing implies that he learned courtliness, or even refined his courtly ways, in her service to make her consider him deserving of her affection.

Two poems of Heinrich von Veldeke—61,33 and 60,13—remain to be discussed. They both can be called songs in praise of love, and they are the only lyrics of Veldeke where the notion of the edifying force of love is clearly discernible. The first stanza of 61,33 begins in an aphoristic style with the assertion that whoever is so wise in the ways of love that he can serve love and bear pain for the sake of love is surely "ein vele minnesâlech man" (61,36). Because everything good comes from love, the poet continues, and because love produces "reinen mût" (62,2), he asks what he would do without love. Speaking of his own love in the second stanza, he claims that he loves his lady steadfastly and that he knows her love is pure. If there is anything false about his love, then there is no such thing as true love. Finally, he thanks her for his love, gives assurances that his singing is devoted to her love, and concludes with the general statement that whoever thinks that love is burdensome is *dump*. Here the man's willingness to accept the *arebeit* associated with true love is obviously connected with the notion that such efforts are worthwhile because of all the good things that come from love, including *reinen mût*. The implication is clearly that the lover becomes a better person as a result of having loved. One must assume, however, that the poet is speaking of mutual love, not unrequited love. Thus it is not possible to cite this poem as an example of the idea that love can have an ennobling effect even if the suitor is rejected.

The so-called duet,[5] 60,13, also offers a fairly clear-cut example of the ennobling power of love. The first stanza, supposedly sung by a woman, begins and ends aphoristically with the statements that whoever knows *blîtscap* without *rouwe* and with *êren* is *rîke*, and that it is good when someone can increase his *blîtscap* with *êren*. Sandwiched between these maxims is the sentence "hê is edele ende vrût" (60,17), presumably referring to the lady's knight. In the second strophe the man says that his beloved, who causes him to sing, should teach him to speak about the thing from which he cannot very well turn his *mût*. His stanza then ends with the statement "sî is edele ende vrût" (60,25) and the repetition of the idea that whoever can increase *blîtscap* with *êren* is doing a good thing. Two passages in this poem have been cited as evidencing aspects of the notion of the ennobling power of love. The first is the statement that "hê is edele ende vrût" which, according to Frings and Schieb, means he is "in seinem sittlichen und geistigen Wert erhöht."[6] Although there is nothing in this line to justify the interpretation that the man has been uplifted in this way, his request in the second stanza certainly seems to point to the idea of the lady as a *Leiterin* and *Erzieherin*. To be sure, it is not specifically stated what he should not turn his mind from, but the proximity of the words "sî is edele ende vrût" would indicate that he is looking to the lady not only as an inspiration for his singing, but also as a model on which to base his own behavior.

In addition to the twenty-seven songs by Heinrich von Veldeke discussed above, there are six poems under the heading *Unechtes* in the portion of *MF* devoted to this poet. One of them, H.S.258,11, has nothing to do with love and hence need not be analyzed here. Three of the remaining five are songs of requited love; these are completely untouched by the idea of ennobling love and present no easy opportunities for its introduction. The speaker in H.S.258,1 says that he has good reason to be joyful when he is with his high-spirited beloved and that he will remain forever in her service because she drives away his sorrows. In H.S.258,24 a lady speaks unabashedly of her desire to hold her lover close to her, to kiss him on the mouth, and to wrestle with him among the dewy flowers. The lady in the

Wechsel, 67,9, is not as eager. Whereas the man speaks of the hope that spring will bring an end to his sadness, the woman tells a messenger precisely how far she is willing to go in her relationship with her suitor. Although it is obvious that the lady is fond of the knight and would like to continue seeing him, she does not want to give in to his entreaties because she fears that the sorrow that may accompany *minne* could cause her to lose her beauty. In none of these songs where the woman's affection for the man is either clear or implied is there any evidence that the woman's love was won by the man having become worthy through self-improvement. And because it is never said what induced the lady to grant the man her favor, no occasion is offered to connect the idea of mutual love with that of the ennobling power of love.

One of the unauthentic songs does present an easy opportunity to introduce the theme under investigation. In V.S.339,1 the speaker believes that whoever attacks women's honor without justification sins, for we all come from a woman. No matter what we say about them, he concludes, many a man derives advantages from them ("manger wirt von in ze vromen," V.S.339,8). At this point the poet could easily have spelled out what these advantages were, including the benefit of ennoblement in the lady's service. But he does not take advantage of this opportunity.

The last poem, H.S.258,17, shares with V.S.339,1 the motif of the advisability of speaking well of ladies. This time, however, the situation does make it possible to think in terms of ennobling love. The speaker says that a man should serve ladies and say the best he can about them, never being angry or trying to take revenge. Such behavior, he feels, might lead to a man's becoming happy. But whether or not he is successful, he says, he will not cease to praise the ladies. If the poet means, as he seems to, that a man should refrain from speaking ill of women and constrain himself not to be angry and vengeful in order to make happiness possible, then one can speak here of conscious self-improvement of behavior to become worthy of the implied reward of love.

17. Engelhart von Adelnburg

The first of the two poems of Engelhart von Adelnburg, 148,1, consists of a central strophe addressed to the lady directly surrounded by two stanzas in which the speaker bemoans his lady's hardheartedness. Although most of the poem seems far removed from the idea of ennobling love, one passage might tempt one to think that the lady's good qualities have an educative effect on the man. The knight begins by claiming that no good woman has ever made him happy and that he does not know how to spend his time because his lady says she will never tire of his distress. He ends the stanza by complaining that, if he does not derive any benefit from "gotes willen" (148,8),[1] it will mean his death. In the middle stanza he appeals to his lady to grant him the *arebeit* of serving her, which he will consider a blessing, and he claims that—besides God—only she can transform his sorrow into joy. At the beginning of the final stanza he says he would sing her praises if he were able, even though she angrily wishes to punish him for what he has never done. The only thing he is guilty of is loving her "mit triuwen" (148,23). He concludes the poem with the exclamation: "seht wie daz ir güete stê!" (148,24).

Almost everything in this poem points away from the idea of the ennobling power of love. The lady's intransigence, indeed, her ill will, reveals no awareness on her part that it is incumbent on her to act as a model for the knight's self-improvement, and the man's inability to think of anything to do shows that he, too, is not conscious of any need to improve himself to become worthy of her love. The only thing that might possibly touch upon the notion of the educative force of love is the man's final statement that his loving her faithfully goes well with or becomes her goodness. If it were possible to interpret this as meaning that his faithfulness is caused by her *güete*, then the lady's goodness would have inspired a virtue in the man. In the present context, however, it seems more likely that her *güete* has attracted him, has aroused his love, and makes her worthy of love, and that the *triuwe* with which he loves her is a natural concomitant of his love. In other words, anyone as good as she is cannot help being loved. At any rate, this is not a clear-cut example of the concept of the educative power of love.

The second poem by Engelhart von Adelnburg, the single stanza

of 148,25, presents an analogue of the notion of ennobling love. It
begins with the question:

> Swer mit triuwen umbe ein wîp
> wirbet, als noch manger tuot,
> waz schadet der sêle ein werder lîp?   (148,25–27)

and continues with the response: "ich swüere wol, ez waere guot"
(148,28). If this should arouse the wrath of Heaven, the speaker con-
cludes, then "die boesen" (149,3) will all go there and "die biderben"
(149,4) will be damned. This brief defense of courtly love service
against those who claimed it could jeopardize one's hope of salvation
is another case of coming close to the idea of the ennobling power of
love without being a genuine example of it. The implication is clear
that someone who courts a woman *mit triuwen* is *ein werder lîp*, and
that something is wrong with the world if such a worthy person does
not go to Heaven. What is missing here is any indication that such a
person has been ennobled by the process.

18. Albrecht von Johansdorf

Of the sixteen poems of Albrecht von Johansdorf, two, 94,15 and 88,19, have nothing to do with love and need not be discussed here. Eight of the remaining fourteen reveal no trace of the idea of ennobling love and offer no particular occasion to think in such terms. Three of these are very brief. In 90,16 the speaker longs to see his beloved and to be able to sing a joyous song; in 90,32 he hopes a lady will reward him for his service, but he is afraid that she does not really care about him; and in 91,36 he expresses his exuberance and goodwill toward anyone who brings him word from his beloved or who praises her in his presence. A fourth, 89,21, is a crusade poem touching on the theme of love only at the very end. Here the crusader says that he knows he should renounce all sinful behavior and leave all mundane cares behind, but there is one thing he cannot give up, namely, his love for a certain woman, and he hopes God will not take this amiss. Such circumstances obviously provide no role for the ennobling power of love.

The other four songs in this group of eight all contain ideas that are directly opposed to the notion of ennobling love. In 86,1 one finds a reversal of the motif of the lady as an educative force. The speaker, after explaining how he could not love more than one woman as some knights do, gives his lady some advice:

> waz möhte ir an ir tugenden bezzer sîn
> dan obes ir umberede lieze sleht,
> taete an mir einvalteclîche,
> als ich ir einvaltic bin? (86,11–14)

In other words, he wants his lady to treat him fairly and honestly without deception; apparently he has reason to believe that this has not always been the case. The lady's behavior has left something to be desired, and the knight has felt it necessary to give her some guidance in the matter. This view is contrary to the idea that the lady's virtues should serve as a model for the knight's self-improvement.

The theme of the knight serving more than one lady also occurs in 89,9, whose first stanza is a lament in which the knight bewails the hopelessness of his situation. The second strophe, which appears to have no intimate relationship to the first, treats a theoretical question of love. The knight asks if it is not to be considered *unstaete* for a man to serve two women. The answer he receives is: "man sol ez dem man erlouben und den vrouwen niht" (89,20). It is not clear to whom the question is directed and, therefore, who supposedly responds. In both manuscript versions the person making the query says "sprechent herre" as he poses the question, whereas the editor of the critical edition, Carl von Kraus, has changed the text to read "sprechet, vrouwe" (89,19).[1] If one assumes that the altered version is correct, the lady is sanctioning a double standard of behavior, an attitude that seems to fly in the face of everything thus far encountered with respect to the idea that the man must be *staete* if he expects to be rewarded for his service. According to this reading, the lady is the direct opposite of a source of inspiration for the man's exemplary behavior. The manuscript texts, on the other hand, do not show the lady's advocacy of the double standard, but rather a male view of the matter, which seems more appropriate under the circumstances. But even if the image of the lady is thus not shattered, the manuscript reading still does not make a positive statement about the role of *staete* in the relationship between lady and knight. It still must be viewed as a negation of at least one aspect of the idea of the educative power of love, for what is being recommended here amounts to saying that the virtue of constancy is not required of the man.

The last two poems containing ideas antithetical to that of ennobling love are crusade songs. In 86,25 one encounters the direct opposite of the concept of the lady as a model of virtue to be emulated by the knight. The poet prays that, when he returns home from the crusade, he will find his beloved has not done anything to sully her honor. If she has, he says, he would rather not come back. This obvious concern about his lady's constancy in his absence is hardly consonant with the notion that the lady should be an inspiration for exemplary behavior. In 87,29 the conflict between the knight's duties to God and to his beloved plays a dominant role, and it becomes clear that the role of the woman is precisely the opposite of that of the lady who inspires the man to fight against the heathens. For here the knight says that he and his lady have been quarreling, that she is angry because he intends to leave her, and that she considers his decision to go tantamount to a renunciation of his love. Although the knight fills the remainder of the poem with his assurances that he will always love her and pray for her, he never says a word that might be interpreted as a criticism of her attitude toward his going on the crusade.

Four of the songs of Albrecht von Johansdorf contain unseized opportunities to introduce the idea of ennobling love. In the brief song, 92,7, the speaker praises his lady's virtues, even though he does not know why she appears to be so indifferent to him; but he misses the chance to mention that her good qualities provide an example for him to emulate in the hope of becoming worthy of her love. In 91,22, a variation of the *Wechsel*-form in which the first three stanzas are devoted to the lady, the missed occasion is connected with the theme of mutual love. After indicating that she has experienced the beginnings of love, the lady sets forth her views on the subject. When two people truly love each other and "ir beider minne ein triuwe wirt" (91,30)—a state that takes considerable time to achieve and that is also characterized as a coming together of "ir zweier muot" (91,9)—no one should separate them as long as they live. If she were ever to lose the affection of such a person who was dear to her, she would never be happy again; she hopes she will never know such an unhappy end to a relationship. If there is anyone who loves her, she concludes, "der sî sîner triuwe an mir gemant" (91,14). In the final stanza the knight speaks as if he were unaware of the lady's feelings. He talks about his devoted service and tells how his happiness and his sorrow lie in his lady's hands. Where the lady sets forth her views on what constitutes love would have been an ideal place to introduce at least some aspects of the idea of ennobling love, but it is clear that these notions are far from her mind. Even the concept of *triuwe* is not employed as a precondition of the lady's reward of the knight, but rather as a basic assumption of a relationship of mutual affection.

In the last two songs in this group, 87,5 and 94,25, the situations that would have lent themselves to the introduction of the idea of ennobling love involve the knight's conflict between his duties to God and his lady. Although the stanza in which the lady speaks in 87,5 is fragmentary, it is clear from the extant text that she is concerned about how her knight expects to fulfill both obligations, for she asks him: "wie wiltu nu geleisten diu beide, / varn über mer und iedoch wesen hie?" (87,15–16). Instead of answering her question, however, the knight tells her not to be so sad and not to worry so much about him, for his soul will go to heaven. There is nothing in either her words or his to indicate an awareness of the idea that the woman's attitude in such a situation should provide an impetus for the man to participate in the crusade.

The lady in 94,25 has at least partially accepted the man's plan to take part in a crusade. In the lady's stanza of this variation of the

Wechsel-form, it is clear that she neither blames him for going nor makes any attempt to restrain him. It is interesting to note, however, that her adjustment to the reality of his departure does not involve a realization that it is incumbent on her to encourage him and that a knight who fails to do his duty to God is not worthy of her love. And just as she shows no sign of an active role, so the knight also gives no hint that he expects this kind of behavior from her. Thus it becomes obvious that, in contrast to Friedrich von Hausen and Heinrich von Rugge, Albrecht von Johansdorf, although he has every opportunity to do so, fails to introduce the idea of the ennobling effect of love into the conflict between the knight's responsibilities to God and his lady.

The ennobling power of love does play a role in two poems of Albrecht von Johansdorf. In 88,33, which offers a theoretical presentation of certain questions related to love, the speaker states unequivocally that whoever loves "gar âne valschen muot, / des sünde wirt vor gote niht geseit" (88,34–35). That such a love has an elevating effect becomes evident as the speaker continues: "si tiuret unde ist guot" (88,36). In addition, it is made quite clear that a man should be rewarded for avoiding evil and loving a good woman: "tuo erz mit triuwen, sô hab iemer danc / sîn tugentlîcher lîp" (89,1–2).

Although no mention is made in 88,33 of what reward the knight might be entitled to, it is precisely this question that is dealt with in 93,12.[2] This poem is an extended dialogue between a knight and his uninterested and hardhearted lady, in which the former confesses his "senden kumber" (93,18) whereas the latter angrily informs him that she will never grant him what he desires. But when the knight finally asks whether all his singing of her praises and all his service to her is to be of no avail, the lady appears to soften; she replies that he will not go away empty-handed, after all. To the knight's eager query as to the nature of his reward the lady answers: "Daz ir deste werder sît und dâ bî hôchgemuot" (94,14). This response contains the only example thus far encountered of the idea that a knight's improvement through his service to a lady is to be considered in and of itself the goal of his service.[3]

The two songs listed as *unecht* under the name of Albrecht von Johansdorf in *MF* both miss the opportunity to introduce the idea of ennobling love in connection with the lady's *güete* or good qualities. The first, 92,14, is a more or less typical lament in which the knight first prays to God for consolation and then appeals to his lady to be merciful and calm the raging of his heart "mit reiner wîbes güete" (92,20). If ever the day comes when he will embrace her, he says, he will be free of care; whether or not this happens depends completely on her *genâde*. There is, however, nothing to indicate that he can obtain his reward by self-improvement inspired by the lady's *güete*. On the contrary, the only function of the lady's goodness appears to be as a source of *genâde*, which does not seem to be something one becomes worthy of, but rather something that can be achieved by arousing the pity of one's beloved.

In the second poem, 92,35, the speaker presents a rare glimpse of the joy of love fulfilled. He begins by praising Fortune, which has crowned him, for his lady, who is "aller güete ein gimme" (93,4), has rewarded him in such a way that he will always be happy. "Frou Zuht mit süezer lêre" (93,11), he concludes, has not abandoned his beloved. Here, too, there is not the slightest hint of the ennobling power of love. The fact that the lady is the epitome of *güete* and *zuht* is not related to any notion of her being a model for him to emulate. Rather, her goodness is emphasized because it is seen as the reason why she has accorded the knight favorable treatment. There is also no indication that the lady has rewarded the knight because he has become worthy of her through self-improvement.[4]

19. Hartmann von Aue

Four of the fourteen songs of Hartmann von Aue dealing with the theme of love have nothing to do with the idea of ennobling love and present no easy opportunities for its introduction. In 206,19 only the woes of love are underscored. The speaker expresses his determination to continue to bear the pain of unrequited love, but complains that he has served his lady too long and to no avail. If he could give up this struggle, he says, he would be a happy man, but, unfortunately, he is not able to do so. Similarly, but with even more emphasis on the hopelessness of the situation, the knight in 209,5 laments the length of his unrewarded service and wonders how his lady would treat an avowed enemy if this is the way he must suffer as her friend.

The third song in this group is the single stanza of 206,10, in which the poet says he has good reason to be sad, for a double sorrow afflicts him—the death of his lord and the pain of unrequited love. There is no occasion in this brief statement of woe for even a trace of the idea of the uplifting power of love. Rather, attention is focused on the poet's utter dejection because a woman he has long served faithfully has refused him *genâde*.

The last of these four songs, 216,29, contains Hartmann's rejection of the idea of love service, which is based upon his lack of success in winning the love of a lady. All he can expect to get by serving noble ladies is tired feet: "bî frowen triuwe ich niht vervân, / wan daz ich müede vor in stân" (216,35–36). What he wants in his relationships with noble women is reciprocity. Because he is convinced he will never find what he is looking for in the world of courtly society, he feels he can spend his time more profitably with "armen wîben" (217,1) where he can find someone to love who will return his affection. In this song, with its renunciation of courtly love, there is clearly no room for the idea of the ennobling power of love.[1]

Only one song of Hartmann von Aue, 214,12, offers a missed opportunity to introduce the idea of ennobling love. After stating that only he who does not know what love is can be happy, the speaker says his distress is the result of his loyalty. Of what use his *staete* will be to his *sêle*, he does not know. He is certain only that it has brought his *lîp* nothing but sorrow and pain. Despite this concentration on the idea of *staete*, there is no mention of any possible connection between the cultivation of this virtue and the hope of receiving love's reward.

Four of Hartmann's songs either hint at or present situations that come close to the idea of the educative function of love. In the first stanza of 213,29 the speaker says he really does not regret being unable to see his lady often for, as long as she refuses to consider him a *friund*, her presence is too painful for him to bear. Despite his lament, however, he remarks that he will never have anything but good to say about his beloved. In the second half of the poem he extends his praises of his lady to a general extolling of good women, ending with the statement:

swaz wir rehtes werben,
und daz wir man noch nien verderben,
des suln wir in genâde sagen.   (214,9–11)

This willingness to offer thanks to good women for whatever men do that is right seems to imply the same kind of situation embodied in the concept of the educative force of love, that is, the woman is a model of exemplary behavior to be emulated by men. Here, however, nothing specifically links this idea with that of love service and the notion of the knight's becoming worthy of a lady's love through self-improvement.

The second poem in this set, 216,1, presents the only example in Hartmann's love lyrics of a woman who is clearly in love with a knight and ready to give him his reward. The lady says that her beloved has earned her love through service and is worthy of everything that a man desires from a woman. No honor is too great for him, she says, and she thinks he is "ein sô bescheiden man" (216,26) that she cannot go wrong in bestowing her love on him. Although the man is considered deserving of the lady's love as far as his character is concerned, there is no indication that she has put any pressure on him to conform to a pattern of exemplary behavior or that he has changed in any way in order to become worthy of her. Hence, this situation comes close to but is not a genuine example of the educative force of love.[2]

In the next poem in this group, 211,20, a short crusade song, the speaker says that, when a lady sends her beloved on a crusade, "diu koufet halben lôn dar an" (211,22), provided that she behaves herself at home. Just as his undertaking will benefit both the knight and the lady, she, too, can contribute to their mutual welfare by praying for both of them while he is away. One might be tempted to see in this brief poem at least one aspect of the idea of ennobling love as it pertains to the crusades, namely, the notion that the woman should inspire the man to participate, for a knight who preferred to stay at home would not be worthy of her love. Although Hartmann does speak here in terms of the woman sending the man, nothing else in the song points in this direction. There is no indication of any reluctance on the man's part, and no mention of the man's becoming worthy by taking part in the crusade. In fact, the song is concerned not so much with the love relationship as it is with the religious benefits that will accrue to both of them by his going and her staying behind and praying. The reason the woman sends the man is not, as was the case in Friedrich von Hausen's poem, 48,13, that no woman of honor could love a man who stayed home, but rather that she can reap some advantage for herself by supporting his endeavor. Under these circumstances it would be difficult to justify classifying this poem as one in which the ennobling power of love plays a role.

The last poem in this set of four, 218,5, is also a crusade song.[3] Although it does not involve a conflict between the knight's obligations to his lady and to God, it is nevertheless of some interest in this study because the poet transfers to a certain extent the terminology of his worldly love songs to the situations in this religious poem. The speaker says, for example, that he is undertaking his journey because he was captured by Love and then set free on condition that he go on the crusade. The service he will perform for the sake of his new love—the love of God—is greater than that of many a man who boasts of what he does for his love. The knight asks his former fellow minnesingers why they cannot serve the kind of love he is now devoted to, for their love will remain unrequited, whereas his is a mutual, reciprocal love: "daz ich dâ wil, seht daz wil alse gerne haben mich" (218,25). Obviously, one cannot speak here in terms of the ennobling power of love in the same sense as in Hartmann's love songs. Nonetheless, it is possible to see in this use of terminology from the realm of earthly love at least a partial transference of ennobling love to the religious sphere. Thus, just as in the worldly arena, the knight's love places certain demands on his behavior, and the fulfillment of these conditions amounts to self-improvement and presumably holds the hope of compensation. Here, however, the reward is purely spiritual—the salvation of the knight's soul.

More or less clear examples of the idea of ennobling love are found in five of Hartmann's songs. In 215,14, the speaker rejoices that he decided to devote his service to a certain lady and that, in an intimate conversation with her, she has given him reason to be hopeful.

How he envisions the outcome of his devotion is expressed in the following lines:

daz schât ir niht und ist mir iemer guot
wande ich ze gote und zer werlte den muot
al deste baz dur ir willen bekêre:
sus ding ich daz sich mîn frôide noch mêre.   (215,18–21)

This is undoubtedly the clearest statement encountered thus far of the view that the knight should consciously strive to improve himself for the sake of his lady and that his hopes of joy are bound up with this endeavor.

In 205,1 the knight comes to the realization that he has only himself to blame—and not his lady—if she has refused to reward him for his service. If she rejects him, it must be because she has found him lacking. The justice of the situation is expressed as follows:

sî hât geleistet swaz sî mir gehiez;
swaz sî mir solde, des bin ich gewert:
er ist ein tump man, der iht anders gert:
sî lônde mir als ich sî dûhte wert:
michn sleht niht anders wan mîn selbes swert.   (206,5–9)

Obviously he feels he has failed to meet a certain standard of behavior expected of him by the lady. Because he has not proved worthy of her love, it is only fitting that she withhold his reward. But, although he still seems to believe theoretically in the idea of self-improvement as a means of attaining love, he appears to have no hope that the scheme will work for him. In other words, instead of inspiring him to ever loftier heights, the notion of striving to become worthy seems here to have had a completely discouraging effect.

The idea that the knight has only himself to blame for his misfortune is also taken up in 207,11. This time, however, it is coupled with the decision to take his service elsewhere. Although he must lament his woe, he is determined not to speak ill of his lady but rather to consider himself responsible. For if she had found him worthy of a reward, she would have given it. After praising his lady and wishing her well, however, he does not say good-bye, as one might have expected. He begins instead to soften his stance and ends by abandoning his resolve to leave her and reaffirming his devotion and loyalty. Thus the sense of discouragement evident in 205,1 and at the beginning of this poem seems to have been overcome. And because the knight, after having stated that he was not rewarded because of his unworthiness, is now willing to persevere, the implication must be that his hopes lie in his ability to become worthy in the course of continued service to his lady.

Perhaps the knight's toying with renunciation in 207,11 was sufficient grounds for his lady to have accused him of disloyalty, for in 211,27 he states that his *unstaetekeit* has caused him to lose "ein staetez wîp" (211,38). Here, too, he blames no one but himself: "Dô sî erkôs   mich staetelôs, / dô muose ouch diu genâde ein ende hân" (212,2–4). What was merely implied in 207,11 about the reasons for his final determination to remain in his lady's service is stated explicitly here. Far from being discouraged by his awareness that he is responsible for his own misery, he now realizes that what has happened has taught him a lesson and he resolves to strive to be *staete* in the hope of attaining happiness: "nû kêre ich mich an staeten muot, / und muoz mit heile mînes ungelückes werden rât" (212,7–8). Thus the educative force of love can be seen clearly at work. The lady's insistence on *staete* has made the knight strive to improve himself, and he seems to be convinced that his altered behavior will make him worthy of her love.

In 212,13—the last of the five songs in this group—the question of *staete* also arises, but here the relationship to the ennobling power of love is not as clear as it was in 211,27. In this poem the knight is separated from his lady, and he wonders how he will be greeted when he returns. His musings about the possibility of his beloved's wavering in his absence develop into an indirect reminder for her to be true to him while he is gone and end with a brief discourse on the advantages of constancy over false behavior. From the speaker's conclusion that the man who practices *staete* will attain lasting happiness it is evident that he is convinced exemplary behavior will lead to a worthwhile goal. What is missing here, however, in contrast to 211,27, is the lady's active role. Indeed, now it is the man who insists on *staete* and reminds the lady of what is expected of her. In this song, then, even though the man is fully aware of the need for self-improvement, the idea of the lady as an epitome of virtue whose excellence is to be emulated is completely lacking.

Of the four poems listed as *unecht* under Hartmann's name in *MF*, one, 214,34, is generally attributed to Walther von der Vogelweide and will be considered in a later section of this study.[4] Two of the three remaining unauthentic poems, which all have in common the motif of the loving woman, contain neither any evidence of the idea of ennobling love nor any easy opportunities for its introduction. The lady in 212,37, which is the lament of a woman who has reason to regret her choice of a friend, does not hesitate to call the man in question a liar and a deceiver. Ultimately, however, she realizes that she, too, is responsible for the unhappy end of their relationship, for she should have been able to see through his sweet talk. Now all she can do is hope that God will alleviate her sorrow as she sadly observes the happiness of other women whose choices were obviously wiser than hers. Clearly the notion of the ennobling power of love plays no role here, for, if the knight had truly demonstrated that he had become worthy by self-improvement, the lady would certainly not have gotten into her present predicament.

In 318,1 a knight speaks of the dilemma confronting him and his lady—even though she values his friendship and knows he should be rewarded for his service, she refuses to sleep with him. But nothing in this discussion indicates that his service to the lady, and her recognition of his right to a reward, involves any improvement on his part to make him deserving of her favor.

The last of the poems in question is 217,14, the much-discussed widow's lament.[5] Ordinarily one might assume that such a poem should be excluded from this investigation, inasmuch as the relationship between man and wife is normally not the theme of the lyric poetry of the period. The lament of the lady in this song, however, is couched in such terms that it would be entirely possible to conceive of its being spoken by any woman who has lost her beloved, not only by a wife who has lost her husband. There is, therefore, no reason to expect anything in this poem that is radically different from the situations found in most of the love songs under discussion, except for the fact that the man has died. Hence it is appropriate to look here for evidence of the idea of ennobling love, particularly because it does play a role in the relationship between spouses in several epic poems of the period, such as Hartmann's *Erec* and Wolfram von Eschenbach's *Parzival*.

The lady in this song laments that she has lost such a man—no woman ever had a dearer lover. She also says he is someone in whom she has always found "triuwe und êre" (217,26) and everything "swes ein wîp an manne gert" (217,27). Although nothing else in the song indicates the nature of the relationship between them and thus cannot point to any awareness of ennobling love, the lady's praise of his good qualities might be seen to at least touch on the topic under investigation. But the poem does not present a clear-cut case of ennobling love, inasmuch as it does not indicate that the lady granted the man her love because of his worthiness or that he earned it through self-improvement.

Several scholars have maintained that 217,14 is not a widow's lament, but rather that of a woman whose lover has left her to participate in a crusade.[6] Indeed, the language of the poem is sufficiently vague to make such an interpretation possible. According to this reading, the crusade context could be regarded as an unseized opportunity to introduce the idea of ennobling love, for the lady gives no indication she realizes that she is obliged to encourage her lover to participate or that a knight who refuses to perform his duty to God does not deserve her love.

20. Heinrich von Morungen

Fifteen of the thirty-three songs of Heinrich von Morungen reveal no evidence of the idea of ennobling love and offer no ready opportunities for its introduction. Although most of the poems in this large group are laments in which the speaker, with varying degrees of patience, talks of the burden of his unrequited love, one of them, 125,19, is a joyous song. The singer's effusive expression of his happiness here, however, is not the concomitant of love's fulfillment, as one might expect, but rather merely the result of something his lady has said that has given him reason to be hopeful. But the speaker concentrates all his energies on his rapture, without revealing that his state of mind and his hopes are connected with the concept of the knight's becoming worthy of the lady's love through self-improvement. Indeed, he has been so wrapped up in his own feelings that, at the end, he seems to offer a tongue-in-cheek explanation of why he has paid so little attention to his lady: "unde enweis vor wunne joch / waz ich von ir sprechen mac" (126,6–7).

In the majority of the songs in this category love is seen to have the opposite of an uplifting result. Again and again, the generally negative and destructive consequences of love are emphasized. In 140,32 the speaker, after describing the incomparable beauty of his beloved, indicates the effect she has on him in the following way:

jâ hât si mich verwunt
sêre in den tôt.   ich verliuse die sinne.
gnâde, ein künginne,   du tuo mich gesunt.   (141,5–7)

These ideas—that love has robbed him of his senses and wounded him or made him sick to the point of death, and that only his beloved can cure him—are encountered repeatedly, either separately or in combination, in the poems under discussion. In 137,10 the knight implores his lady to save him, for he is sick, his heart is wounded, and he will soon die if she does not look at him and properly take note of his distress. Similarly, in 141,37 he says that she has wounded him right through his soul "in den vil tôtlichen grunt" (142,1) by refusing to grant him a kiss, and in 133,13 he claims that her glances, which cause him torment and great grief, have almost destroyed "daz herze und den lîp" (133,14).

The theme of the loss of the wooing knight's senses, together with that of sickness, debilitation, or death, is found in a number of the poems in this group. In 135,9 the man speaks of the completely be-numbing effect the sight of his beloved has on him; unable to utter a word in her presence, he cannot tell her personally how much she has lacerated his heart. In a similar fashion, in 141,15 he complains that, although her eyes have wounded him and her entry into his heart has made him sick, he can only speak to her through his songs, for in her presence the sound of her voice leaves him "vil gar âne witze" (141,35); thus he does not know where to turn. And in 129,14 he asks anyone who has been able to control his senses at the sight of his lady, who has just made an appearance at a window, to go to her and plead his (the suitor's) case with her, for both the joy and the sorrow of love will soon bring him to his grave.

The motif of death also appears in 147,4. Here the speaker feels that his lady intends to do him in, for he calls her a sweet, gentle murderess. But death is not seen as a release in this song. The lover informs the lady that she will not be able to get rid of him if she causes him to die because he contemplates continuing the relation-ship after death. His soul, he maintains, will serve her soul in heaven "als einem reinen wîbe" (147,16). Obviously the attitude im-puted to the lady here leaves no room for the idea of the educative power of love. For instead of being a source of inspiration for the knight's betterment, the lady is actively desirous of his destruction.

One also looks in vain for the concept of ennobling love in 143,4, where the idea of *huote* plays a prominent role. After complaining about the loss of so many joyless days and years as a result of his beloved's neglect, the knight wonders whether the distance that has grown between them has been caused by the fact that his lady is "mit valscher diet behuot" (143,17). He rebukes her gently for letting such an obstacle get in the way of love, and he expresses the hope that she will be able to deceive those who keep such a careful watch over her.

Two of the songs presently being examined express only disap-proval of the lady's behavior. In these the speaker uses sarcasm to underscore his criticism. Even a forest would have given some re-sponse, he says in 127,1, if someone had shouted into it as much as he has complained about his misery to his lady. She, however, ap-pears to have slept through all the din, or so it would seem, at least to judge from the reaction he has received. Even a parrot would have learned to say the word "love" in all this time, he continues, so why can she not understand his pleading? He concludes that, unless God works a miracle on her, he could more easily cause a tree to bow down by his entreaties than he could persuade her to give him a favorable hearing. In 134,6 he asks why his heart, her beauty, and Love have conspired to bring about the death of his joy, and he asks Love to give his beloved a part of his distress. But, he bitterly concludes, he had better not wish her the pain of love, for such words might anger her because nothing she has ever *said* has caused him to suffer. In neither of these songs, with their sarcastic attack on the woman's refusal to react in any way to his plight, is there a place for the idea of the ennobling or educative power of love. The lady's complete lack of concern makes it impossible to conceive of her as a model to be emulated by the knight. She can hardly serve as a source of inspiration for moral betterment when she herself is viewed as being heartless and cruel.

The last songs in this group—143,22, 139,19, and 130,31—present not the cold and hardhearted lady of the laments, but the picture of a woman in love. None of them gives any indication of what motivated the woman to bestow her favor. Thus they do not present an easy opportunity to introduce the theme under investigation; rather, they so emphasize certain aspects to the exclusion of others that one is not tempted to think in terms of ennobling love. In 143,22, a *Tagelied*, with its concentration on the joys of physical love, the rapture of the man in contemplating the nude body of the woman, and the pain of parting at dawn, it is not surprising that the educative force of love is absent. The second song, 139,19, consists of three brief scenes in which the poet encounters his beloved. In the first she is dancing with others in the meadow, and he joins in joyfully; in the second he finds her alone in a room where she has been crying because she thinks he is dead; and in the third she has called him to her high up on the battlement where, he says, he could have taken advantage of her when his passion burst into flames so that he thought he had set the world on fire. In this poem, too, the predominance of the passion of love leaves no room for an appearance of the theme of ennobling love. The third song of requited love, 130,31, is a *Wechsel* in which a knight and his lady take turns speaking about their mutual affection and the obstacles that make it difficult for them to be together. In the first stanza the knight implies that he has chosen her as his love and his lady above all others because of her physical charms, whereas in his second strophe he curses those who speak ill of her and who are responsible for his having to keep away from her. The lady speaks first of the pain of their latest leave-taking and her longing for her lover, and then of the hypocrites who are pleasant to her beloved in his presence but who abuse him verbally

behind his back. Given its concern with those who are bent on pre-
venting the union of the lovers, there is obviously no place for the
idea of the ennobling power of love in this poem.

Seventeen of Heinrich von Morungen's songs present situations
that would have lent themselves easily to the introduction of the
motif of ennobling love. In one of these the occasion to make such a
connection arises when a woman who has lost her beloved offers
advice to another woman. The first stanza of 142,19, a *Wechsel*,
presents a knight who rejoices in his choice of a noble lady whom he
has vowed to serve forever, for he has never seen such a good
woman. It is not this lady who speaks in the remaining two stanzas,
however, but rather the one he has apparently abandoned for his
new love. She not only bewails the loss of the man she loves, but
also makes it very clear that she does not have the same high opinion
of her rival as her beloved. The expression of her disapproval is pre-
ceded by the following words:

> Gerne sol ein ritter zîen
> sich ze guoten wîben: dêst mîn rât.
> boesiu wîp diu sol man flîen:
> er ist tump swer sich an si verlât;
> wan sin geben niht hôen muot.   (142,26–30)

This would have been the ideal place to introduce the idea of the
educative effect of love—only in the service of a good woman can a
knight improve himself by striving to emulate the model behavior
she represents. In this case, however, the lady does not take advan-
tage of the opportunity. She only emphasizes that "boesiu wîp" can-
not offer "hôen muot," that joyous soaring of the spirit which is the
concomitant of love, but which is not necessarily dependent on or
connected with the knight's self-improvement.

A second song in this category, 127,34, is generally critical of the
speaker's lady, although it does take a more or less optimistic turn at
the end where it misses an opportunity to connect the idea of worthi-
ness with that of ennobling love. In this poem the knight bemoans
his having yielded to the lady's whims about his singing or not sing-
ing, and he complains bitterly about all the time he has lost in her
service, for which he has received nothing but the occasional privi-
lege of gazing at her. He also speculates on the value of *triuwe*. Any-
thing that is rare, he remarks sarcastically, increases in value—except
a loyal man. His own experience has shown him that "er ist verlorn,
swer nu niht wan mit triuwen kan" (128,38). Thus it is clear that he
does not believe in the proposition that loyal devotion will neces-

sarily be rewarded. It is also interesting to note that nothing here indicates that the man's loyalty must be considered an improvement in his behavior. Finally, despite his bitter lamentations, the knight concludes the poem with an assertion of his determination not to give up hope and to sing his lady's praises until the end of his days. The best thing that could happen to him in this world would be for her to consider him deserving of *genâde*, he says. Again, however, nothing in the poem implies that her deeming him worthy has anything to do with the concept of the ennobling power of love.

Another song containing a missed opportunity is 134,14. Its basic theme is that the knight has chosen too high a goal for himself; therefore, his service has been scorned and his suffering has gone unnoticed. Although he realizes that it would make better sense for him to turn elsewhere, where his service would be more welcome and the hope of reward more certain, he seems to be determined to persist in his apparently hopeless devotion to his lofty lady. This inability to act in what he himself clearly recognizes to be a reasonable fashion must be viewed as another variation of the notion of the paralysis caused by love, a state symbolized in the last stanza of the poem by the image of the knight intently gazing upward at his lady, his sun, which has risen too high, and wishing that evening would finally come to bring her closer to his reach. The extent to which he has been rendered incapable of any activity other than staring rigidly at his lady is expressed in the concluding line: "wand ich mich hân gar verkapfet ûf ir wân" (135,6). Although the knight's selection of a lofty goal lends itself well to introducing the notion that the heights to which he aspires might have an inspirational effect on him so that, by emulating the object of his striving, he might improve himself and hence become deserving of his reward, such an opportunity remains unseized here. On the contrary, the loftiness of his goal leads only to discouragement and despair.

The next two songs in this group have in common the theme of *huote*. The knight in 136,25 curses first those who keep his beloved hidden from view and thus rob him of his sunshine, and then the institution of *huote* in general. *Huote* makes good women turn to devious ways and deprives the world of one of its joys, "wan durch schouwen   sô geschuof si got dem man" (136,39–40). In 131,25,[1] the man bemoans his utter isolation from his lady and says that, if those who guard her so zealously were deaf and blind, he would be able to plead his case with her successfully. But this not being so, he wishes that she could read his mind from afar and smile at him in response. Then, quoting from an earlier poem (127,1) about the parrot and the starling, which would have learned to say "minne," he asks that his lady say the same—for which he would be eternally grateful. Next he complains that people who bitterly bewail things they do not really feel in their hearts are thought to behave just as properly as those who suffer and weep alone without being able to tell anyone about their misery. Then, after playing with distinctions between the words *liebe* and *minne*, he says that "diu guote" (132,23) gives him "hôhen muot, dar zuo freud unde wünne" (132,24), but that he does not know what love (*liebe*) can do; he only knows that he is always filled with painful longing for it. In the final strophe the knight says his lady should not smile at others the way she smiles at him, and she should not make herself so appealing for others to gaze at, for no one has the right to see such things in her, to whom he has dedicated his life and who holds his happiness in her hands.

One looks in vain in these two poems for any evidence of the ennobling power of love, although there are several places where it could have been easily introduced. Thus, for example, in 136,25 the speaker says God created woman so that man could gaze at her beauty, but speaks not a word about her also being a model of virtue to be imitated. Similarly, when the speaker in 131,25 tells of the things that *diu guote* "gives" him, inspiration for improvement— namely, her being the epitome of goodness that he should imitate— is not one of them.[2] And when he wonders what the effects of love might be, all he can state with certainty is that his longing for love constantly imbues him with sadness.[3]

In the remaining songs in the category of unseized opportunities the theme of praise of the noble lady plays a more or less important role. The speaker devotes almost the entire song 122,1 to extolling his lady who, he claims, far outshines every other woman in the realm where German is spoken. He praises not only her beauty and her demeanor, but also her "tugent reine" (123,1) and her goodness, which, he says, envelops her just as the moonlight embraces the earth on a clear night. In lauding her goodness and her virtues, however, the speaker says not a word to indicate that the lady's character might be a source of inspiration for the improvement of his own.

Although only the last stanza of 145,1—a song in which the speaker bemoans the changing of his initial joy into sorrow in the course of his courtship—contains the motif of praise, the degree of this glorification makes up for its brevity:

> Hôer wîp von tugenden und von sinne,
> die enkan der himel niender ummevân,

sô die guoten diech vor ungewinne
fremden muoz und immer doch an ir bestân.　　　　(145,25–28)

Nowhere in the poem, however, is there a hint that the lady's virtues are supposed to spur the knight on to self-betterment.

In the other poems extolling the lady, such praise is tempered, to a greater or lesser extent, by the knight's criticism of the way he has been treated. After jokingly stating at the beginning of 145,33 that he is undertaking a campaign against his lady, and after calling upon his friends to help him make her aware of his pain and suffering, he turns to praising her virtues at length. Everything she does, he says, bespeaks her good qualities, and good words and deeds are her companions. But if he may be allowed to say so, he continues, she should treat a friend like a friend if she wants to truly achieve perfection in her youth. After this bit of advice he concludes by saying: "ich hân hôchgemüete" (146,39), implying that her *güete* has produced this state in him. However, nothing in the poem indicates that her goodness has, or is supposed to have, a salutary effect on his development. On the contrary, instead of being inspired by her behavior to improve his own, he feels compelled to admonish her to become even better than she is.

Praise and criticism are mixed in eight additional poems. Although in 144,17 the knight, who at first resolves not to be gloomy any longer, does not directly criticize the lady, his disapproval of her behavior is certainly implicit in his ultimate conclusion that, as long as she will not put an end to his misery, he will be found in sadness "bî der ungemuoten / schar" (144,36–37). Thus, even though she is "ganzer tugende ein adamas" (144,27) and "ein wunnebernder süezer meije" (144,29), this is not sufficient for him to be "in hôhem muote" (144,33), as was the case in 145,33. In 132,27 the speaker begins by indirectly accusing his lady of being hardhearted toward him and ends by mixing praise with censure. The only unwomanly deed for which he can rebuke her is her failure to reward him for his service. But he seems willing to be patient and to wait for her to be possessed by love as he is. This same patience and readiness to persevere is found in 140,11, in which the knight's joy, based on the hope that the lady will reward him, and his sorrow, resulting from her unwillingness to console him, are contrasted and mingled with only an intimation of criticism. If he should ever speak ill of a woman, he says, his beloved would probably deserve a reprimand for her attitude regarding his singing. But he refrains from actually doing so and ends by calling her "des liehten meien schîn" and his "ôsterlîcher tac" (140,15–16) and by wishing her nothing but the best. Finally, in 123,10 the speaker's disillusionment and despair far outweigh any implied praise of the lady. He laments bitterly that she first said she did not want to hear his singing, but now complains that he is silent. Her treatment of him, he feels, can only be interpreted as scorn and hate, and, if he is to sing again, she will have to give him something to be happy about. Despite his displeasure with her conduct, however, he is determined to continue in her service, no matter what the outcome may be. The only faint praise that can be heard here is in the next to last stanza, where he addresses the lady with the words "vil wîplîch wîp" (124,8) and appeals to her "wîbes güete" (124,18) in his efforts to convince her to console him. In none of these four poems, however, is a connection between the lady's virtues and the idea of the educative function of love even hinted.

Four of the poems combining praise and criticism underscore the negative and ruinous consequences of love. The lady in 130,9 is likened to a *rouberîn* who attacks without having declared war and makes a prisoner of any man that looks at her. In this way the speaker has also been assaulted and left "siech an lîbe / unde an herzen sêre wunt" (130,26–27). If one asks what is responsible for all this destruction and havoc, one finds the following answer: "daz machent alle ir tugend und ir schône" (130,15). Thus it is clear that the lady's good qualities, which might have been expected to inspire his self-improvement, have had the reverse effect.

The destructive aspect of love is expressed in 126,8 first by means of the idea of magical enchantment. The speaker has been bewitched by love and his lady, just as many a man has been cast under a spell by looking at elves. The debilitating consequences of this situation become clear in the second stanza when he expresses the wish to spend three days and several nights alone with his beloved. Then, he says, he would not lose "den lîp und al die maht" (126,21). And her treatment of him has had the following effect on his heart: "und ir fremden krenket mir daz herze mîn / same daz wazzer die vil heize gluot" (126,26–27). Although hardly any of the poem is taken up with praise of the lady, the singer does have this to say about her:

und ir hôher muot,   ir schône, ir werdecheit,
und daz wunder daz man von ir tugenden seit,
deist mir übel und wirt noch lîhte guot.   (126,28–31)

Thus here, too, the lady's good qualities have not had an ennobling effect; instead, they have resulted in his misfortune. To be sure, he still hopes the situation can be reversed. But there is no indication that the good that might lie in store for him has anything to do with the notion of his being rewarded for having become worthy of the lady's affection through self-improvement. Finally, in the last strophe, the idea of the paralysis caused by love—that is, the inability of the knight to function because of his obsession about seeing his beloved—is conveyed by the image of the knight standing and waiting for the chance to have his lady's glance fall on him, just as the little birds await patiently all night the coming of day.

In 124,32 love's negative effects have reduced the knight to such despair that he yearns for death as a release from the pain he has suffered since he began serving his lady. Here he has contemplated taking his own life, but rejects the possibility because it is against God's will. It should also be observed that the reason he took the lady into his heart is stated at the beginning of the poem:

> Hete ich tugende niht sô vil von ir vernomen
> und ir schône niht sô vil gesên,
> wie wêre si mir danne alsô ze herzen komen?   (124,32–34)

Again it is obvious that the lady's good qualities have not led to any ennoblement, but rather to disaster. That the lady would be relieved if he were dead is also implied in this song when, in the concluding stanza, the speaker imagines a unique form of revenge for the torment she has caused him. If she thinks she will be free when he is gone, he says, she may be deceiving herself, for he hopes that someday his son will be so handsome that she will fall in love with him and he will break her heart.

The knight's yearning for death also plays a role in the long retrospective poem, 138,17. After stating that no one but his beloved, whom he calls "diu guote" (138,19), would weep for his grief (if she were to hear his lament), he looks back to the time when she first sent a *hôhgemüete* into his heart, of which her goodness and her radiance were the bearers. When she looked at him with her sparkling eyes and secretly smiled at him, he says, his spirit soared as high as the sun. Now, when he is alone, he imagines that she comes to him right through the walls, comforting him with her words and leading him off high over the battlements. He even says she is a noble Venus because she can do so much, taking away his pain, his joy, and all his senses, and shining in on him through a window like the radiant sun.[4] In the last stanza, however, he realizes that his belief is blasphemous and that his beloved has never taken him seriously; he asks why he does not beg God to free him from this life. He is like a swan, he concludes, that sings when it is dying. Although the speaker in this song refers to his lady as *diu guote* and says that when he first recognized her *güete*, it filled his heart with joy, it is clear that her goodness no longer has even this beneficial effect on him. And nowhere is there any indication that her good qualities have had an ennobling result. On the contrary, his love has brought him such misery that he longs for death as a release.[5]

One other poem, 137,27, should be discussed in conjunction with those combining praise with criticism, because here the knight questions whether he has been correct in attributing so many laudable qualities to his lady. After stating that his beloved should punish him if he has been wrong to love her, and after pleading with her to help him cast off the burden of his ever-growing sorrow, he looks back at all the good things he has said about her and wonders whether perhaps he has misjudged her. If he has been right, then he still has reason to hope for happiness. His doubts are summed up in the final verse: "in weiz niht waz schoener lîp in herzen treit" (138,16). Obviously, he hopes he has been accurate in assessing her goodness because this will ultimately be responsible for making her realize that she must reward him. But there is no trace of the idea that her good qualities should serve as an inspiration for him to improve himself.

Only one song of Heinrich von Morungen, 136,1, contains passages that might tempt one to think in terms of the idea of ennobling love. The poem begins with the theme of the knight's inability to communicate in his beloved's presence. Although the sight of his lady is a joy for his eyes, it brings death to his heart, for she never offers him aid or consolation and he is never able to speak when he is with her, despite the fact that he knows exactly what he wants to say. In addition to the motif of the knight being struck dumb when he is face-to-face with his lady, the idea of the man's constancy also plays a role in this poem. He is not changeable like the wind, he says, for he has been true to his beloved since his childhood, no matter how much she has hurt him. Initially, one might associate this emphasis on his faithfulness with the concept of the educative function of love. A closer examination, however, reveals that the knight's loyalty does not represent any improvement in his character because he has been "vil stête her von einem kleinen kinde" (136,11). Similarly, the bitter statement with which the song concludes—"dêswâr mirn ist nâch werde niht gelungen" (136,22)—might be taken to mean that, despite his having become worthy of a reward, he has not been adequately compensated. However, nothing in the poem indicates that he has *become* worthy. It is stated only that he has not been treated in accordance with his merits.

A clear example of the idea of ennobling love is found in only one poem of Heinrich von Morungen, 122,1, which was also discussed above in the category of unseized opportunities. In the course of lavishly praising his lady, to which almost the entire poem is devoted, the knight calls her the one "durch die ich gar alle unstête verkôs" (122,24). As noted earlier, the requirement that the knight be faithful in his devotion if he expects to be rewarded for his service places a certain demand on him to behave at least in one respect in an exemplary way. And because the man says here that he has given up inconstancy for the sake of his lady, one can speak of such a beneficent effect. Nothing is explicitly stated, however, to indicate any expectation that he will become worthy of her love as a result of such betterment in his behavior.[6]

21. Reinmar von Hagenau

Of the thirty-four poems of Reinmar von Hagenau in *MF*, eight neither contain a trace of the idea of ennobling love nor present any easy opportunities for its introduction. Three of these reflect, or seem to reflect, a relationship in which the knight's love is returned by the lady, who appears to be willing to fulfill her beloved's desires; two of the three are variations of the *Wechsel*-situation, in which both parties express their feelings. In the first half of 152,25 the lady, after complaining about the apparent impossibility of pleasing everyone and expressing her wish to behave properly in society, speaks about the knight who has been serving her. She hopes that God, who can see into his heart, will help her know his true thoughts because she fears that his actions toward her have not been sincere. If she were convinced that his intentions toward her were serious, she says, she would be willing to commit herself wholly to him. In the second part of the poem the knight, who is not aware of the lady's affection for him, bemoans his failure to win her favor, but states both his determination to continue in her service and his resolve to ask for her love. The idea of the ennobling power of love plays no role in the relationship depicted here. The lady is hesitant to bestow her love not because she feels he has not yet become worthy, but rather because she is uncertain about the sincerity of his feelings. And the knight does not seem to be aware of any need for self-improvement to win her love. Rather, he counts on the efficacy of the service-reward concept and the boldness of his determination to press his case.

In the other *Wechsel*-like poem, 154,32, the knight complains that he knows only sorrow. The dawning of a new day, he says, cannot fill him with joy as long as his beloved shows no signs of affection for him. He feels his absence from her, which has pained him deeply, has not made any impression on her. Not only has she not missed him, she has even been happy without him: "Si was ie mit fröiden / und lie mich in den sorgen sîn " (155,23–24). But despite her apparent indifference and even her refusal to believe in his devotion, he is determined not to give up hope. That the knight has more reason to be optimistic than he realizes becomes evident in the last stanza. It seems that he is completely misinformed about the lady's real feelings, which she now expresses in a monologue. She appears oppressed with woe from which only the man she loves can free her. His staying away from her, she says, will be the death of her; if he were lying close to her, all her troubles would disappear. However, neither his lamentations about her supposed lack of concern nor her secret longing for him has anything to do with the idea of ennobling love.

It appears as if the lady is willing to fulfill the knight's desires in the remaining poem, 156,10. The knight has been away, and as he contemplates his return his heart leaps up with joy in anticipation of being with his beloved again. He prays that God may allow him to see her so that they can rid each other of their cares. The poem ends on an extremely optimistic note: "owol mich danne langer naht! / wie kunde mich verdriezen?" (156,25–26). But the certainty of the coming reward is in no way connected with the idea of the ennobling power of love.

The fourth song where one looks in vain for the idea of ennobling love, 175,1, is a lament in which the speaker complains that his misery is not taken seriously. It disturbs him that everyone says he can do nothing but complain, and he wants to know why it is not clear to all that he has no reason to rejoice. Only if he receives his reward, he says, will he be able to look forward to the coming of a new day. He also regrets the many good words he has wasted on his beloved because she has caused him nothing but grief. Indeed, his words were the best any man has ever spoken and could never have been uttered except in truth. At the end of the poem he returns to his relationship to those around him, stating in the future he will be more careful who is with him when he expresses his feelings. There are too many *ungefüege liute*, he says, and, from his past experience, he is afraid that his words will be misinterpreted. Moreover, he is at a loss to explain how people who hate him could act as if they were glad to see him because God knows he would never do anything to harm anyone. The song concludes with a plea for kinder treatment, for many people who now think they can do nicely without him will mourn him after he is gone. This poem, which emphasizes the poet's pride in his own accomplishments and his bitterness about the lack of understanding shown by his audience, clearly has little room for the idea of the ennobling power of love. To be sure, the poet does feel he deserves a reward, but there is nothing to indicate that he believes he has become worthy of it through self-improvement.

Another song that offers no opportunity to think in terms of ennobling love is the single stanza, 194,34. The speaker asks in a playful tone whether anyone can help him, for he is at a loss what to do—

neither his talking nor his silence has been of any avail. So far, all he has found is "nein und niht" (194,38), but now he is going to look for what she has hidden away, "daz vil süeze wort geheizen jâ" (195,2).

In still another song in this category, 172,11—a variation of the *Wechsel*-form—love's effects are the opposite of ennobling. The man complains that he is getting old in his lady's service because she has treated him so poorly. Nonetheless, he cannot see renouncing her, for without her he knows he can never be happy. Thus, she will have to abuse him more than any woman has ever misused a man before he will give her up, even though he can attest that she, and she alone, has robbed him of everything he had, particularly his joy and all his senses. If she wishes to deny it, he is confident that right is on his side. The lady responds angrily and haughtily to what she perceives to be his threats by saying he is mistaken if he thinks she is defenseless. If he attacks her, he will think he has met up with an entire army. The man has the last word in the final stanza where he repeats his determination to persist in his devotion to the lady, for he was born to live in the hope of serving her and having her end his sorrow. In this song nothing indicates an awareness of the idea of ennobling love. On the contrary, the destructive aspects of love are underscored. The lady's mistreatment of the man is causing him to turn gray, and she has deprived him of his senses and his happiness. In addition, his depiction of her, as well as the characterization of her in her own stanza, hardly reveals her to be in any frame of mind to act as a guide for him to follow along the path of self-improvement.

The last two songs that lack any evidence of the idea under discussion are not really love poems and hence need not be of serious concern in this investigation. One is a lament on the death of Duke Leopold, 167,31, supposedly spoken by his widow. It deals exclusively with the lady's feelings of pain at the loss of her beloved husband and offers no information about the nature of the relationship between them that might bear on the problem of ennobling love. The other is a crusade song, 181,13, in which the knight speaks of his difficulty in keeping his thoughts on his holy mission. His *gedanke*, he says, "wellent allez wider an diu alten maere" (181,28) and want him to devote himself again to joy. But because the conflict in this poem is expressed only generally as one between duty to God and a desire to return to a worldly existence, and not specifically as one between service to God and devotion to a lady, the conflict has nothing to do with the idea of participation in a crusade as a means of becoming worthy of love.

Eighteen of the songs of Reinmar von Hagenau present unseized opportunities to introduce the idea of ennobling love. In three of these the situation that would have easily lent itself has to do with a woman who is in love with her suitor, but who is unwilling to fulfill his uttermost desires. The first of these, 178,1, is a *Botenlied* in which the lady tells the messenger to go to her knight and inform him that she is always glad to hear that he is well and happy, but that he should never do anything that would bring about their separation. Although she tells the courier how much she loves the knight, she is reluctant to let her beloved know this until the messenger is sure that the knight truly loves her. If this is indeed the case, he may tell him whatever will please him, as long as it is consonant with her honor. And if the knight wishes to come see her, he must desist from the plea he recently made. What he desires can never be granted, for "des er gert daz ist der tôt" (178,29). The love he wants men call *minne*, she says, but it would best be called *unminne*: "Wê im ders alrêst began!" (178,35). In the final stanza the lady regrets having spoken so freely about such delicate matters and forbids the messenger to tell her beloved anything of what she said.

The same situation is also dealt with in 177,10, where it becomes clear from the lady's conversation with a messenger that her knight has made a request of her that she feels she cannot grant, and she asks that the subject not be raised again. Here, however, it is evident that she is faced with another dilemma, for her knight has resolved never to sing again unless she bids him to. If she does give the command, she fears some harm might come of it. But if she does not, she will lose her "saelde an ime" (177,29) and incur the wrath of society for depriving it of its joy. The end of the poem does not resolve this matter; rather, the lady complains that women are not able to win "friunt mit rede, sinwellen dannoch mê" (177,35), and she emphasizes her desire for a platonic relationship with the words: "in wil niht minnen" (177,36).

The last of these three songs, 186,19, is a monologue in which the lady bemoans her sad predicament—she must reject the man she loves because of her honor. She tells how sorry she was for her beloved when she saw how miserable he seemed after she had angrily demanded that he refrain from further entreaties of the kind he had previously made. The pity she felt for him, however, was not sufficient to induce her to yield to his pleas, and she is determined not to let their relationship develop into *minne*, for "minne ist ein sô swaerez spil / daz ichs niemer tar beginnen" (187,19–20). In the final stanza she praises him by saying that, of all the men she has ever heard or seen, "der keiner sprach sô wol / noch von wîben nie sô nâhen" (187,22–23). She also wishes him well and concludes that there is no reason why he should not continue to sing—it cannot do anybody any harm, "sît er niht erwerben kan / weder mich noch anders niemen" (187,29–30).

Considering the attitude of the lady in these three poems, it is not at all surprising that there is no trace of the idea of the man's meriting compensation because of self-betterment. Indeed, from what the lady says it is clear that the knight *is* deserving of her love, although it is neither stated nor implied that he *became* worthy in her service. But deserving or not, he will not receive the reward he seeks, for her reluctance to yield to his pleas has nothing to do with this notion. One aspect of the concept of ennobling love that one might expect to find in these songs, where the reasons for the lady's refusal to requite the knight's efforts on her behalf are stated so explicitly, is the theory that the refinement of the man in the service of the lady is its own reward. Like the woman in Albrecht von Johansdorf's poem, 93,12, the lady of Reinmar's songs could have pointed out to her knight that, even though she cannot grant what he desires, certain benefits do accrue to him as a result of his courtship. However, not a word is spoken about such a possibly uplifting effect of love. The lady appears to be so completely caught up in her own emotions and the dilemmas confronting her that she gives little thought to the needs of her suitor. She concludes that he should continue to serve her through poetry not because *he* might profit from it, but rather because *she* derives pleasure from his singing, which she feels cannot do anyone any harm.[1]

The missed opportunities in five songs in this category are connected mainly with the notion that the knight derives—or might derive—some benefit from his wooing even if his love remains unrequited. The speaker in 174,3 indicates that, at least in one respect, he has changed for the better since he has known his lady, for he says: "sît daz si mîn ouge sach, / diu mich vil unstaeten man betwungen hât, / der mac ich vergezzen niemer mê" (174,26-28). This transformation from *unstaete* to *staete*, however, is not explicitly related to the idea that it will help make him deserving of her love. Instead, the man concentrates on the misery resulting from his lady's refusal to offer him hope of ever achieving his goal or even to take seriously his claims that he is serving her. Indeed, far from expressing any optimism concerning the effectiveness of his course of action, he wishes he had never become involved with her. In a spirit of resignation, he concludes that even if he never receives any reward from her, at least he will always have his memories of the lady who pleased him more than any other woman he has known. Here, where he assesses his predicament of unrequited love and establishes that he has derived something worthwhile from his endeavors, one certainly might expect him to consider the improvement in his character mentioned earlier as a benefit achieved despite his lack of success in attaining his original goal. There is, however, not even a hint of this idea in the song.

In 158,1 the speaker states how difficult it is for someone who is happy in love to believe him when he says he can never know joy. Those "den ir gemüete hôhe stât" (158,12) make fun of him because he has bemoaned his sorrow for such a long time. What do they want him to do? he asks. Can someone who is unfamiliar with joy sing about it? Should he lie about his condition? That would only be a useless form of self-deception, he feels, and he asks why "they" do not want to let him go on striving to achieve his goal. Because he is certain that his only hope of happiness lies with his lady, he is determined to continue his suit. If it should turn out that what "they" say about "verlorner arebeit" (158,35) applies to him, he will, of course, be miserable, but he does not see that he could have done otherwise, and at least he has learned the meaning of "sende nôt" (158,30). In the context of a statement concerning his having received something for his efforts, even if it was not exactly what he had expected, one might anticipate the idea that he has benefited from his service by having become a better person in some way. But there is not a trace of this, or any other aspect of the notion of ennobling love, in this poem.

The speaker in 153,14 wonders what it must feel like to be successful in love: "Wiest im ze muote, wundert mich, / dem herzeclîche liep geschiht?" (153,14–15). This query is closely followed by a reference to *staete*, but the idea that the man's behavior has improved or that his constancy will lead to a reward does not appear. *Staete* is mentioned only in connection with the hypothetical case of the man who has experienced *herzeclîche liep*—the speaker would like to know how this person conducts himself, "ob er iht pflaege wunneclîcher staete" (153,19) as he should. The same view of *staete* is reiterated in the final stanza when the speaker says that, if he ever reaps the benefit of his lady's constancy, he will compensate her for it with the same attitude: "sol mir ir staete komen ze guote, / daz gilte ich ir mit semelîchem muote" (154,27–28). Thus it would seem that in this poem *staete* is viewed as a quality characterizing a relationship of mutual affection rather than as a prerequisite for winning a woman's love.[2]

Between the first and the last strophe of the same song the speaker mentions, among other things, his decision to refrain from any further active pursuit of his goal, which until now has caused him only grief, and to resign himself to a love of which no one need be jealous, because, as he says, his lady resides "in mînem sinne / und ich die lieben âne mâze minne, / nâher dan in dem herzen mîn" (154,9–11). Far from regretting his having taken her into his *sin*, he considers that he has profited from it. If one asks in what way, however, one receives only the vaguest of answers. Apparently the mere contemplation of her good qualities is enough to give him pleasure:

> Got hât gezieret wol ir leben
> alsô daz michs genüegen wil,
> und hât ze vröiden mir gegeben
> an einem wîbe liebes vil.   (154,23–26)

In such a situation, where the man praises the lady's good qualities so highly and where he almost seems to be resigning himself to a kind of platonic relationship from which he claims to derive some good, one might expect the appearance of one aspect of the ennobling effect of love, namely, the notion that, even if he does not win the lady's love, he at least becomes a better person for having tried. But neither this idea, nor any relationship between her exemplary behavior and his character, is evident in the poem.

Although the speaker in 166,16 says he finds his sorrow sweet, he still would like to see it transformed into bliss, and he calls upon his friends, as well as anyone who has heard of his misfortune, to advise him what course of action to take. When he receives no reply, he concludes on his own that there is no hope for him because the woman he loves apparently hates him. He then speaks about "ein rede der liute" (167,13), which disturbs him so much that he cannot accept it with forbearance. People have mockingly asked him how old his lady is, implying that she must indeed be getting on in years if he has been serving her so long. He only hopes that she, the best of all women, will let him derive some advantage from their "zühtelôser vrâge" (167,21). For, apparently recanting his earlier conclusion that she despises him, he now says he cannot believe she esteems him as little as she appears to, and he affirms his intention of pressing his suit. If others rejoice in their happiness, he will find joy in his sorrow; if he cannot obtain anything else from her, he will love "ir güete und ir gebaerden" (167,3). Instead of ending on this note of resignation, however, he suggests in a final stanza that his lady submit to an experiment to see whether she could love him—she should hold him close and treat him as if she really cared for him. If they were both pleased with the situation, she could continue it, but if he should not gain her favor as a result, the arrangement could be abandoned as if she had never submitted to his embrace. In this song, too, where the man speaks of perhaps having to be satisfied with less than he had originally desired, one might expect the ennobling effect of love to be one of the benefits of his service. But there is no indication that this is the case, even in his wanting to love her *güete* and her *gebaerden* if he cannot have anything else. Nowhere is it said or implied that his contemplation of her virtues will make him a better person.

In the remaining song in this group of five, 190,3, the speaker begins with the question: "Wie tuot diu vil reine guote sô?" (190,3). He cannot understand how someone so good could let him go to ruin or could not reward "ir lieben unde ir friunden wol" (190,10). Although he has not yet received any consolation from her, he clearly bases his expectations on her good qualities and reputation: "si hât tugent und êre: dâ von mac es werden rât" (190,18). But if she does not bring him joy, he, *tumber man* that he is, will only be able to lament that he cannot make up for the many days he has lost in her service. This regret over his wasted time would have easily lent itself to the introduction of the idea that, if nothing else, he has at least derived some benefit from his years of service. But no such counterbalancing notion is to be found here. Another missed opportunity in this song occurs when the knight praises the lady's virtues; this could have been the place to indicate that they should act as a model for him to improve himself and thereby become worthy of her. Instead, attention is focused on her goodness as the reason why she could not continue to let him suffer much longer.

The next four songs in the category of unseized opportunities have in common the theme that the knight has done or is willing to do whatever is necessary or whatever his lady commands to win her favor. In 165,10 the speaker says his friends are annoyed by his lamenting, and he agrees: "des man ze vil gehoeret, dem ist allem sô" (165,13). Yet he assures them that he does not deserve to suffer the way he does and, if he does not get to lie with his beloved, no one will derive any benefit from his joy. In addition, he complains that the *hôhgemuoten* do not take him seriously, for they accuse him of not loving his lady as much as he claims. This is simply not true, he says; even though she has never given him any consolation, she has always been as dear to him as life itself. He then begins an encomium of the fair sex, saying that nothing is as praiseworthy as a woman when she applies herself to true goodness and that whomever she loves faithfully has every reason to love life.[3] Because women give the whole world *hôhen muot*, he wants to know why he cannot also be granted a little bit of joy. This seems to imply that, if his beloved were truly good, she could not make him suffer so. But he also realizes that her *werdekeit* might be diminished if she yielded to him, and he is torn between wanting her and not wanting to see her discredited in any way. In the final stanza, however, he appears to be just as certain as he was at the beginning of the song that he has not merited the poor treatment he has been accorded; indeed, he has done everything that by rights should have gained her favor. He concludes by returning to speak of those who have refused to believe his sincerity; he asks them to listen to his words again and determine whether anything he has ever said has not come straight from his heart. The statement that he has not deserved to be treated so shabbily and that he has done everything possible to win his lady's love is precisely the point in the poem where one might look for an indication that he has become worthy through self-improvement. But there is no hint that this is the case, for no specific actions on his part are mentioned. A second missed occasion to introduce an aspect of ennobling love arises in connection with the lavish praise of women in general and the concentration on the value of a woman's true goodness in particular. Conspicuously absent here is any reference to the notion that a man should adopt a woman's virtues.

In 196,35 the speaker says that, if his beloved would show him *genâde*, he could renounce sorrow forever and ignore many things that people have been saying about him and his lady. He cannot understand why some have taken it amiss because he has sworn that she is dearer to him than all other women, and he reaffirms his oath, claiming to be willing to live "swie si gebiutet" (197,7). Bitter about the bad treatment he has endured, he complains that "ungefüeger schimpf" (197,9) constantly bombards him. They say that he talks too much about her and that the love of which he speaks is a lie. In response to this mockery he can only reply with the wish that they would esteem his lady the way he does and leave him and her in peace. The only place in this song where the ennobling power of love could have played a role is in the man's announcement of his intention to put his life in his lady's hands and to live as she commands. There is, however, not even a hint here of the idea that, under her guidance—or at least following her example—his character will be improved and he will thereby become worthy of her love.

The speaker in 170,1 expresses his desire to hurry to his beloved, even though he does not seem to believe that the fulfillment of his hopes is imminent. He says he is determined to persist in his suit and to serve her in such a way that she will have to alleviate his suffering "âne ir danc" (170,6). Why he is so insistent on continuing to woo her becomes clear in the next two stanzas where he says that everything good he ever heard about her has turned out to be true. No other woman can hold a candle to her. He realizes that his joy lies solely in her hands, for she is his "ôsterlîcher tac" (170,19). The generally optimistic tone of the first three stanzas is missing in the final two. Here he laments that his lady has scarcely heard his complaints because the presence of other persons prevents him from getting close enough to her to give vent to his feelings. He concludes by remarking sarcastically that no one would take it amiss if such people would desist from spending time where they really have no business. One place in this poem that would have lent itself nicely to the introduction of the idea of ennobling love is the passage in the first stanza where the speaker says he is going to serve his beloved in such a manner that she will have to reward him whether she wants to or not. Here one could easily expect to find the notion that he will become worthy of her love in the course of his courtship by means of self-improvement. Nothing in the poem itself, however, points specifically in this direction, and there is no reason to assume that anything more is involved than the man's belief in the feudal concept that service must be rewarded. Another unseized opportunity in this poem—as was the case in the two songs just discussed— occurs when the speaker extols his beloved as the best of all women. This, too, is not related in any way to the idea that the woman's good qualities should serve as a model for the man.

In 195,10 the speaker complains that his lady seems to show no consideration for his misery, even though he serves her "swie sô si gebiutet" (195,15) and she knows he has endured everything he is supposed to in order to win her favor. Before saying that he should be more optimistic because she has always behaved toward him like a woman "an der triuwe und êre lît" (195,27), he also states that she would have rewarded him if she had considered him *wert*. But any hope seen earlier in the poem is dispelled by the pessimism of the concluding stanza. If she does not end his sorrow, he says, he will have to be sad until he dies. In this song the speaker's declaration that he has suffered whatever he should have to gain his lady's affection and that he has done whatever she commanded would have been the place to make a connection with the idea that what she desired of him was improvement. Yet because nothing specific is said about what he felt obliged to do to win her love and what she demanded of him, it cannot automatically be assumed that his efforts in her service were directed toward self-betterment. A second missed opportunity in this song arises when the man states that his lady would have compensated him if she had thought him deserving. Because he thinks she does not believe he is worthy—an assumption that does not necessarily mean he has been trying to earn his reward by becoming a better person—one might expect some hint of what further action he could take in this regard. But there is no mention of any such possibility, and one is definitely left with the feeling that the speaker is not relying on the theory of the ennobling power of love to help him achieve his goal, but rather on the hope that his lady, in light of her goodness and sense of fairness, will ultimately be touched by his lengthy suffering.

Another unseized opportunity is provided in 159,1. The speaker says he will not be overly concerned about his lady's seeming indifference to him. He will persist in his courtship in the hope that a miracle will take place. Occasionally, he says, his *lîp* has advised him to turn elsewhere, but his heart would not listen to such counsel; he thanks it for having chosen so well and granted him such sweet *arebeit* that he must remain devoted to his beloved forever and rejoice in the prospect of continuing to serve her. In addition, he is confident that she will reward him when he tells her of the distress he suffers because of her. The song concludes with a playful stanza in which he says that, if he ever succeeds in stealing a kiss from her and she is angry about it, he will be only too happy to put it back where he found it. In this song one might expect a reference to the idea of ennobling love when the man speaks enthusiastically of his sweet *arebeit*. But there is no intimation that this involves conscious improvement on his part or that he counts on its efficacy to bring about the desired results. On the contrary, he seems to rely on a miracle or on the fact that his beloved will be deeply moved when she learns of his great torment.

The unseized opportunity to introduce the idea of the educative power of love in the next two songs in this group—163,23 and 187,31—involves the speaker's emphasis on his ability to control himself. At the beginning of 163,23 he complains that women do not seem to find him appealing even though he delights in their praise and has never spoken a harsh word against them. Nonetheless, they will continue to enjoy his service as a result of his devotion to a certain lady whom he cannot help loving despite her apparent indifference to him. To be sure, he finds some small consolation in a kind of fatalistic attitude ("swaz geschehen sol, daz geschiht," 164,2) and in the coming of summer, which seems to have renewed his hopes and inspired him to extol his lady above all others. But when he remembers the joy of having seen her, he also recalls the pain of having had to leave her again and the agony of having been unable to speak in her presence. Indeed, the memory of the misery of those days prompts him to say that he could never have survived had he not been able to bear his sorrow "mit zühten" (164,32). If he were to give vent to his true feelings of woe, he says, the people who used to like to spend time in his company would desert him. So he must force himself to appear cheerful as long as he is in society. In the last stanza, however, a mood of despair predominates. The poet has had enough of bringing joy to the world through his art. Having received no reward for his service to society, he now intends to remain silent unless his beloved commands him to sing once more.

In 187,31 the speaker laments that those who have never truly been under Love's sway make light of the woes he so sadly bemoans. If they had to bear his burden, they would feel the same pain as he does and they would no longer doubt his sincerity. But even though they constantly ask him why he is in such a miserable state, he decides he cannot tell them, for "swer wîbes êre hüeten wil, / der bedarf vil schoener zühte wol" (188,29–30). He concludes that, love for him having meant only pain, even the beauties of summer cannot help alleviate his sorrow—his thoughts are so gloomy that for him it must always be winter.

In both songs the man's capacity to control himself could have been regarded as a form of exemplary behavior that might have made him worthy of the lady's love, as will be the case in two other poems—162,7 and 160,6—to be discussed below.[4] Here, however, the opportunity is left unexploited by the poet, for not a word is spoken about the possible efficacy of this attitude in winning the woman's favor. Instead, in 163,23 the man's ability to control himself is considered not only a means of surviving the darkest days of his despair, but also a social necessity—if he had moaned and groaned in public, his joy-seeking companions would have fled him like the plague. And in 187,31 the man's self-control is prompted not by his wish to hide his misery and act cheerfully in public, but rather by his reluctance to reveal the true cause of his unhappiness in order to protect the honor of women—presumably by not saying anything detrimental about them. (Whether this kind of forbearance can be related to the idea of ennobling love is doubtful, inasmuch as nothing here justifies the assumption that the man's ability to control himself represents an improvement in his character.) As far as the rest of the poems is concerned, the focus on the debilitation of the man who knows love only as pain points away from any notion of love's uplifting power.

The last examples of unseized opportunities occur in four songs that will be discussed in the main in other categories below.[5] In two poems the poet fails to use the occasion of praising the woman's good qualities to at least hint that they should be a model for the knight to follow in his endeavor to become worthy of the lady's love. The man is so discouraged in 160,6 that for a moment he even wishes he could free himself from her, but he abandons the idea when he contemplates her excellence—without saying a word, however, about the latter's possible role as an example for him to follow. In 151,1 the speaker claims not to mind suffering for the sake of "einen alse guoten lîp" (151,19) and expresses confidence that she will not deny him recompense for his steadfastness, for she could not behave so badly as to mistreat him in this way. But instead of providing an inspiration for a betterment in his behavior, her goodness merely assures him that she will not leave his service unrewarded.

In 179,3 the man compares himself to a wild falcon that has flown too high and returned without its prey, for nothing he has ever said has made an impression on his lady and his having informed her too boldly of his innermost desires apparently has made her angry. In using the falcon-metaphor to express the notion that the goal he has set for himself is perhaps too high, the poet would have had a perfect opportunity to introduce the idea that the loftiness of the lady might inspire the man to become like her. Instead, however, one finds only the negative view that the man's attempts to reach such a pinnacle are doomed to failure.

Finally, in 170,36, the speaker offers a summary of the proper behavior for wooing a lady. Women are pleased when "man si staeteclîchen bite" (171,11), and whoever wants to win their favor, "der wese in bî und spreche in wol"(171,15–16). Conspicuously absent is any mention of the idea that the knight could become worthy of love through self-improvement.

Eight of the poems of Reinmar von Hagenau contain passages that either tempt one to think in terms of, or present situations that come close to, the idea of ennobling love. In 152,15, a variation of the *Wechsel*-form, the lady complains in the first strophe that she seems to have no power to make her beloved fulfill her wishes, and she asks the messenger she is addressing to inform her knight of her displeasure and her fear that the *triuwe* they once shared no longer exists. From the knight's three stanzas it becomes clear that her concern is unfounded. If he has seemed distant and changed it is only because he has been unable to show his true sentiments in public. He is still steadfastly in her service, and the assurance of her continued loyalty is sufficient to make him as happy as someone "der bî vrowen hât gelegen" (152,24). In this song both the knight's concern with how he should behave and the lady's complaint that she cannot make him do her will tempt one to think of aspects of the idea of ennobling love. Here, however, the man's altered behavior has nothing to do with the notion of self-improvement, but merely results from his fear of attracting attention and exposing their relationship to public scrutiny. And when the lady complains that he does not do what she wants, she is not alluding to any attempt to induce him to improve his character and hence become worthy of her love; rather, she is merely expressing her desire to have him visit her more often.

The speaker begins 157,11 by stating that he knows from his own experience how much woe love can bring. He maintains that no man with only hope to go on has ever sung as much as he has. But now no one should be surprised if he can no longer sing, for the uncertainty of his situation has robbed him of his art. Although he grows older from day to day, he declares, he is no wiser now than he was last year, inasmuch as he is unable to give himself any good advice. He also claims to know what has done him so much harm—he has told his beloved of his plight so often that she no longer wants to listen to him. For this reason he now intends to be her silent vassal and just hope for her *genâde*. He would not continue serving her if he did not know that she could make him *wert* "vor al der welte" (157,32) if she wanted to. Finally, realizing that she will not react positively to his pleading, he hopes that she will at least let him be her fool and not take his words amiss. This song might seem to be referring to the idea of ennobling love when the man says his lady could make him *wert* if she so desired. What the speaker means by this, however, is not that he would be morally uplifted under her guidance and hence become worthy of her love, but only that his stature would increase in the eyes of the world if she bestowed her favor upon him. Indeed, almost everything in the song emphasizes the negative and debilitating effects of love. His sorrow in love and his doubt of ever winning her affection have paralyzed him as a poet; love has prevented him from making wise decisions about his own predicament; and love has reduced him to wanting to play the role of a fool at his lady's feet.

In five of the six songs containing situations that come close to the idea of the educative function of love the concept of *staete* plays a more or less significant role. The *Wechsel*-like poem, 151,1, begins with a woman lamenting that a knight whom she desires stays away from her, whereas those who envy other people's good fortune are all too often in her presence. The second strophe reveals that the knight is unaware of the extent of her affection for him, for he states that he has long served his lady to no avail. But he does not mind suffering for the sake of such a good person, he claims, and is confident that she will reward him for his *staete*, for she could not act so poorly as to abuse him in this way. In the third stanza the lady now appears convinced of his true feelings for her and promises to reward him with her love. The final strophe shows the knight in a state of *hôhgemüete*, undoubtedly the result of his having received her *genâde*. In this song the knight's certainty that his lady will reward him for his constancy approaches the notion of ennobling love by showing an awareness of the need to conform to a high standard of behavior. What is missing here, however, is an indication that his *staete* represents an improvement in his character that would make him deserving of her love. Indeed, nowhere in the poem is there any sign that her willingness to requite him is based on the principle of his having become worthy of her. The only reason she gives for granting her favor is his confidence in her: "sît daz er mir getriuwet wol, / sô wil ich hoehen sînen muot" (151,27–28).

After stating in 189,5 that it would be untrue if he said he had succeeded in his courtship, the speaker says that, fool though he may be, he will lament anew the misery his lady caused him when she deprived him of joy. But, he continues, he is not so foolish as to persist in loving her steadfastly. Then, however, he begins to take back some of the negative things he has said. Thus, although his love's labor appears to have been lost, he will still show honor to all women because one woman did give him joy *mit gedanken*. And if she ever expects him to sing with joy again, she will have to say "yes" to his entreaties. Yet he fears that, if he has to wait too long for his reward, it might come too late to do him any good. Indeed, he has waited so long already that he often despairs of attaining his goal. What keeps him going, however, is his belief in the system. Someone who is characterized by *triuwe* and *êre* cannot help rewarding service such as his. And his faith in the efficacy of constancy to win the lady's love, which seemed to be wavering earlier in the poem, appears to be fully restored at the end: "ouch ist ez wol genâden wert, / swâ man nâch liebe in alsô lûterlîcher staete ringet"

(190,1–2). There is no doubt that he feels his *staete* makes him worthy of her *genâde*. But just as in 151,1, it is not clear that this represents an improvement in his behavior.

In 170,36 the speaker declares that, even though no one's misfortune could be greater than his, he makes every attempt to appear happy in public. In addition, he is careful to refrain from speaking ill of women, for he considers that to do so would be *unstaetekeit* and he knows that ladies like to be wooed with constancy. He is also aware that to win the favor of women one must spend time in their company and speak well of them. But evidently he is disillusioned about ever attaining his goal; he has followed the prescribed course and has not been rewarded. Although at first he says that his misery is greater than he deserves, he ultimately realizes that he is foolish to think that his lady is responsible for his plight, inasmuch as he has no one to blame but himself: "mir machet niemen schaden wan mîn staetekeit" (171,31). Although here, too, the man's consciousness of the need to maintain a high standard of behavior comes close to the idea of ennobling love, it is obvious that he no longer believes his constancy will be effective in obtaining the lady's favor and hence bring him joy. On the contrary, it is his very *staetekeit* that is causing him such woe.

The poet's loss of faith in *staete* is even more pronounced in 162,7, which begins with some general remarks about the advisability of not making too many reproaches to someone whose friendship one desires to keep. In the second stanza he directly addresses his own problem, asking why the lady he loves causes him such pain when he has not pressed his suit in a dishonorable fashion and when every word he has spoken about her has come from his heart. If it turns out that his *triuwe* is to be wasted, he says, no one should be surprised if he is angry once in a while. He then proceeds to rail against *staete*: even though people say it is the mistress of all virtues, as far as he is concerned it has destroyed his joy and he will never praise it again. In addition, he expresses his bitterness about the fact that those who know how to rant and rage in their wooing have more success with the ladies than those who cannot conduct themselves in such a fashion. He complains that he only knows the sorrow of love, while the way leading out of misery into joy remains closed to him. But then, after proclaiming his desire to be known as a master of the art of bearing pain, so that all will agree that "niht mannes sîniu leit   sô schône kan getragen" (163,9), he acknowledges the necessity of suffering if one wishes to know happiness. At the same time he seems to replace his abandoned faith in *staete* with a belief in a certain attitude toward enduring his woes. Torment must be born "mit bescheidenlîcher klage   und gar ân arge site" (162,38). He feels that nothing is as good as "guot gebite" (163,1) and he places his hope of finding joy in patient waiting.

Although the poet's awareness of the need for the man to conform to an exemplary standard of behavior does approach the idea of ennobling love, the situation in this poem cannot be viewed as a genuine example of the phenomenon under investigation. If the poet's restrained reaction to the lady's indifference and his calm forbearance in the face of his troubles could be considered an improvement in his character, and if this change for the better helped make him deserving of the lady's love, then one certainly could say that love represented an uplifting force. But there is no evidence that this is the case. Nothing indicates that the lady's favor could be gained in this way; on the contrary, the poet seems well aware that those who do not control their emotions in public fare better with the ladies than he does. Moreover, everything appears to suggest that the poet is constitutionally unable to behave in any other way. One is certainly not left with the feeling that he has deliberately trained himself to become a master of self-control in order to win his lady's love; rather, it appears that this is simply the way he is. Thus it would seem that he is making a virtue out of a necessity. Because he cannot help himself, he is compelled to hope that his forbearance will ultimately achieve the desired results—even though he admits that the lady has given him no reason to assume he will succeed.

The themes of *staete* and patient waiting are also found together at the end of 160,6, although they are not treated as broadly as in 162,7. After praising the lady and boasting of the opportunities for success with other women he has passed up, the poet in 160,6 complains that his beloved has asked him what form of *genâde* he desires from her. If she claims not to know what he wants, he wonders of what use all his efforts and all his torment have been. He is so discouraged that for a moment he even wishes he could free himself from her, but he abandons the idea when he contemplates her excellence. Because he has always been honest with her, he cannot understand at first why she has made him suffer so much. Then he realizes, however, that perhaps it is precisely because he has been forthright and revealed his vulnerability that she has caused him so much pain. But when he finally asks himself whether she actually could be as cruel as he has imagined her to be, he answers that she must have another motive for acting the way she does: "sin getet ez nie wan umbe daz / daz si mich noch wil versuochen baz" (161,29–30). In the final stanza he laments that *Frau Gnade* has not offered him consolation. She should take note of his *staete* and help him overcome his sorrow, for he has waited "sô kûmeclîche" (162,4) and "mit schoenen siten" (162,3). If his lady does not understand this, then he will be lost entirely.

In contrast to 162,7, where the poet's belief in the efficacy of his good manners and self-control replaced his faith in *staete*, here both his constancy and his ability to behave decorously while awaiting his reward are clearly the reasons why he feels he deserves *genâde*. If the lady is proving him, as he is inclined to believe, he seems to think she need not continue to do so, for it is implied that he has shown he is worthy of her love. One might be inclined to view this explicit discussion of the lady putting the man to the test as clear evidence of the uplifting power of love in this song. There is, however, no more reason to assume so than in the case of 162,7, because here, too, nothing suggests that the knight's character has improved in the service of the lady. The trial in itself does not indicate the presence of the educative force of love, for it is not sufficient for the man merely to demonstrate during the process that he merits the lady's affection. Only if the knight was not worthy of the lady but became so through self-betterment in the course of his courtship could one say that love had exerted an ennobling force. All that can be stated here is that the poet, by showing an awareness of the need to conform to a certain standard of behavior, comes close to the idea of the educative power of love.

In the last song in this group, 179,3, the speaker begins with a statement to the effect that he hopes the joy he ultimately is granted will correspond to the manner in which he conducts his courtship and the quality of his love. He continues with the complaint that certain persons have denied him access to his lady. Let them watch over her until they go mad, he exclaims. And he bitterly asks what they think they are going to perceive by observing her so closely. No one need envy him the favor she has shown him, for the only thing she has ever given him is that feeling of *hôhes muotes* he experienced when he dared to woo "ein wîp mit alsô reinen siten" (179,17). After reprimanding himself for speaking regretfully about the *arebeit* he has had to bear in the course of his service and hoping that God will perform a miracle by making her his, he says he would rather not have her favor if it meant having to share it with others. He then likens himself to a falcon that has attempted to fly too high and returns without its prey, for nothing he has ever said has touched his lady deeply and his having expressed his desires too boldly apparently has aroused her wrath. The only reward he has ever received has been in his imagination, and anyone who cannot refrain from commenting about that is committing a sin. But he says he does not really care what such a person thinks. He concludes by wishing that whoever woos as he does may live "in hôhem muote" (181,9).

From the way this poem begins one might expect the idea of ennobling love to be strongly in evidence, inasmuch as how the speaker goes about his wooing seems to be vitally important to him. But after this initial statement there is little to indicate that his behavior as a suitor includes a conscious effort at self-improvement. To be sure, he rebukes himself for having complained about the *arebeit* he has had to suffer and vows not to do so again, which might be viewed as self-betterment. However, his expression of regret represents only a temporary wavering from what apparently has been an exemplary attitude toward *arebeit*, for when he promises to stop grumbling he also says: "ich muoz leben als ich pflac" (179,26). Furthermore, it must be remembered that the ability to endure distress stoically, even though it might be praiseworthy and a prerequisite to the achievement of anything worthwhile, is not in itself a sign of the uplifting force of love. Only if the knight shows a change in his conduct, only if he was previously undisciplined and then, in order to become deserving of the lady, subjects himself to a program of improvement can one say that love has had an educative effect on the suitor. Aside from the man's recovery from the short lapse just mentioned, nothing in the poem shows that such a transformation has taken place. The most that can be said here is that the man's awareness of the need to conform to a high standard of behavior comes very close to the idea of the elevating force of love without being a genuine example of it.

More or less clear examples of the idea of ennobling love are found in only three of Reinmar's songs. In the first stanza of 150,1 the poet speaks of his beloved as one who is always in his thoughts, whose *êre* he proclaims in his songs, and whom he will always rank above all other women. The only sorrow he seems to know results when he is absent from his lady. At first glance, the second stanza appears to have little or no connection with the first. Here the poet says that a man "der sinne hât" (150,10) and whose heart strives for "niht wan êren" (150,13) can become "saelic unde wert" (150,11) if he associates with "den liuten" (150,12). A knight, he says, should strive for "manger güete" (150,15), and if anyone is envious because of it, he (the poet) is ready to bear such a *schade* willingly. This kind of envy, he goes on to say in the last strophe, is not easily concealed. Many a man asks why he (the poet) makes a fool of himself, and he could give an answer if he wanted to. But anyone "der pflaege schoener sinne" (150,25) should not have to ask in the first place, for there isn't anyone who will not find "sînes herzen künneginne" (150,27).

Whether or not this poem has anything to do with the notion of the ennobling power of love depends primarily on how the second stanza is interpreted. At face value Reinmar seems to be extolling the benefits that accrue to a man who spends his time with "den liuten." Because his becoming *wert* appears to be one consequence of this association, it could be said that society has an educative effect upon him. But the stanza does not mention the lady's role in this process, although it certainly could be assumed that she would play some part in society's influencing of the knight. If, however, one takes the expression *mit den liuten umbegân* to be used "verhüllend . . . für den Umgang mit der Geliebten," as von Kraus suggested,[6] then one could speak with more assurance about the lady's elevating effect on the man. Bert Nagel also assumed that Reinmar was talking about the ennobling effect of love service in the last two stanzas. Even though he did not specifically agree with von Kraus's interpretation of *liute*, Nagel based his assumption on Reinmar's general tendency to make use of "gedämpften Ausdrucks" and claimed that what appears in the poem as an exposition of general ethical behavior really alludes to the specific "sittlichen Qualitäten, die der höfische Frauendienst fordert."[7] Because the first stanza clearly deals with love and the last two lines of the poem return to the theme of *minne*, it does seem reasonable to suppose that the uplifting influence on the knight referred to in the song represents at least a veiled example of the ennobling power of love. Nowhere, however, is there a connection implied between the man's becoming *wert* and his striving to be good, on the one hand, and his being rewarded with the lady's favor as a consequence of his behavior, on the other.

In 173,6 the speaker, after stating his determination to persist in the service of his lady, says that, if ever a good and faithful man received his reward, then he, too, will know joy. He also explains to some extent what he means by being *guot*, for he devotes almost two stanzas to assuring the lady that he intends to be upright and honest in his dealings with her. This certainly seems to indicate an awareness of the notion that, by maintaining a high standard of behavior, he can hope ultimately to attain his goal. Although he does not specifically state that he is attempting to become worthy of her love, he seems to imply it. In the final strophe, however, it becomes obvious that the speaker has some doubts about reaching his objective: "Wie mîn lôn und ouch mîn ende an ir gestê, / dast mîn aller meistiu nôt" (173,34–35). Thus it is not at all clear that he believes his endeavors to act in an exemplary fashion will have the desired effect on his beloved.

At the beginning of 197,15 the speaker says that perhaps he should give up his love; the pain he is suffering will lead to his death if it lasts too long. But such a renunciation is impossible, he asserts, because it would mean abandoning his only hope of bliss. His joy and his sorrow being inextricably bound up with his lady, he has no choice but to be sad as long as he is prevented from seeing her. The notion that the man's behavior has improved as a result of his love is clearly expressed in this poem: "Waz sol ein unstaeter man? / daz was ich ê: nu bin ichz niht" (197,26–27). And a relationship between this change and his hope of reward is at least implied, for his question "Was sol ein unstaeter man?" immediately follows the statement "Mich wundert sêre wie dem sî / der vrouwen dienet und daz endet an der zît" (197,22–23) and the wish that he, too, might know some happiness.

In addition to the thirty-four poems by Reinmar von Hagenau discussed above, thirty-five songs are presented under the headings *Unechtes* and *Aus den Anmerkungen* in the section of *MF* devoted to Reinmar.[8] Of these, eleven contain no evidence of the idea of ennobling love and no situations that would readily lend themselves to its introduction. In two songs the participants are depicted in a more or less humorous way. One of these—H.S.313,V.S.435—is a *Wechsel* in which the man says his lady's mouth robs him of his senses and drives him wild. Once she bit him when he kissed her, and he is determined to get his revenge. Indeed, he is convinced she will come crawling to him when she learns how angry he is. The lady, for her part, makes light of his threats. Although her friends, fearing she will be wounded by his *spieze*, want to protect her, she is unafraid and even eager to meet him on the meadow, where they can test each other's strength. The second poem—H.S.308f.,V.S.431—is a variation of the *Wechsel*-form with an introductory stanza in which a quarrel between an old man and his wife unfolds. The woman implies that the husband has no cause to beat her, for he has been just as unfaithful as she. In the next two strophes the wife says that her old husband is angry because she loves a young man. She will not be dissuaded from her purpose, however, even if it means kicking the horrible old man out on the street. She even wishes he would drop dead so she could be rid of the old fool. The final stanza presents the husband's prayer that God might make his *frouwe* of gentle spirit and without malice. He concludes by expressing the hope that she will give up her shameful behavior for his sake, for otherwise he knows no way he can keep watch over her. Obviously there is no room in either of these clearly uncourtly situations for the idea of the ennobling power of love.

In only one song in this category—195,37—does a woman in love play a serious role. The lady in this poem gives vent to her passions, saying she is unhappy because she is being prevented from meeting with a knight whom she loves. Yet she is pleased that he has promised to come to her, and she is determined to give herself to him. If he does not lie close to her on many a summer day, she maintains, it will be the end of her beauty. But if he consoles her, no one will see her crying very often. Nowhere in this song does the woman say—nor is there any easy opportunity for her to do so—what induced her to bestow her love.

Five songs in this group share the theme of the speaker's relationship to society or, at least, to certain people around him. In 168,30 he says the only thing that is preventing him from being completely happy is "ein rehte herzeclîchiu nôt" (168,32). To be sure, people say that joy must depress him, but this, he maintains, is simply not true. It is as dear to him as ever, and he wants to be happy to please his friends and annoy his enemies who think their hate will make him miserable. He concludes by stating that he does not wish to have anything to do with those who have no use for him, but if he could find people who would be loyal to him, he would gladly serve them for their favor. This song, with its merely implicit reference to an unhappy love affair and its emphasis on the speaker's difficulties with his contemporaries, neither gives any evidence of, nor presents any opportunity to introduce, the notion of the ennobling power of love.

The clear hostility of certain persons in the poet's environment is also reflected in 203,24 and H.S.312,V.S.434. After rejoicing in the passing of a joyless winter, the speaker in 203,24 states that people should not hate him if he is cheerful, for he is not doing anyone any harm and it should not be anyone else's business if his beloved should treat him well. If he has to hide his joy, he says, he would have to become a thief. In the concluding stanza the speaker expresses concern that his *frouwelîn* might fall and hurt herself while playing ball. If that should happen, he claims, the harm would be half his. In the single strophe of H.S.312,V.S.434 the speaker says he does not know what to sing because, if he laments his old woes, the *valschen* will be very pleased. Thus he decides to send his cares to his beloved so that they will tell her heart to help end his misery, for his love has brought him nothing but distress. He closes the poem by asking when the happiness of love will finally bring him joy. Nowhere in these songs is there any hint of the idea of the uplifting force of love.

In the fourth of these songs involving social relationships, 193,22, the speaker says he is afraid that people will take it amiss because he is so sad. He cannot help it if what he says reflects his depressed state of mind. When he was happy, he spoke "vil mange rede guote" (193,32); perhaps someday he will be able to do so again if he is treated properly. Those who seek only joy, he complains, seem to think they can do without him, but they will wring their hands when he is gone. They should be ashamed to think of him as they do, for the only way he has offended them is by directing his thoughts to love. Toward the end of the poem the speaker appears to regret his dedication to his beloved and all the woes it has brought him. But when he asks himself why he cannot turn elsewhere, he concludes that he does not wish to because he can find joy only with his lady. In this lament, too, there clearly is no trace of the notion of the educative power of love. The poet's decision to continue his suit despite the devastating effect of his devotion is not connected in any way with the idea that self-improvement will make him worthy of her love.

The last of the poems depicting the speaker's relations with people around him, 185,27, reflects more or less sympathetic reactions to his dejection rather than antagonism. Here he says that, because people have told him that sadness does not become him as much as joy, he will try to be high-spirited and hopeful. But any such effort seems doomed, he continues, for the only thing that will make him happy is the love of his lady. If she ever decides to reward him, he may no longer be alive or, if he is, he will be too old to appreciate it or to be of any use to her. He concludes by musing that she, too, will be old by then, and she may be sorry that she did not give herself to him. Although the speaker does discuss the possibility of his beloved's yielding to him some day, there is no indication of what will induce her to do so, and certainly no sign that the achievement of such a goal would be the result of his having become worthy through self-improvement. Indeed, instead of any uplifting effect of love, only the destructive aspects of his hopeless courtship are shown here.

The last two songs that are devoid of the idea of ennobling love and that lack any occasion to introduce it are more or less typical laments of unrequited love. In 201,12 the speaker says he should have stayed where he was wanted instead of directing his attention to a woman who has caused him nothing but pain. After asking why he is wasting his time in such an unpromising situation, he laments that others, unlike him, have the chance to talk with her. He concludes by saying that, if someone else receives a reward where he has been rebuffed, he will never serve a lady again in the hope of obtaining her love. Because this song does not indicate either why he presumably was successful in earlier courtships or why this time he has wooed in vain, it clearly offers no opportunity to think in terms of the ennobling power of love. In contrast to the dejected knight in 201,12, the man presented in the single strophe of H.S.303,1,V.S.423 is in a considerably more optimistic frame of mind. But although the speaker says that all his sadness would disappear if his beloved kissed and embraced him, here, too, there is no occasion to expect the appearance of the idea of the ennobling effect of love.

Ten of the poems under the headings *Unechtes* and *Aus den Anmerkungen* contain unseized opportunities to introduce the idea of ennobling love. In three of these the major occasion not made use of arises in the context of certain benefits a man derives from love. In 182,14 the speaker says his heart is as high as the sun because of a lady who has freed him of sorrow. She gives him joy and *hôhen muot*, and he would follow her to the ends of the earth. The only true happiness he has ever known has come from his lady, who has granted his every desire since she took him into her *genâde*. Similarly, the man states in 183,33 that his beloved has rid him of his cares. She is responsible for his being "vil wunneclîchen wol gemuot" (184,7) and her *güete* has banished his woes. Even though some people disapprove of his interest in the lady, he is certain their efforts to thwart him will be in vain, for they do not know "wiez ergangen ist / in kurzer frist" (184,29–30). In contrast to 182,14 and 183,33, the man in 195,3 is discouraged about the prospects of a happy outcome of his relationship to a lady. But his dejection does not become apparent until the second stanza, for at the beginning he speaks only in general terms about how good it is to be blessed by the love of good women, who are the source of the world's *wunne* and *heil* and whose "güete wunder geben kan" (195,9). The second half of the song tells of the man's sadness caused by his lack of success in courtship. He concludes by wondering about the reasons for his failure, thinking that perhaps he has been obliged to pay for having had only one love or for having been too eager for success. In both the poems in which the man sings of the joy of love, as well as in the lament of unrequited affection, the notion of self-improvement is conspicuously absent from the discourses on the benefits of love. In addition, in the two songs where the lady's *güete* is mentioned, the poet misses the opportunity to make a connection with the concept that the woman's virtues serve as a source of inspiration for the man. Finally, when the speaker speculates in the lament about what went wrong in the relationship, one might expect him to consider the possibility that he had not become worthy of the lady's love.

Praise of the lady's good qualities is likewise the point where the poet might have introduced the notion of ennobling love in H.S. 312,10, which is also a song of fulfilled love. Here the speaker begins by extolling his lady, who has separated herself from the *valschen*. He dares not speak fully about the reward he has received from her, for he must consider her honor and protect her "kiuschen wîpheit" (H.S.313,12) by seeing to it that gossips do not find out about their relationship. But just as the man's having won the lady's favor is not connected in any way with his having become worthy of it by means of self-improvement, so, too, no attempt is made to relate the lady's goodness to the idea of ennobling love.

Another song in which the missed opportunity concerns the lady's goodness is 169,9, where the speaker laments a distress that "an daz herze gât" (169,19) and whose end he cannot foresee. He says he could use the advice of wise people but cannot find loyalty among those he has served, although he would be willing to do anything for good people. He then praises his eyes and his heart for their role in directing him to a woman who "hât sich underwunden / guoter dinge und anders niet" (169,29–30), and he affirms that he gladly endures suffering for the sake of his lady. In the final strophe he indicates that, even though an evil person will never think well of him, any such criticism can only redound to his credit.[9] In this song, too, nothing is said about the lady's good qualities guiding the man toward self-betterment, just as it is not evident that the man's willingness to suffer is related to the idea of ennobling love, for there is no indication that the acceptance of pain is part of a process of self-improvement leading to the attainment of his goal.

In two songs the unseized opportunity is offered by the statement of the man's readiness to do what his lady demands of him. The two stanzas of 203,10—a woman's monologue—show the lady's spirit soaring to new heights of joy because, as she says, "ein ritter mînen willen tuot" (203,12), and she is determined to practice "wîbes triuwe" (203,16). One might suppose that at least part of what she wants him to do involves self-betterment, but nothing in the poem even hints that this is the case. And from the rest of the song, in which all she does is talk about how wonderful it is when he lies in her arms and holds her close, one has the impression that his doing her will primarily entails making love to her.

The knight's willingness to do what his lady wants is seen from the man's point of view in 201,33. Here the knight is discouraged by his inability to act toward his lady as he should. The problem is not that he cannot do what she demands of him, but that he is not wise enough to know what she desires that would enable him to reap the reward for his efforts. Because everything he has suffered does not seem to have helped him achieve his goal, he declares he will never trust a woman again. No sooner has he said this, however, than he seems sorry and wishes to retract it, for he asserts: "jâ sint si guot. / ich hoere sagen daz si niht alle   haben einen muot" (202,5–6). He continues by claiming he would do "waz ir wille waere" (202,7) if he only knew what it was. In fact, he would do anything she desired except desist from his wooing, as only she can console him. And because he is sure that any joy he is to know must come from her, he hopes she will give him what he has requested. The song ends on a bitter note when the knight says he never saw a woman "sô staete" (202,19) who mistreated a man in the way she has behaved toward him. Sadly he concludes that all his pleas have been in vain and that she is out to deceive him "alse ein kint" (202,24). In this poem the idea of the ennobling power of love seems conspicuously absent. The song offers a perfect opportunity for its appearance, for the knight is eager to please his lady in the hope that he will be rewarded for doing so. Yet he has no idea how to please her. He seems to be totally unfamiliar with the notion that he should strive to improve himself to become worthy of her love.

In another two songs, the poet's emphasis on the feudal nature of the relationship between the lady and the knight would have easily lent itself to the introduction of the theme of ennobling love. The speaker begins 194,18 with the statement that he was filled with joy when he first saw his beloved, who entered through his eyes and settled in his heart. Then addressing the lady, he asks why she is attacking him there. He begs for *genâde*, for he cannot defend himself against her, and because his heart is in her power, he has no choice but to hope for her mercy and to wait for his reward. In H.S.304, V.S.425 the knight is dejected because he is unable or reluctant to plead his case with his lady. Although he looks to his beloved as his source of joy, he says he hopes for her help only like the vassal who refuses to let himself be freed from his obligations at any cost. He realizes he entered into her service of his own free will, but he dares not press his claims for a reward. In both poems the underscoring of the bond between lord and vassal could have been connected with the notion that, by becoming worthy in the course of his service, the knight could expect to be rewarded. But here—as has been the case so often elsewhere—the man's expectation of his reward is based on the views that the lord should have mercy on a suffering vassal and that the *dienestman* has a right to compensation for service rendered. Nowhere is there even a hint that self-improvement is the lady's condition for granting her favor.

The last song in this category, 190,27, is a lament in which the knight says his lady's failure to fulfill his request is to be interpreted as blameworthy. He cannot understand why she is ungracious toward him, for she knows that no one loves her more than he. Furthermore, he believes he deserves his reward; even if she does not love him, she should grant his desires "dur ein wunder" (191,3). The song concludes with the statement that he would renounce anything in this world before he would give her up. Here, the man could have easily explained *why* he deserved a reward—namely, that he has become better and hence worthy of her love. But instead, the only basis offered for his feeling meritorious appears to be his belief that he loves her more than anyone else.

Five of the poems under Reinmar's name in *MF* in the sections marked *Unechtes* and *Aus den Anmerkungen* contain passages that either approach the idea of ennobling love or tempt one to think in such terms. Mutual love plays a role in three of these songs. In 198,4, a *Wechsel*, the lady complains that she has not seen her beloved for too long and expresses her longing to be with him as soon as possible. The man states that he has never known such joy before and that he wants to raise her spirits and reward her with good because she is herself so good. This sentiment appears to come close to the notion that the man is inspired to become better by his lady's good qualities. But here too much should not be made of his desire to do good, for it seems likely that this merely means he wants to be nice to her because she has been kind to him. In no way is it intimated that an improvement in his behavior was a condition of his winning her love.

In 199,25 the lady says she would be without sorrow except that she longs for her beloved's *güete* when he is not with her. As far as she is concerned, he can have anything he wants, for "man so guoten,   baz gemuoten, / hân ich selten mê gesehen" (199,39–200,2). While she has him she has little need of anything else, and she is ready to do his bidding and to suffer for his sake the hatred of "boeser liute" (200,17). She also dwells on the joy "der beste man" (200,24) gives her when he lies with her, and she says she would be true to him no matter what he did as long as he loved her. He recently departed from her, she states, but she will not forget him and she will wait "mit êren" (200,40) for him to return, for "wîp mit güeten   sol ir êre hüeten / schône zallen zîten, / wider ir friunt niht strîten" (200,36–39). Finally, after praying that God might protect him wherever he goes, she concludes the song by saying that no man has ever tried to attain a woman's reward "alsô schône" (201,7) as he has and that knowing so much about his *êre* has brought her *herzesêre*.

In this poem several things tempt one to think in terms of the idea of the educative force of love. It is evident that the woman is impressed by her knight's good qualities and it can be assumed that her appreciation of them played some part in her decision to grant him her favor. There is no indication, however, that the deportment she admires represents any improvement on his part. On the other hand, her statement at the end of the song that he strove for her love "alsô schône" might tend to support the view that he was consciously making an effort to act in a way that she found pleasing. But the words "alsô schône" are quite vague and do not necessarily imply that what was pleasing to her had anything to do with an improvement in his behavior. Another factor that might work against taking the notion of ennobling love too seriously here is the lady's explicit willingness to do what he commands and to be loyal to him no matter what he does, providing that he continues to love her. Given such an attitude, it is difficult to imagine that she cared very much about his self-betterment as a means of becoming worthy of her love. On the contrary, one almost has the feeling that, as far as the educative force of love is concerned, the roles are reversed; in other words, it is the lady who appears to be trying to behave in an exemplary fashion, or at least in a way that will not antagonize her beloved.

The lady of 192,25—the third song of mutual love—has not yet yielded to the entreaties of her knight. At the beginning of the song she claims she cannot do what he wants, and she calls upon those who guard her to protect her from temptation. When she first allowed him to serve her, she did not realize the suffering it would soon entail. Now she wishes he would desist from his suit and from desiring that she venture both her *êre* and her *lîp*. Although she used to think that death would be better than surrendering herself to him, she finally makes up her mind to give in to him because she feels she will lose him if she does not. She seems to rationalize her judgment with the following words: "ein als schône redender man, / wie möhte ein wîp dem iht versagen, / der ouch sô tugentlîche lebt als er wol kan?" (193,5–7). This justification of her decision shows that she is familiar with the idea that the knight's generally virtuous conduct makes him deserving of the reward of love. However, nothing in the poem points to the notion that he has consciously striven to improve himself to become worthy. Again one is dealing with an instance that comes close to, but is not the same as, a genuine example of the ennobling power of love.

Another song that makes one think of an aspect of ennobling love is 184,31, in which the singer's ability to alleviate the suffering of others plays a role. Here the speaker says that, when he was happy, he freed 100,000 hearts from woe. Now, because his lady refuses to console him, he finds himself among the lovelorn. If he were to regain his joy, however, he is certain he would still be able to comfort them in their distress. In this case it could be argued that the joy of love has an edifying effect on the poet in that he is able to serve others, which he cannot do when he is depressed. Although this is true, such betterment is quite different from that encountered elsewhere, for here the uplifting is not the result of a conscious effort to become deserving of love, but rather the consequence of love's fulfillment.

In the last poem in this category, 176,5, the speaker asks his lady to make his heart leap up. He reaffirms that she is his *frouwe* and he her servant, whose joy is fully in her hands. He maintains that he does not deserve the poor treatment he has had to endure, for the only thing he ever did to her was to look at her furtively and to blush whenever he heard her name. Finally, he says he has suffered for her sake more than any other man has ever done for his love, and he pleads with her to be kinder to him and to save him. Here one is tempted to argue that the man's belief that he does not merit the lady's disfavor because he has behaved impeccably toward her in public indicates an awareness of the notion that a certain standard of behavior is a prerequisite to the attainment of love. But because it is not clear that an improvement in his deportment is involved, this situation also must be classified as one that comes very close to the idea of ennobling love.

More or less clear examples of the idea under investigation are found in seven of the poems presented under the headings *Unechtes* and *Aus den Anmerkungen* in the sections of *MF* devoted to Reinmar von Hagenau. In 180,28, a crusade poem, the speaker touches on the theme of ennobling love in a way quite similar to that observed in one of the crusade songs of Friedrich von Hausen (48,13) and in Heinrich von Rugge's *Kreuzleich* (98,28). After turning away in the first stanza from the singing of worldly joys for the sake of God, whom he recognizes as the source of all the happiness he has known, he claims in the second stanza that there is more reason to be joyous now than ever before, for a man can attain what he desires, "lop und êre und dar zuo gotes hulde" (181,1)—presumably by participating in a crusade. But one must remain cheerful in the pursuit of these goals, he warns. In the final strophe he speaks of those who remain at home and think they can have their will with the ladies. These stay-at-homes will not have it so easy, he asserts, if they believe they can sway a woman "diu sinne und êre hât (181,8). God knows, he concludes, a good woman's ring cannot be acquired easily. Clearly it is implied here that a good woman would not give her love to someone who had shirked his duty to serve God as a crusader. Thus the attitude imputed to the ladies can be seen to have an educative effect on the knights—to become worthy of the ladies' affection, they must fulfill their obligations as crusaders.

The speaker begins 191,34 by declaring that he will not lose courage because of "swachen nît" (191,35) and that, when "iht leides" (191,36) befalls him, he bears it secretly "mit fuoge" (191,37) and hopes for the best. Even though his woe is often so great that no one can assuage it, he puts a happy face to the world. This behavior should not be interpreted as a lack of constancy, he says, for it is appropriate for a "sinnic herze" (192,9) to lament its trouble to itself. But, he continues, those who do not give much thought to how they live molest him and make fun of him. Such people he considers evil, whereas he is good; he would never hate a "rehten man . . . so er rehte tuot" (192,16–17). He concludes the song first with the statement that no one can attain "staeten lop" (192,18) by pleasing everyone, and then with the sentiment that a man should be more concerned with honor than with other things and take pains to do good. Because all allusions to sorrow in this poem are quite general and because there is no direct reference to a knight's courtship of a lady, it cannot be stated with certainty that the speaker's efforts to behave in an exemplary fashion should be categorized as an example of the educative power of love. Still, the echoes of love service are so strong that it seems likely that the song indeed deals with the phenomenon under investigation.

Two of the songs in this group are concerned, at least in part, with the theme of *staete*. In 172,23 the speaker, after a pessimistic opening regarding the sad state of the world and a personal complaint about his unrewarded service to a lady, expresses doubts about the efficacy of *staete*. Even though he has attended to his beloved "mit guoten triuwen" (173,1) since the time he first heard of her, his constancy has not helped him, for she has left him without joy. But he decides not to renounce her because it would mean losing too much. Here it seems to be implied that, at least in one respect, the man's behavior improved in the service of his lady in that he became *staete* after he was attracted to her. Clearly he believed she would reward him for becoming steadfast. The fact that she has ignored him, however, has caused him to lose faith in the principle of self-betterment as a means of attaining the goal of love. Similarly, in 191,7 the speaker connects a lament about unrewarded service with the idea of the importance of *staete*. In contrast to 172,23, however, the suitor here seems to persist in believing in the possibility that constancy will have the desired effect when he says:

> Ze rehter mâze sol ein man
> beidiu daz herze und al den sin
> ze staete wenden obe er kan:
> daz wirt im lîhte ein guot gewin.   (191,16–19)

From his speaking here of *turning* to *staete*, it is evident that the notion of self-improvement as a way of becoming worthy of love plays a role in this song.

The theme of the ennobling power of love is developed in 202,25 in the context of other people's animosity toward the speaker, who complains at the beginning about "der werlde unstaete" (202,25). No matter how much he would like to do right, he maintains, people who do not care about honor and joy prevent him from acting the way he wants to. He also says he is wiser in many respects than he used to be—he despises those whom he ought to, and he honors good women for the sake of the one who should free him from care. If he has to suffer because of the loftiness of his spirit and his admiration for a man "der daz beste gerne tuot" (203,1), then he is afraid he might lose heart. On second thought, however, he casts off such doubts and affirms that "boeser liute klage" (203,3) cannot really bother him. And if some day he should succeed in winning his lady's favor, no one would see him sad any more. Here the speaker's desire to act properly is evident; it is also clear that he believes his behavior has improved. Although no explicit connection is made between his striving to be good and his prospects of winning his beloved's favor, one can assume that such a relationship is implied in this context.

In 198,28 the speaker, after stating his confidence that in the end suffering will be turned to joy and declaring that anyone who strives for honor is bound to meet with pain, he asserts that "man sol sorgen: sorge ist guot; / âne sorge ist nieman wert" (198,35–36). In addition, although he is pleased that he so zealously desires what will make him happy, he seems to imply that the struggle itself is worth the effort, for even if he is unsuccessful, he says, no one will ever have failed in a more praiseworthy way. Furthermore, he appears to be sure it is not possible to have "liep ân arebeit" (199,8), and he reiterates his certainty that, no matter what woes he may have to endure, he will ultimately know joy. But just at this apparent apex of confidence he turns from hope to doubt with the words: "Wê waz spriche ich! jône touc zer werlte niht / dienest âne saelekeit" (199,9–10). From here on he dwells on his sorrow, lamenting that he must do without joy, for the only love he has does not want him. He concludes by saying that, nonetheless, he will serve his beloved as long as he lives, whether the result is joy or sorrow.

The first half of this poem, where the speaker praises the benefits of bearing pain and cares, offers a fairly clear example of the ennobling power of love. If *sorge* is good and no one can be *wert* without it, and if *liep* cannot be achieved without *arebeit*, one cannot help associating the notions of becoming worthy through sorrow and the attainment of love through the expenditure of great effort. Even though it is never explicitly stated that the reward of love depends on the man's becoming worthy by means of self-improvement, it is certainly implied. Moreover, even the idea that the endeavor itself has merit without the expected compensation is present here. However, the second half of the song clearly shows that the knight's belief in the efficacy of self-betterment as a means to an end and in the value of *arebeit* for its own sake has been thoroughly shaken.

The last song in this group presents the knight in a considerably more optimistic frame of mind. In the first two stanzas of 183,9 the speaker states clearly that he hopes he will be successful if he is deserving. In addition, he goes on to say in what way he will be able to merit his beloved's reward, for he declares that she promised him "vil des guotes" (183,17) on condition that he be the enemy of all "valschen dingen" (183,18). This clear example of the educative force of love seems to be further reinforced by the speaker when he says:

"ich bin von ir genâden wol gezogen" (183,20). Because there is no evidence in the poem that he has already been granted the lady's favor, this statement probably means that he has become *wol gezogen* in the hope of receiving her *genâde*. If so, this is one of the most explicit statements thus far encountered of the idea that the man can become worthy of the lady's love by means of self-improvement.[10]

22. Walther von der Vogelweide

Because the vast body of songs by Walther von der Vogelweide spans a period of some forty years, it is customary to organize his literary production chronologically as well as thematically. In keeping with tradition, as well as for the sake of convenience, this study will follow the general groupings outlined in Halbach's handbook.[1] Only those poems dealing with the topic of *minne* will be examined for evidence of the theme of the ennobling power of love.

Of the nine poems classified as Walther's earliest songs, three—all songs of unrequited love—contain unseized opportunities to introduce the idea of ennobling love. In 115,6, where there is more emphasis on the knight's hope of attaining joy than on any present sorrow, the speaker says his lady is his ultimate source of *fröide*. Her heart is so full of good qualities that she cannot prevent him from rejoicing "nâch ir güeten" (115,21). But although the contemplation of her goodness may make him at least partially happy, the actual sight of her incapacitates him, for when he is in her presence, she completely robs him of his senses.

The knight's sadness is more evident in 13,33, where he begins by stating that those who doubt the sincerity of his laments do not know what true love is. Love, he insists, is "aller tugende ein hort" (14,8), and no one can be truly happy without it. After these generalizations he speaks specifically about his relationship with a lady. He expresses the hope that she cares for him as much as he does for her, basing his confidence on her goodness, which will not fail to treat him well as soon as she realizes his true state of mind. His optimism is followed by a pessimistic note as he recognizes how difficult it is for a woman to know who really loves her, "sît man valscher minne mit sô süezen worten gert" (14,25). At the end of the song he pleads with his beloved to let him earn the greeting "der an friundes herzen lît" (14,37).

Like 115,6, the third of these laments, 109,1, shows the knight eager to receive joy. He knows his beloved can free him from sorrow, and he confesses that never before has he been afflicted by love in this way. After addressing *Minne* and acknowledging her great power, he implores her to ask his lady to direct her *wîplîch güete* toward him so that he will be rid of his cares. In the final stanza he says he will always be pleased to serve such a good woman in the hope of love's reward, and if his misfortune comes to an end, he knows that no man will ever have experienced greater joy.

Common to all three of these songs is the theme of the lady's *güete*. But whereas in 115,6 her *güete* and *tugende* make him rejoice, in the other two poems the speaker relies specifically on his lady's *güete* to reward him, the implication being that her goodness will prevent her from mistreating him once she realizes the genuineness of his feelings. It is interesting to note, however, that nowhere does the idea appear that the perfection of the lady should act as an inspiration for the man to become like her and thereby become worthy of her love. One might also expect the notion of ennobling love to appear when the knight in 13,33 entreats the lady to let him earn a greeting appropriate for lovers. But here, too, the opportunity to be explicit is missed, inasmuch as he does not even hint at what he intends to do to deserve his reward. It should also be mentioned that in 115,6, where the knight is rendered senseless in the presence of his beloved, love's debilitating effect, rather than any edifying influence, predominates.

Three of the earliest songs—two *Wechsel* and a woman's monologue—present the figure of a loving woman and contain situations that come close to the idea of ennobling love. In one *Wechsel*, 71,35, both the man and the woman express their love for each other and rejoice in their happiness. Although the man does not extol his lady's virtues in his two stanzas, the woman describes her beloved as someone who lives "mit valschelôser güete" (72,9), whose *staete* gives her joy and whose *tugend* has won him the highest place in her heart. The second *Wechsel*, 119,17, introduces a pair of lovers who are having problems getting together. The man says he knows his lady loves him, but he is miserable nonetheless because she is unable, or unwilling, to fulfill his desires. He laments the sad state of the world from which joy has fled. The woman reveals in her first stanza that she indeed loves a man whom the whole world praises and would gladly do what he has asked of her if she had the opportunity. From her second strophe, however, it becomes apparent that social pressure more than anything else is preventing her from being happy with her *gesellen*. In the woman's monologue, 113,31, the speaker faces a similar dilemma. Indeed, she could easily be the same woman as in 119,17. At first she confesses that she secretly loves a knight and that she can no longer say no to his entreaties. But in the ensuing three stanzas her seeming willingness to yield to his desires is countered by her feelings of fear and guilt, and she appears to conclude that she must refuse him—she must preserve her "wîbes êre" (114,10). That she loves him dearly, nonetheless, becomes clear in the final strophe, where she says she has given him a place in her heart that no one else has ever held because "die besten jâhen / daz er alsô schône künne leben" (114,17-18).

In all three of these poems involving a loving woman—in 119,17 implicitly and in 71,35 and 113,31 explicitly—the woman indicates that the man has won her love because of his good qualities. In 71,35 she speaks of first-hand knowledge of his *güete*, *staete*, and *tugend*; in the other two songs she talks about the praise he has been accorded by everyone or *die besten*. But nothing in these poems suggests that the man's exemplary behavior, which obviously made a strong impression on the woman, is the result of an effort to improve himself in order to become worthy of the lady's love. It could just as well be that the lady fell in love with a man already distinguished by excellence. If this is the case, the situation depicted here is not a genuine example of the educative effect of love, but, rather, only approaches the idea of the ennobling power of love.

Clear examples of the notion of ennobling love are presented in four of Walther's earliest songs. Two of these are *Botenlieder* reflecting the initial stage of a relationship between a knight and a lady. The first two stanzas of $MF214,34^2$ present a conversation between a messenger and the lady. The former says a knight who wishes to do "daz beste daz sîn herze kan" (*MF214,37*) has offered her his service in the hope of attaining her *genâde*. The lady wishes the knight well, but suggests he turn his attention elsewhere, for she does not know him well enough to entertain thoughts of granting him the kind of reward he seeks. In the remaining stanzas, the knight bemoans her lack of interest in him and states that love has so enslaved him that he cannot abandon his service. He concludes by saying that anyone who considers *minne* sinful should think carefully about the matter, for "vil manic êre" (L.217,12) is associated with love, and *staete* and *saelikeit* are its consequences. In addition, he says, it is painful for love "daz iemer ieman missetuot" (L.217,15).

The second *Botenlied*, 112,35, presents only a dialogue between the messenger and the lady. The former implores his master's beloved to free the knight from sorrow, to give him *hôhen muot*. If she makes him happy, he will sing her praises and thereby bring joy to others as well. And if she desires it, his sadness, which teaches him to gladly do *daz beste*, can be changed to joy. The lady's response, with which the poem concludes, is hardly encouraging. She says she cannot rely on the knight to behave properly and she prays that God may help her to do the right thing and to keep her from going astray.

The messenger in MF214,34 emphasizes that the knight wishes to do his best in the hope of winning the lady's favor; in the final strophe, the knight himself affirms his belief in love as a source of good things and an inspiration to good behavior. In 112,35 the educative effect of the knight's service is revealed when the messenger speaks of his master's sorrow as something "daz in lêret / daz er daz beste gerne tuot" (113,21–22). Interestingly enough, in both poems it is the man who is conscious of the idea that striving to do good might help him in his quest for love, whereas the lady appears to be unaware that she is supposed to play an active role as an inspiration and even feels the knight is proposing something that can only lead to sin.[3]

The third example of ennobling love is found in 111,22, a *Wechsel* generally considered a part of the literary feud between Walther and Reinmar von Hagenau.[4] In the first stanza the speaker talks about a man who bids so high in a game that he thinks no one can outbid him and who says that, when he sees a certain lady, she is his "ôsterlîcher tac" (111,26). He then asks what would happen if the rest of the people were to agree with this (overlavish praise of one lady— Reinmar's—at the expense of all others), and he concludes the stanza by stating that he is the one who will oppose this position. It would be better, he says, to offer the lady a gentle greeting.[5] That is his answer to the claim (made by Reinmar) that one lady's perfection "checkmates" all others. In the second stanza a lady—presumably Reinmar's—says that she is a respected and honorable woman who can protect herself from thieves. Whoever wants to obtain a kiss from her (she says with reference to the robbing of a kiss mentioned by Reinmar) should strive to attain it "mit fuoge" (111,37). But if such a person should get it suddenly ahead of time, she concludes, she will always consider him a thief. Although nothing in the first stanza points to the theme under investigation, the woman's strophe does touch on the problem in that the lady is urging a man to strive to achieve the reward of a kiss by conforming to a high standard of behavior. Thus the poem offers one of the relatively rare examples— even if it is in a playful context—of a woman taking an active role in guiding a man to become worthy of at least one of the rewards of love.

The final poem containing evidence of the edifying effect of love is 13,33, a song discussed in the main under the category of missed opportunities above. Among the generalizations about love at the beginning of the song is the statement that love, in addition to being the prime cause of happiness, is "aller tugende ein hort" (14,8). This idea, namely, that love is the source of all virtues, is, like its counterpart in *MF*214,34, a variation of the notion of the uplifting power of love found only rarely in the works examined thus far.

The next set of poems to be discussed is made up of seven songs classified by Halbach, along with the nine earliest ones just reviewed, as *Frühe Lieder*. Two of these are laments of unrequited love that contain unseized opportunities to introduce the idea of ennobling love. In 97,34, after lamenting youth's lack of interest in the true *fröide*, which can only come from women, the speaker complains about being separated from his lady. He emphasizes that, nonetheless, his heart is with his beloved, a fact resulting in his often being considered *sinnelôs*. Although he accuses the *merkaere* of being responsible for his isolation, it becomes clear that his lady's attitude toward him also must be involved, for he turns to *Frau Minne* at the end of the song and asks her to attack and oppress his lady in the same way she has afflicted him.

The idea of the man's isolation also plays a considerable role in 99,6, which begins with the contention that, because true joy comes only from women, one should honor them all. Inasmuch as no one is worth anything without it, the speaker says he seeks such joy from a woman whose *güete* his heart has always proclaimed whenever his eyes have sent it to her. He adds, however, that it has been a long time since he has actually seen her. Yet he can view her with the eyes of his heart—the thoughts of his heart, as he puts it—which can penetrate walls and contemplate her wherever she may be. Thus it does not matter to him how her keepers try to protect her from him, for his "herze wille und al der muot" (99,33) can see her "mit vollen ougen" (99,32). He ends the song by asking whether he will ever be so happy that his beloved will be able to see him without eyes. If that were to happen, he would then know that she also loved him.

In both songs, which emphasize that love is the source of life's true joy, it would have been appropriate to mention another benefit to be derived from love, namely, the acquisition of worthiness in the course of a man's service to a lady. But in neither case is the knight's desire to have his beloved return his love coupled with the notion that he has become worthy of her favor by means of self-improvement. Indeed, in 97,34, instead of any uplifting effect, the debilitating power of love is underscored with the image of the man rendered helpless while his heart has gone off to be with the distant beloved. And in 99,6, although the lover's heart is aware of his lady's *güete*, there is no indication that the latter should serve as an object for the suitor to emulate.

The remaining five songs in this set of seven to a large extent contain generalizations about true love and are either imbued with, or at least clearly reflect familiarity with, the ennobling power of love. One, 91,17, takes the form of exhortations to a young man, who is urged to be *hôhes muotes* for the sake of "diu reinen wol gemuoten wîp," (91,18) and to make himself worthy ("wirde dînen jungen lîp," 91,20). The poet tells him he will never know complete joy if he does not acquire "die werkekeit von wîbe" (91,22).[6] Because true joy can come only from good women, the young man is admonished to strive for *herzeliebe.* He is sure to profit from it, the poet says, for even if he fails to win the love of the lady in question, he will be all the more worthy for it. Indeed, he will become "alsô wol gemuot" (91,33) that he will be pleasing to other women. If, however, he should succeed in his suit, "halsen, triuten, bî gelegen" (92,1) will bring him untold joy. In the final stanza the speaker confesses that he has not been fortunate enough to attain the bliss he has just described. This poem presents one of the clearest statements yet encountered of the uplifting power of love. One even finds here the notion that the man's service to the lady is of value in itself because the man is ennobled by it, even if he is unsuccessful in love. Nevertheless, the attainment of love's reward is still to be viewed as the ultimate goal—if not with one woman, then with another.

Very similar sentiments are found in 92,9, where the speaker uses his own hopes of obtaining joy in his relationship to his lady as a springboard for launching a discussion of true love. What pleases him even more than the coming of spring, he says, is the fact that wherever *wîbes güete* was measured, his lady took the prize. She is more beautiful than a merely beautiful woman, he claims, for it is *liebe* (grace, graciousness, amiability, kindness) that makes a woman truly beautiful. But what renders a woman most desirable is the joining together of *liebe* and *schoene* with *tugende.* Such a combination increases a man's worth (*werdekeit*), and whoever knows how to bear "die süezen arebeit" (92,30) appropriately for the sake of such a woman has a right to speak of *herzeliebe.* Having thus delineated his ideal woman, the speaker proceeds to wax eloquent about the joy to be had by anyone who is rewarded with the love of such a woman, concluding that nothing can be compared with the happiness "dâ liebez herze in triuwen stât, / in schoene, in kiusche, in reinen siten" (93,2–3). In the last stanza he implies that a man who does not desire to woo "ein reine wîp" (93,8) is not worth very much. And even if a suitor's efforts are unrequited, his service ennobles him ("tiuret doch wol sînen lîp," 93,10). But he does not have to be satisfied with such ennoblement as a reward, for if the woman he first served rejects him, what he has done for her sake—presumably his attempts to improve himself—will please other women, one of whom will ultimately make him happy.[7] The poem then closes with the lofty sentiment: "swer guotes wîbes minne hât, / der schamt sich aller missetât" (93,17–18).

Here, in addition to the aspects of ennobling love found in 91,17, one encounters in the final words of the song an uncommon variation of the notion of the elevating force of love, which has been seen only twice before in the works surveyed.[8] Whereas generally the self-improvement of the man in the service of a lady was considered either as an end in itself (if only rarely) or as a means of achieving the reward of love, the last statement in this poem reveals what might be called the reverse assumption. In other words, it is not the hope of gaining love that inspires the man to excellence, but rather the possession of it—the man who *has* the love of a good woman is ashamed to act improperly.[9]

In the other three songs in this group of five the ennobling power of love does not play as prominent a role as in the two just examined. Most of 93,19 is concerned with the speaker's reaction to his lady's inaccessibility. She is, he says, cut off from him in two ways: by those who guard her as well as by her loftiness. But while the former vexes him sorely, the latter only arouses his yearning for her, and he wishes he had the keys that would give him access to both her person and her *tugend*. Even if he cannot overcome the problems caused by her keepers, however, they will never be able to make him cease loving her.

This discussion of the man's difficulties in approaching his lady is preceded by a stanza in which, as in 91,17 and 92,9, generalities about the nature of true love are presented. Nothing in the world, the speaker maintains, can better bring joy to a longing heart than a woman, and nothing can guide a person to live a better life ("stiuret baz ze lebenne," 93,22) than the lady's "werder lîp" (93,23). Indeed, nothing can surpass the happiness that results when such a woman loves a man "der ir wol lebt ze lobe" (93,26). Despite the fact that only the beginning of the poem deals with the question of ennobling love, this single stanza contains one of the clearest statements yet encountered of the idea that a woman of noble qualities can—and even should—serve as an inspiration, a guiding light, so to speak, for the man who seeks to live an exemplary life. And it is likewise evident that the man lives such a life to please the lady.

In the first two stanzas of 95,17 the speaker laments his lack of success in love in the course of the summer when he had high hopes, and he asks that those who were more fortunate than he not mock him in his misery. The mention of such lucky people in the first part of the song becomes the point of departure for the following discussion of the value of love. First, the speaker lauds the happiness of any man and woman whose hearts are joined *mit triuwen*. He is certain that "ir beider lîp / getiuret und in hôher wirde sî" (96,1–2). But he also maintains that a man who perceives their *tugende* in such a way that "ez in sîn herze gêt" (96,6) is likewise *saelic*, and a reasonable woman should not deny such a man her goodwill. This praise of true lovers is then contrasted with a condemnation of those who think they can lead a good life without devoting themselves to good women. Such fools, the speaker claims, cannot see that true joy and *wirde* can result only from service to a good woman —on whomever she looks favorably, "der hât mit fröiden wirde vil" (96,18).[10] In the final stanza he even curses those who seek love outside the convention of *dienest*. He says that "ein saelic wîp" (96,24) would not grant her favor to anyone who was unworthy—she observes "guotes mannes site" (96,25) and excludes *die boesen* from her consideration.

This poem offers yet another variation of the idea of ennobling love. Whereas usually it is the man who is ennobled by his service to his beloved lady, the poet speaks here of both loving partners being *getiuret*. And, concomitantly, this pair of lovers, rather than just the lofty lady, is held up as a model of behavior.[11] *Their* good qualities should penetrate a man's heart and, presumably, make him worthy of love. This song also contains an example of a rarely encountered aspect of the notion of the uplifting force of love, namely, the presentation of the woman as an *active* participant in the procedure. By discriminating between proper and improper behavior the woman exerts an educative effect on her suitor, for he will consciously strive to meet her standards.

The last of the five poems in this group in which ennobling love plays a role, 96,29, focuses on the idea of *staete*. Here the speaker is concerned more with his own problems than with generalizations about love. He claims his constancy has caused him nothing but sorrow since Love commanded him to practice this virtue; if Love does not take his *staete* into account, it will be his undoing. Despite his lack of success, he says, addressing his lady directly, his steadfastness has been of the purest kind, and he pleads with her to consider how long he has suffered. Then, after praising her lavishly, he concludes by telling her that she should let him benefit from having pressed his suit "sô rehte" (97,33).

In keeping with the lack of broad generalizations about love in this poem, the theme of the elevating power of love is restricted here to the relationship of the man's *staete* to his belief in his right to a reward. Although it has cost him great pain and effort, he has consciously cultivated a specific virtue presumably because he feels his lady demands it of him as a condition for winning her love. Thus he has, at least in one respect, striven to improve himself to become worthy of his lady's favor.

The next group of songs to be analyzed is made up of twelve poems possibly composed between 1198 and 1203.[12] Four of these contain no trace of the idea of ennobling love and present no easy opportunities for its introduction. One, 114,23, has such a tenuous connection with the theme of love that it need not be considered in much detail. The speaker begins by reporting that winter is finally giving way to spring and that he has informed his lady of this fact. He goes on to say that, if he had died, it would have been a great loss for good people who strive for joy and would like to sing and dance; if he had missed this splendid day, he would have deserved to be cursed. At the end he asks God to bless his audience; he also asks the audience to wish him good fortune.

The three other songs in this category share the motif of extreme dissatisfaction with the lady's treatment of the devoted knight. The speaker begins 40,19 by complaining that he has celebrated his lady so well in song that many people praise her. If she now dishonors him with abuse for having increased her stature, then he has been a fool. But instead of continuing to find fault with his lady, he blames *Frau Minne* for this predicament. Lady Love has dealt unfairly with him, he maintains. Even though he has been her undaunted champion, she has wounded him through the heart whereas his beloved remains unscathed. He therefore begs Lady Love to either shoot her in the heart as well, or heal his wound. If she does not help him win his lady, however, he threatens to renounce his allegiance to her.

In 69,1 the knight's bitterness is expressed both indirectly and to the lady herself. At the beginning he asks someone to tell him what love is, and then proceeds to give his own definition. As he understands it, love is something that brings pleasure. If it causes pain, it should be called something else. According to him, *minne* is the joy of *two* hearts—one alone cannot encompass it. Having thus clearly stated his view of the need for mutual affection, he pleads directly with his lady to help him before it is too late. If she does not care for him, he says, she should say so clearly and he will give up the struggle and become a free man. She should keep in mind, however, that no one is better able to sing her praises than he. In the final stanza, speaking again indirectly, he asks whether his lady thinks he is going to continue to present her with joy in return for sorrow, to glorify her in song while she abuses him. If he were to put up with such treatment, he says, there would have to be something wrong with his sight. At the end, however, he appears to retract his harsh words by asking: "wê waz sprich ich ôrenlôser ougen âne? / den diu minne blendet, wie mac der gesehen?" (69,27–28).

The knight's discontent in 54,37 is also expressed to *Frau Minne* as it was in 40,19. After asking why he makes others happy when they do not show their appreciation or pay attention to his sorrows, he describes his hopeless predicament for which he holds her responsible. Love has entered his heart and displaced his *sin*, sending it to his beloved where it has been unable to accomplish anything. He pleads with Lady Love to go to his lady, force access to her heart, and afflict her the way he has been afflicted. In the last strophe he acknowledges Love's great power and says that, as long as Love has conquered him, he thanks God that the object of his devoted service is so worthy. He will never cease to serve her, and he begs Love to allow him to dedicate his life to his beloved.

In these three laments, where the man's dissatisfaction with the state of his relationship with his lady plays such a prominent role, the predominating feeling is the opposite of the uplifting effect of love, namely, the destructive or debilitating consequences of the knight's apparently hopeless quest for his lady's favor. Whereas in 40,19 great emphasis is placed on the knight's distress and illness resulting from the wound Lady Love has caused by shooting him in the heart, in the other two songs it is the knight's senses that have been adversely affected. Blinded by love in 69,1, he is *ôrenlôs* and *ougen âne* and hence no longer able to make sound judgments; in 54,37 love has invaded his heart and displaced his *sin*, leaving him unable to function properly.

Six of the songs composed between 1198 and 1203 contain unseized opportunities to introduce the idea of ennobling love. The first half of 51,13 is a lively portrayal of the wonders of May and its rejuvenating spirit, without any specific connection with the theme of love. At the beginning of the fourth stanza, however, the poet shifts abruptly and reproaches his lady's red mouth for taking delight in his misery. Then, addressing the lady directly, he calls her an *ungenaedic wîp* who is alone responsible for his depressed state; if she who is so rich in *genâde* refuses to treat him graciously, then he cannot say that she is *guot*. He concludes the song by asking her to give him just a little bit of joy so that he, too, can participate happily in the glories of May. This May song, even though it turns into a lament of unrequited love of sorts, clearly has nothing to do with the idea under investigation, inasmuch as it never relates the lover's hope of reward to the notion that he has become worthy of it through self-improvement. The one occasion that might possibly have lent itself to bringing in an aspect of ennobling love—the mention of the woman's (supposed) goodness—is not made use of, for here the lady's goodness is viewed as a reason for the man to hope for generous treatment, rather than as a source of inspiration or a model for emulation. As has been seen so often before, the assumption is that it behooves the lady to exercise *genâde* if she lays claim to being considered *guot*.

Five songs in this category share the theme of high praise of the beloved lady and/or joyous hope or anticipation of love's fulfillment. In 110,13 the poet praises the occasion that he met "die reinen, die lieben, die guoten" (110,21), whose beauty and goodness have so overwhelmed him that he cannot think of giving her up. Her beauty, her goodness, and her red mouth that laughs so charmingly have given him what joy he has known on this earth; he hopes that whatever he can expect from her *hulde* will redound to their mutual benefit.

The poet's joy is much more explicit in 118,24, where he says he is so happy he could almost perform miracles; if he should win his lady's love, his *sinne* would soar higher than the sun. The sight of his beautiful lady, he continues, has never failed to make his eyes radiant with joy. Thus he has sung this happy song in her honor, and for her sake he is ever ready to increase the world's pleasure through his singing. For this, he says, she owes him thanks. He knows, of course, that she can wound his heart, but it does not matter as long as she also has the power to undo whatever sorrow she causes. No one can persuade him to give up his hope, for he is certain he would never find another woman as lovely and good as his beloved, who is more beautiful and more praiseworthy than Helen and Diana.

The other three songs in which praise of the lady and the wish for fulfillment play a role also share the theme of the decay of courtly society. The poet begins 42,15 with a complaint about the young and the wealthy who have abandoned joy, and he reproaches *frou Saelde* for mismatching his poverty with his *hôhen muot*. But the poet advises anyone who bears secret cares to turn his thoughts to good women and summer days—that will offer relief. At the end of the song the speaker tells his lady that, whenever he thinks of her excellent qualities, she reaches right into his heart where love resides. No matter what happens to him, he assures her, she is dearer to him than anything in the world.

At the beginning of 117,29 the poet quotes his complaint in 42,15 about the lack of joy in society and expands upon the theme, lamenting that his lady's good qualities and beauty appear to be wasted in such wretched times as these. After this discussion of the miserable state of the world the speaker comes to the defense of winter. It, too, has its advantages, for if the days are short, at least the long nights offer lovers the chance to free themselves from care as they lie together. But at the very end of the song the poet seems to recant—somewhat whimsically perhaps—saying that maybe he should keep silent about such things if he hopes ever to enjoy a similar intimacy himself.

Almost the same elements are found in 112,3, only in reverse order. The speaker's wish for physical fulfillment is encountered in the first stanza, where he expresses his desire to pick roses with his beloved. He would then disport himself with her in such a way that they would be friends forever. In the second strophe he despairs of being happy in a world where no one strives to achieve joy. Of what use are art, beauty, and wealth, he asks, when one does evil without fear and "triuwe milte zuht und êre" (112,14) are no longer valued?

The idea of the ennobling power of love is conspicuously absent in these five songs, even though there are several occasions when one might expect its appearance. In all but the last poem the lady's good qualities or her *güete* are mentioned, but nowhere is there any indication that they exert an educative effect on the man by inspiring him to improve himself to become worthy of love. On the contrary, at least in 110,13, the lady's *güete* has a debilitating effect inasmuch as the poet speaks of his senses, "der si mich hât mit ir güete verdrungen" (110,16). In 42,15, too, a similar result might be observable in the poet's description of what happens to him when he contemplates his lady's *tugende*: "sô lâ stân! dû rüerest mich / mitten an daz herze, dâ diu liebe liget" (42,25–26). Such an outcry would seem to imply that he is completely overwhelmed by the experience.[13] Finally, none of the poet's complaints about the degeneration of courtly values is linked specifically with the disappearance of the belief in the ennobling force of love.

Although none of the songs composed between 1198 and 1203 present clear examples of the idea of ennobling love, two poems contain situations that might be interpreted as coming close to it. In 112,17 the knight speaks first of the powerful effect of his lady's *ougenblicke* on his heart and wishes he could see often the one whom he serves as if he were her bondsman. Then he says he carries in his heart *eine swaere* because of her, from whose service he cannot desist and with whom he would like to be intimate both night and day. This desire cannot be fulfilled, however, because his lady does not wish it. In the final stanza he expresses his irritation with the situation in which he finds himself. If he has to pay for his *triuwe* in this manner, he says, then no man should ever trust her again. It seems, he claims, that she would rather be scolded than praised. He ends the song by asking why she whom he loves so much acts this way. The prevailing impression conveyed by this poem is, to be sure, the opposite of any edifying effect of love—the destructive result of the knight's devotion is made clear by the devastating impact the lady's glances have on his heart. But there is one hint of the idea of the ennobling power of love—the speaker's comment that no one should trust his lady if he has to pay for his *triuwe* by being rejected. The implicit assumption here is that his *triuwe* deserves a reward. But because there is no indication that this quality represents an improvement in his behavior to make him worthy of the lady, it is not possible to consider this as a clear-cut example of the educative force of love.

In 63,8 the speaker refuses to join those who despair of all good things, for he still hopes that the lady to whom he has lamented his sorrow will bring him joy. If she makes him happy, he says, he does not care what evil people say. Indeed, he would be glad to bear the envy and hatred his lady's favor would arouse, and he implores her to make *them* unhappy by pleasing *him*. What he would like as far as she is concerned, he continues, is to have a "friundîn unde frowen in einer waete" (63,20). If she would be his lover and his lady at the same time, he would be her "friunt und geselle" (63,30). Although little in this plea for mutual love points to the ennobling power of love, one might consider the man's explanation of why he wants to be able to call her his beloved as well as his lady: "friundinne ist ein süezez wort: / doch sô tiuret frowe unz an daz ort" (63,24–25). The use of the word *tiuret* might make it appear as if the lady has an edifying effect.[14] Even though this could refer to the idea of the man being ennobled by his service to the lady, it is not at all clear that this is so. It could very well be that here *tiuret*, as it so often does, refers to a raising of the man's esteem; in that case, the poem would be dealing with the notion that the man merely derives honor from being able to consider the lady his *frouwe*.[15] It is, of course, also possible that both meanings of *tiuren* are involved.[16]

The poems Walther composed when he was at the height of his

powers are divided by Halbach into several groups. The first set of six primarily contains what he calls "höfisch-festliche Hymnik" and "hochhöfische Tugendlehre."[17] Three of this set show no evidence of the idea of ennobling love and do not offer any opportunities for its introduction. Two of them, 53,25 and 45,37, emphasize the visual impression made by women. In the former the poet indulges in an enthusiastic description of his lady's appearance that clearly reveals a yearning for sensual fulfillment. Because only the lady's external charms are praised—not a word is said about her *tugende* or her *güete*—there is scarcely any occasion for the presence of the ennobling power of love. As might be expected, only the physical effects of love are mentioned—the poet wishes he could get close enough to her to see himself reflected in her eyes, which would rejuvenate him; if he could kiss her on the mouth, he would be cured of his sickness.

In 45,37 the poet asks whether anything can compare with the wonders of nature in the month of May. He then proceeds to answer his own question by depicting a beautiful noblewoman as she makes her entrance at court. Nothing is more *wünneclîch* than her *minneclîcher lîp*, he says; indeed, if he had to choose between the two, it would be May he would give up. Here, just as in 53,25, the concentration on a woman's outward appearance does not present any opportunity to think in terms of the ennobling power of love.

The third song without a trace of the notion of the educative function of love is 56,14, Walther's famous *Preislied*, in which he speaks as a messenger who has come with news for which he expects to be rewarded. He says he is going to speak about German women in such a way that they will please people all the more. But for doing so he does not want any recompense other than their friendly greeting, for they are, after all, *ze hêr* in relation to him. His travels abroad, he continues, have convinced him that *tiuschiu zuht* surpasses anything he has ever seen, and he swears that, if he has any ability to judge beauty and good behavior, the women in the German-speaking lands are better than women elsewhere. German men, too, are worthy of praise for their courtliness, and anyone who insults the Germans must be misinformed. Whoever seeks *tugend* and *reine minne*, he claims, should come to his country, and he concludes his general praise with the personal wish that he might live there for a long time. In the last stanza he turns to his own problems, speaking of his relationship to a lady whom he has served and hopes to continue to serve. Even though he has no intention of desisting from his suit, he says, she causes him great pain. He ends the strophe with the wish that God might forgive her for mistreating him and the hope that she might possibly change her mind. Because the main part of the poem does not deal seriously with the relationship between men and women, it is not surprising that there is no room here for the idea of ennobling love. But even in the last stanza, where the poet complains about the treatment accorded him by the lady he has been serving, no mention is made of any elevating force of love. On the contrary, the passage emphasizes love's destructive and debilitating effects on the poet's "herze und den muot" (57,20) on which the lady is so well able to inflict wounds.

All three of the remaining songs in this set of six present clear examples of the idea of ennobling love. Two of them, 43,9 and 85,34, take the form of conversations between a man and a woman, and in both cases proper behavior is the major topic of discussion. The man speaks first in 43,9, assuring his lady he will always serve her because he has heard tell of her many good qualities. He says his *werdekeit* would have been diminished if he had not met her and, because he is *tump* and would like to be *deste tiurre*, he asks her for advice on how he should conduct himself. The lady responds modestly, saying that he praises her wisdom too much. Nonetheless, she is willing to counsel him, but before she informs him about women's desires she wants him to tell her what men expect of women. He complies by asserting that a woman's *güete* is crowned by *staetekeit*. In addition, she should be joyous in an appropriate fashion and friendly in her greeting. A woman's "minneclîcher redender munt" (43,37), he says, makes a man want to kiss it. In the final stanza she tells him what kind of a man pleases the ladies, namely, one who can distinguish between good and evil and who speaks well of women. If such a man knows how to be properly *vrô* and to aim at goals that are neither too high nor too low, he can achieve what he desires, for what woman would deny him anything ("einen vaden," 44,9)? A good man, she concludes, is worth good silk.

The idea of the ennobling power of love obviously plays a prominent role in this song. The man clearly looks to the lady, who is distinguished by her many good qualities, as the source of inspiration for improving himself. One also sees here a rarely encountered instance of the woman playing an active part, through her rendering of advice, in the process of the man's betterment. It is likewise apparent that the man expects something in return for becoming the type of person that would please the lady. What is not clear in this poem is the precise nature of the reward, as the exact meaning of the woman's words in the last stanza cannot be determined. If, as one group of scholars asserts,[18] the lady is alluding to the giving of herself when she says a man can attain the goal he desires, then the song illustrates the "standard" situation where the lady's love is viewed as the man's reward for having become worthy by means of self-improvement. But if, as others maintain, the conclusion of the poem amounts to a whimsically expressed rebuff on the lady's part, in that she considers him only as a good vassal who deserves the gift of a rich garment, rather than as a suitor who is entitled to the lady's love, then it is an example—or at least a variation—of the idea that the man's self-betterment is of value in itself. Although this is not specifically stated in the song, it is implied, inasmuch as the reward of love is not connected—at least in the lady's eyes—with the man's desire to improve his conduct.

The second of these conversations, 85,34, begins with the knight's appeal to the lady that he be allowed to speak with her. He says he would gladly be counted among the best if she would reward him. In addition, he tells her she is beautiful; if, as he suspects, she possesses *güete* as well, then she is truly worthy of esteem. The lady assures him that, by praising her so charmingly, he has earned the right to say whatever he wants. She does not know whether she is beautiful, she says, but she would very much like to think she has *güete*; she asks him to teach her how she can preserve it, for "schoener lîp entouc niht âne sin" (86,14). The knight then expresses his willingness to instruct her how to behave in society. She should honor noble people, he says, and look at and greet them in a friendly way. But she should also give herself to one man and accept the gift of his life in return. At this point he drops the impersonal tone of the teacher and offers himself to her in the type of exchange he has just described. Although the lady is happy to heed his advice concerning her social behavior, she says he must be content to be only her *redegeselle*, for she does not know anyone from whom she would want to take *den lîp*. To this the knight replies that he is willing to take whatever chances are necessary; if he loses his life in the process, it will be a gentle death. The lady then concludes the poem by asserting that she wishes to live and that she does not need the sorrow that might result from this kind of give-and-take arrangement.

The idea of the ennobling power of love is encountered at the very beginning of this song when the knight says: "möhte ichs wider iuch geniezen, / sô waer ich den besten gerne bî" (86,1–2). With these words he openly offers to improve himself in return for some benefit he might receive from her; that the reward he has in mind is her love becomes obvious in the course of the poem. An unusual aspect of this particular manifestation of the educative force of love is its presentation in the form of a proposition by the man. It would appear that this knight is not willing to subject himself to the discipline of self-betterment unless he has some strong assurance that he will be compensated for his endeavors by her love. One is almost tempted to go a step further and interpret 86,1–2 as an example of the reversal of the standard conception of the uplifting power of love, that is, the man says he is ready to improve if the lady will give herself to him. In other words, instead of love being the reward for exemplary behavior, the promise of the knight's improved conduct is looked upon as a kind of inducement for the lady to grant him her favor. Unfortunately, it is not feasible to support this view conclusively based on the text. It does, however, remain an interesting possibility that is consistent with the generally aggressive role played by the knight in the poem. In this connection, another feature of this song is clearly in opposition to the usual presentation of the motif under investigation. Whereas normally the knight looks to the lady for guidance or inspiration, here it is the lady who seeks advice from the man concerning proper behavior. In keeping with this reversal of roles, there is no hint in this song of the idea that the man's improvement is a worthwhile goal in itself. Certainly the knight is not of this opinion, and the lady does not say or imply anything of the sort when she tells him that their relationship must remain on a platonic level.[19]

In the third song containing clear evidence of the idea of ennobling love, 46,32, Walther begins by addressing *Frowe Mâze*, whom he considers the source of all *werdekeit* and whom he asks to teach him how to woo with moderation (*ebene*). For no matter whether he seeks love *nidere* or *hôhe*, he comes to grief. Lack of moderation (*unmâze*) constantly causes him distress, he says. He was almost *tôt* because of a love that was *ze nidere*, and now he is again *siech* because he is directing his attention *ze hôhe*. In the second stanza he explains what he means by the terms *hôhiu* and *nideriu minne*. The latter kind of love is demeaning in that the body strives after lowly pleasure (*kranker liebe*). Such love causes pain that is shameful (*unlobelîch*). *Hôhiu minne*, on the other hand, is inspiring and causes the spirit (*muot*) to soar in search of *hôher wirde*. It is such a love that now beckons him, he says. He has met a woman who has attracted him; if *herzeliebe* makes an appearance, he is afraid that he will be hurt—unless *mâze* comes to his aid.

Whatever difficulties may be connected with interpreting this much-discussed poem,[20] the question of the ennobling power of love does not seem to be problematical here. The uplifting effect of love is clearly associated with what Walther calls *hôhiu minne* when he says

its result is "daz der muot nâch hôher wirde ûf swinget" (47,9). Al-
though the details of the educative force of love are not spelled out
in this song, it is clearly implied that the man, presumably in the
service of a lady, is incited to strive toward goals that will increase
both his inner worth and his esteem. Whether such an effort to
achieve *hôhe wirde* is worthwhile in itself, or whether it is a means to
an end, namely, the reward of the lady's love, is simply not stated in
the poem. It might be argued, however, that Walther at least implies
that the difficulty he sees in his experience of love that is *ze hôhe* is
the pain of unrequited love. This certainly would point toward dis-
pleasure with the view that self-improvement as the concomitant of
hôhe minne is a satisfactory goal in itself.

The next set of poems, called by Halbach the *Preislied-Zyklus*,[21]
consists of five songs more or less intimately related to 56,14.[22] Three
of these contain unseized opportunities to introduce the idea of en-
nobling love. At the beginning of 70,1 the speaker tells his lady that
it is not his fault he greets her so rarely in person, and that people
who love each other can also be angry with one another from time
to time. Then, in the second stanza, he expresses dismay at how
quickly his days are slipping away from him; he suspects that, wher-
ever they are going, they will not be treated as well as when they
were with him. In the final strophe he again addresses his lady. He
tells her there is one thing she must not say, for it would not be in
accord with her *güete*. If she were to act like the *boesen* who, when it
comes time for payment, say, "If he were blessed by fortune, I would
help him," then he would have to find her behavior hateful. The
poet's dissatisfaction with the lady's conduct here has nothing to do
with the idea of ennobling love. He does not indicate that the time
he feels he has been wasting has been spent in an effort to improve
himself, and he does not base his appeal for a reward on the notion
that he has become worthy. The one occasion that might possibly
have lent itself to introducing an aspect of ennobling love—the refer-
ence to the lady's *güete*—is not made use of, for instead of its being a
source of inspiration, it is regarded as the basis for his expectation
that she should not mistreat him.

In 52,23 the knight comes close to rebelling against the lady. He
says she is cruel because she has not acted properly toward him.
When he entered her service, he maintains, he was young and
happy. But when he asks himself what he has received in return, all
he can answer is: nothing but the sorrow he bears. Although he has
never seen a more beautiful head than hers, he has never been able
to look into her heart. There, he fears, he has been deceived in spite

of his devotion; he swears that he would have obtained the sun, the moon, and the stars for her if he had been able to. Then he expresses deep regret for the many days he has spent in vain in her service. He cannot understand her behavior, he continues, for she seems to hate her friends and to be on intimate terms with her enemies; nothing good can come from such unjust treatment, he predicts. In conclusion, he says his lady should not be offended if he rides to other lands and inquires about women of beauty and high esteem, although, he assures her, none of them could ever cause him pain by rejecting him.

This song shows not a trace of the idea of the ennobling power of love, despite the fact that there are several places where its appearance might have been appropriate. Although the knight feels he is entitled to a reward for his long years of devotion, there is no indication that any effort at self-improvement was involved in his service to make him deserving of her love. Concomitantly, the notion that his becoming a better person is, even at least partially, a kind of recompense in itself is singularly lacking here, for he states clearly that the *only* result of his endeavors has been his *kumber*.[23] It is also interesting to note that, when he asserts that there is nothing he would not have done for his lady, the type of things he mentions—even though they are in the realm of the fantastic—do not hint at the concept of self-improvement, but rather point toward the acquisition of things that would please his beloved. Finally, the general tone of the song, with its emphasis on the bitter, demoralized state of the poet who sees his joy destroyed and his time wasted, seems to be the opposite of any uplifting force of love.

The poet begins 100,3 by saying that extolling good women never fails to bring him some joy and dispel love's sorrow, and he is pleased that his words are able to both raise their spirits and offer him some comfort. Then, in the second stanza, he speaks more intimately about his own problems: the lady whom he serves, and who could see to it that he was never sad again, does not thank him even though she clearly enjoys his praise. In the last strophe he says that women he does not really know well express their gratitude to him, but that such thanks cannot compare to the reward he would hope to get from his lady. He finishes the song by stating that, no matter what her intentions might be, his are good; he only regrets that his deeds are sometimes not in accord with his thoughts.

The idea of the ennobling power of love is conspicuously absent in this poem. Inasmuch as the question of service and reward are clearly touched upon, there would have been ample opportunity to introduce the notion that the man's endeavor to improve makes him worthy of the lady's love. Here, however, the man seems to base his hope of reward solely on his singing of the lady's praises. As he puts it, she forgets him when it is time for thanks, "und hilfet mich vil kleine / swaz ich sie geloben mac" (100,12–13).

In addition to the unseized opportunity just discussed, the poem also contains a passage that might possibly hint at some awareness of the idea of ennobling love. It could be argued that the last lines of the song, in which the poet speaks of his good intentions, might show a conscious effort on his part to do good. But this seems doubtful; when he says "mîn wille ist guot" (100,22), he does so in direct contrast to the words "si hab den willen den sie habe" (100,21). Moreover, the meaning of *wille* is so vague in the context that it is not possible to say that it goes beyond the very general sense of "his intentions toward her are good or honorable."

Only one song in the so-called *Preislied-Zyklus*, 70,22, clearly deals with the question of ennobling love. In the first stanza of this song, which combines the conversation and *Wechsel* forms, the man pleads with the lady to let him live just for her. But, he continues, she must allow him one thing to help him pass the time while he is waiting for her favor. Although he does not come right out and say what he is referring to, his hints are clear enough to the lady, who responds indirectly in the next strophe. She says if she ever has a lover, she will want him all for herself. Her "friend," however, loves other women and she is not willing to share him. The knight replies, also indirectly, that his lady is too perturbed about his making friends elsewhere. After all, he says, despite his doleful entreaties she has never commanded him to live only for her, as she now seems to imply. Because she does not react to his laments, he asks what good it has done him to love her above all others. If she wants him to give up other women, she will have to be more responsive to his words. In the final stanza the lady addresses him personally, admitting that she has not paid much heed to his pleas. She has failed to show an interest, she explains, because she knows he has said the same things to others as well. Anyone who wants to win her affection, she concludes, will have to avoid such inconstancy.

This song offers a clear example of what was only suspected in 85,34, namely, a reversal of the usual idea of the ennobling power of love. It is expressed in the knight's attitude toward the concept of constancy. He seems perfectly eager to renounce other women for the sake of his beloved, but he is not about to do so until she gives him some sign that she returns his affection. In the meantime he wants to be free to attend to others as well. In other words, he is not willing to improve his conduct until after he has been rewarded, or at least until he has been given some assurance that he will be recompensed for his service. The lady, on the other hand, believes in the "standard" version of the theory. She wants to see some improvement in his behavior before she pays serious attention to his wooing. It should be noted, however, that the entire discussion of the issue is restricted to the one question of the man's faithfulness.

Halbach's next set of poems in the larger group of those written by Walther at the height of his powers is divided into two subgroups. The first of these consists of two songs, 90,15 and 72,31, where the idea of ennobling love plays a role—in one explicitly, in the other by implication. In 90,15 Walther laments the sad state of society and his position in it. Fortune, he says, does not smile on someone who practices *triuwe*; this being the case, he wonders if there is any hope for himself. Not only does his *zuht* not benefit him, he complains, but also he is even made a fool of because of it. The old values are out of fashion and only evil people achieve wealth and reputation. But it is the women who are responsible for the men's wicked behavior, he maintains. Previously, "dô ir muot ûf êre stuont" (90,33), the world was happy in anticipation of their favor and praised them for their *fuoge*. Now, however, it is obvious that one can win their love with *unfuoge*. What bothers him most when he goes to see the ladies, he continues, is that the more *zuht* he displays, the less he is esteemed. The ladies simply scorn "wol gezogenen lîp" (91,5). Of course, a "wol bescheiden wîp" (91,6) would not do such a thing, he concedes, and he wishes good fortune to whatever good women and men still exist. To them he pledges his service. He concludes with a warning that he will renounce his singing if the state of the world does not improve.

The decline of courtly values lamented by the poet is patently related to the idea of the ennobling power of love. When Walther blames the women for the way the men conduct themselves, he is clearly criticizing the breakdown of the concept of the uplifting force that can be exerted by women. Although he does not supply all the details, the implications of his complaints are fairly obvious. Formerly, when women insisted on a certain standard of behavior—on *fuoge*—men tried to live up to their expectations in the hope of winning their favor. Now that this is no longer the case, it is the men who lack good breeding who succeed in their wooing. In other words, love has ceased to have an educative influence because women no longer are taking the proper initiative.

In 72,31 the poet finally breaks with his lady in a most uncourtly fashion. After stating that he has decided to resume his singing despite his earlier intention to remain silent, he says a certain woman no longer wishes to see him. Although he has made her famous and esteemed through his songs, she does not seem to realize how dependent her repute is on his praise, or that people will curse her if he ceases to sing. Now that he has seen that she is not *guot*, he continues, he is not inclined to treat her with deference. He will now behave toward her the way she does toward him. If she frees him from distress, she will enjoy honor through him; if he dies, however, then she, too, will be dead. If he is getting older in her service, he concludes, she is not getting any younger, either; if she now prefers a younger man to him, he hopes such a young fellow will avenge him by taking a switch to her old hide.

In such a context of deliberate coarseness it is not surprising to find no hint of the idea of the ennobling power of love. The situation here is not unlike that in 90,15, where the poet's dissatisfaction with the state of courtly society was intimately connected with the notion of the educative function of love and, specifically, with the lady's particular role in it. But whereas in 90,15 the poet dealt mainly with generalizations, here he concentrates on his personal relationship to his lady and his bitterness about her failure to accord him the treatment he thinks he deserves. Even though the topic under discussion is not mentioned in 72,31, the generally assumed connection of this poem with 90,15 might make it reasonable to suppose that everything he said in the latter concerning the breakdown of the idea of the elevating power of love is also implicitly valid here, and that his lady is an example of the type of woman he was complaining about in the previous song.

The second of the subgroups contains three songs, 44,35, 47,36, and 58,21. Of these, only one, 44,35, lacks any clear connection with the idea of ennobling love. The pitiful condition of society, which was the theme of 90,15, is also the topic of discussion at the beginning of 44,35. Here, however, a different approach is encountered as the poet reports the views of both men and women about the cause of the present state of affairs. The men say it is the women's fault because they are no longer joyful as they once were, and the women blame the men for not giving them any reason to be *hôhes muotes*. After presenting this dilemma, the poet turns to his personal dispute with his lady, claiming that she has arrogantly accused him of being at the end of his powers as far as praise is concerned. He asserts that she is foolish, if not crazy to say this, for he is just as capable as ever.

He has stopped lauding the ladies merely because he is wary of praising those who deserve it in front of those who do not. For him one thing is clear—he will never again praise them all indiscriminately. As if to show that he still knows how, he then lavishly extols a certain woman he knows who is not jealous when other commendable women are similarly praised. At the end of the poem, he generalizes about the damage priests and women do to themselves by not wanting people to distinguish the good from the bad among them.

Unlike 90,15, which combined criticism of society with the idea of the ennobling power of love, 44,35 has a different focus of attention and avoids any discussion of the issue. Whereas in 90,15 it was women's failure to insist on proper conduct in men that led to a deterioration in men's behavior, in 44,35 it is women's reluctance to allow distinctions among themselves that is causing the problems—primarily the drying up of the source of ladies' praise upon which they are so dependent to maintain a joyous state of mind. It is also interesting to observe that, when Walther demonstrates that he still knows how to extol women, he does not touch at all on the subject of women's role in the educative function of love; rather, he mentions only the lady's beauty and goodness in a very general sense, and, specifically, only her lack of envy when others who are praiseworthy are also lauded.

In the two remaining songs in the second subgroup, the idea of ennobling love is found in only one small portion of the poem. At the beginning of 47,36, which contains Walther's renunciation of love service to noble ladies, he says that, no matter how uncouth he may be, he does possess good breeding in two respects: he shows consideration for those around him by not being sad when others are merry, and by not laughing when they are crying. And just as he adjusts his demeanor to the mood of his environment, he also adapts his poetry to the conditions at hand. That is why his songs are no longer full of joy. But as soon as *unfuoge* disappears, he says, his singing will again become courtly. He then gives the reason for the sad state of society. Women no longer distinguish between good men and bad, which deprives men of joy and honor; women likewise do not like men to make distinctions among them. Expanding on the idea of differentiating among women, he continues with a discourse on the relative merits of the terms *wîp* and *frowe*. He prefers the former to the latter, he says, because *wîp* encompasses the womanly virtues, which are not necessarily associated with *frowe*. The end result of this is the elevation of *wîp* over *frowe* and with it the nobility of character over that of birth. At the end of the song he says he is no longer content to wait in vain for a reward from the ladies whom he has praised. Henceforth he will treat them the way they treat him. After asking the question: "What do I get from these overbearing ladies?" he states his intention of turning his praise to women who know how to thank him for it.

Like 44,35, a large part of this poem is concerned with the idea of making distinctions among women. But the theme of the ennobling power of love also makes an appearance here. Its treatment is essentially the same as in 90,15, only in a much briefer form. In this case, the poet blames the ladies for the deterioration of society by not distinguishing between good and bad men. Although there are even fewer details here than in 90,15, the implications are basically the same—by not caring about the behavior of their suitors, the ladies' function of encouraging an improvement in men's conduct has become inoperative. In turning away from the service of noble ladies, Walther also implies a loss of faith in the efficacy of the concept of the educative force of love—at least as it had been conceived in the context of the traditional love-service relationship between a knight and a noble lady.

In 58,21 the poet touches on many of the themes found in the other songs in this set. He begins by telling those who complain that there are no more singers around that the dearth of song is directly related to the present state of the world. Then he defends himself against the *lôsen* who criticize him for not speaking well of the ladies. No one has ever spoken better of German women, he declares, but they hate him because he insists on differentiating between the good and the bad. After apostrophizing *haz* and *nît* in the third stanza, he returns in the fourth to his own predicament, saying that anyone who woos a good woman as he does must possess many good qualities. Unfortunately, he maintains, he has only two such qualities to offer, *scham* and *triuwe*; although they used to be valued highly, today they are detrimental to success. Nevertheless, he is not going to change his ways. Next he responds to those who say that no one is without faults by claiming that his lady has only two—she causes her friends pain and she does no harm to her enemies. Finally, he says she also has two good features—*schoene* and *êre*—and she could not ask for more.

The idea of the ennobling power of love appears in this song only in the fourth stanza when the poet says a man must have many *tugende* if he desires a good woman. This is clearly a variation of the notion that a good woman will not consider a man's suit if he does not conform to a certain standard of behavior. There is, to be sure, no specific mention of the view that the man should strive to improve in order to become worthy of the lady's love. But the poet's statement in no way excludes the idea of the man's *becoming* virtuous, even if he actually speaks only of his *being* in possession of good qualities.[24] In addition, Walther's bitterness about his lack of success, despite his adherence to the theory of the educative power of love, is quite evident. He indicates here, as he did in other songs in this group, that, because the old values are no longer held in esteem, the concept of the ennobling power of love can hardly be very meaningful.

Halbach labels his next group of songs *Ebene Minne: I*, consisting basically of the two poems, 49,25 and 50,19, but also including 115,30. The first two, which are clearly directed at women of a lower social standing than that of the ladies addressed or referred to in the poems already discussed, both contain unseized opportunities to introduce the idea of ennobling love. In 49,25 the poet calls his beloved *herzeliebez frowelîn* and hopes God will always bless her. He complains, however, that people reproach him for aiming his songs *sô nidere*, and he curses those who are interested only in wealth and beauty for not understanding what true love is. One should not be too eager for beauty, he warns, for *haz* is often connected with it. *Liebe* is better for the heart, he says. It can make women beautiful, whereas beauty cannot make a person *liep*. After this discussion of the relative importance of *liebe* and *schoene*, the poet turns again to his beloved whom he loves no matter what people may say. If she has *triuwe* and *staetekeit*, he will not worry about her deliberately causing him sorrow. But if she does not possess these qualities, he concludes, he hopes she will never be his.[25]

In 50,19 the poet is not at all certain of his beloved's feelings. He complains to her that she does not look at him, and he hopes that she has some good reason for ignoring him thus in public. He can accept her behavior if she is avoiding his eyes for fear of revealing her feelings in the presence of others, but he suggests that she give him some sign of her favor, even if it consists only of casting her glance down to his feet. For his part, he says, even though there are many women of greater wealth and higher station who by rights ought to please him, he has chosen her as his *frouwe* because she is *guot*. He concludes the song by reminding her of the necessity of mutual affection in a love relationship: "eines friundes minne / diust niht guot, dâ ensî ein ander bî" (51,7–9).

Neither of these songs in which the lady is not of the highest social standing reveals an awareness of the ennobling power of love, even though both contain situations that would have easily lent themselves to its introduction. Unlike 92,9, where the poet also discusses the relationship between *liebe* and *schoene*, 49,25 does not touch upon the benefit of self-improvement to be derived from service to a woman possessing the perfect combination of qualities. Rather, the poet concentrates only on the direct advantages he sees accruing to himself from his beloved's virtues. In other words, if she is truly good and kind, she will not make him suffer. In 50,19 the lady's goodness is also emphasized as perhaps her most attractive feature, but here, too, there is no indication that her good qualities are supposed to have an educative effect on him.

The third poem in this group does contain an example of the idea of ennobling love. Although at first glance it might seem that the poet's beloved returns his affection in 115,30, a closer look reveals that this is not at all certain. He begins by wondering what a particular woman sees in him that would prompt her to cast a spell over him. He is, after all, not the handsomest of men. But if he is not good-looking, he says, he does possess some *fuoge*; if she prefers that to beauty, she is *wol gemuot*. If that is indeed the case, then everything she might do for him would suit her well, and he would bow to her in gratitude and fulfill her every wish. What need has she of magic, he asks, for he is already her bondsman. Besides, he concludes, the powers she does have are not supernatural, but are merely her *schoene* and her *êre*, and her ability to cause joy as well as sorrow. Thus by the end of the poem it becomes clear that she has not deliberately enchanted him because she loves him and that he is not at all sure of her feelings.

This song clearly touches on the theme of the ennobling power of love when the poet speculates about what might attract his beloved to him other than his external appearance. He obviously would approve of her way of thinking if she valued the quality of his behavior more than his looks, and he would find it appropriate if she should show him her favor. The lack of such an attitude on the part of women is precisely what the poet complained about in several of the poems in the group just discussed. However, there is no real indication here that the woman in question shares this frame of mind. The speaker merely says he hopes this is so. Furthermore, as in 58,21, the notion that the man should attempt to improve himself in order to merit the woman's love is not specifically mentioned. Thus the situation is presented from the point of view of completion rather than from the standpoint of development. But the idea that a woman expects a man to live up to a certain standard necessarily includes the possibility of his striving to better himself so that he will conform to her expectations.

The next set of poems, called *Ebene Minne: II*, has as its nucleus the two songs 39,11 and 74,20. It contains, in addition, a number of poems more or less closely related to these in a variety of ways.[26] Both of the primary songs, which deal with the theme of love's physical fulfillment, as well as one of the four related poems to be discussed here, show no evidence of the idea of ennobling love and offer no easy opportunities for its introduction. In 39,11 a girl recalls a rendezvous with her lover under a linden tree where they enjoyed love's delights on a bed of roses that he had made before she arrived. In 74,20 a man offers a wreath of flowers to a girl participating in a dance and invites her to help him pick flowers for an even better one in a nearby meadow. The bliss he experiences with her in the grass under the trees amidst a shower of falling blossoms turns out to be only a dream, however, and he resolves to spend the summer looking for his dream-girl among the dancers he meets.

That neither of these songs shows any trace of the idea of the ennobling power of love is, of course, not surprising, inasmuch as neither of the relationships depicted gives any indication of having been developed within the context of love service. Although the idea of a reward is mentioned in 74,20, it can hardly be taken as a serious sign of love service; the gift of the wreath and its accompanying compliment constitute the extent of the activity for which recompense is desired. The portrayal of the mini-courtship makes it perfectly clear that there is no room here for the idea of love's morally elevating power.

The other song in this category, the fragmentary 110,27, has little to do with the theme of love. The speaker says it is difficult to please people with his singing because everyone seems to want to hear something else. If he knew what they wanted, he would sing it, for he is familiar with both joy and sorrow. The summer delights him, he says, but the uneasy doubts (*zwîfelwân*) he has about how he will fare with his beloved make him sad. In view of the limited concern with a love relationship in this song, the absence of the idea of ennobling love is hardly unexpected.

Only one song in this set, 65,33, contains a situation that would have lent itself to introducing the idea under investigation. Here the speaker's doubts about his ever winning his lady's favor cause him to consider leaving her service. But a ray of hope keeps him from taking this drastic step, he says. He measured a blade of straw with his fingers, as he saw children do, and no matter how often he did it, the prediction was always the same: he will find *genâde*. In the final stanza he implies that his new-found optimism has made it possible for him to more easily tolerate the fact that others are also in his lady's service. Although he cannot believe that one of his rivals would gain her favor, he concludes by expressing his annoyance at how long she continues to pay attention to those who only boast about their successes. The missed opportunity in this song arises in connection with the clear emphasis on the concept of service and reward. Although the omen of the straw makes the man hopeful that he will win his lady's love, no indication is given that his expectation is based on the notion that in the course of his service he will have become worthy of his reward by means of self-improvement.[27]

The idea of ennobling love plays a more or less clear role in two of the songs in this set. In 184,1 the poet states that he wants to be happy in the expectation of being granted his lady's favor. When he is not feeling particularly cheerful, he says, he likes to indulge in wishful thinking and daydreams that often improve his mood. He then gives an example by imagining what it would be like to lie so close to his beloved that he could see himself in her eyes. The dream of joy is followed by his assertion that all the suffering he has endured has brought him nothing. If she does not want to reward him for his sorrow, then he will attempt to behave better (*gehaben baz*) on the chance that she prefers a happy mien to a sad one. He decides that, even if neither pleases her, he would rather act joyful than unhappy.

Whether or not the idea of the ennobling power of love is involved in this song is debatable. At the end the poet does talk about improving his behavior in the hope of pleasing his lady and winning her favor, which certainly sounds like one of the primary aspects of the theory of the educative effect of love. It turns out, however, that he merely resolves to compose himself, to hide his sorrow behind a mask of gaiety in case his lady is more likely to react favorably to a bright face than to a moping one. If one were convinced that the speaker considered his change of bearing a true improvement directed at acquiring a noble characteristic, such as *fuoge* or *zuht*, and that he realized this would help make him worthy of the lady, then one could easily view this as a genuine example of the phenomenon under investigation. But nothing in the poem itself really points in this direction. What predominates here is the feeling that the man, thinking that suffering (and showing it) would earn him a reward, bore his pain (and yet complained about it audibly). When it finally dawned on him that he was getting nowhere, he decided that perhaps feigning joy would be a more effective approach. It would therefore be difficult to take this instance seriously as evidence of the presence of ennobling love if 184,1 could be considered by itself. Its generally acknowledged close relationship to 61,33 (+ 184,31), however, makes it necessary to examine this song also before reaching a final determination.[28]

The first stanza, 61,33, refers unmistakably to a previous poem, half of which, according to the poet, has been bitterly attacked. His critics have said that others may sing such songs, but he should in future pay more attention to propriety and practice moderation. (What they have found so offensive is presumably the stanza in 184,1 where the poet had conjured up a vision of a tryst with his lady.) He feels, however, that he has indeed desisted from many things for the sake of what they call *zuht*.[29] And if things are so bad that he derives no benefit from it, then he will withdraw from the world. In the second stanza, 184,31, he says he intends to complain to *rehter hövescheit* that so many people have treated him so harshly. The real reason they have done so, he intimates, is that they are jealous—they, too, would like to be where he had imagined himself in 184,1. But no matter, he concludes; whoever can maintain his *zuht* deserves a headdress of silk.

The discussion of *zuht*, *mâze*, and *hövescheit* in this poem makes it easy to suspect the presence of the idea of ennobling love. To be sure, the poet and his critics have conflicting definitions of these terms. Assuming that in 184,1 the poet is referring to his deliberate attempt to cover his sorrow with a facade of joy, one must surmise that he is saying he has given up his gloominess and that he considers this ability to compose himself as an example of these qualities. His opponents, however, view his portrayal of his daydreams as a sign that he lacks them. It is also evident that the poet believes some benefit should be derived from this endeavor to maintain *zuht*—not only when he complains that he has gotten nothing from it, but also when he generalizes at the end about how a person deserves a head covering of silk for preserving it. It is clear that the main ingredients of the educative effect of love are here—the conscious effort to improve one's behavior and the expectation of some recompense for so doing. If it could be assumed that the lady's love is meant to be a reward, the case would certainly be more convincing. That it is possible to do so has been shown by von Kraus,[30] who takes the position that the silk *schapel* of the last line refers to its original wearer, that is, a lady, and that the poet is really referring to himself in his final generalization. The poet therefore is implying that, because of his *zuht,* he is worthy of the reward of love as depicted in the imagined rendezvous of 184,1. As far as the latter poem is concerned, it can now be seen that the doubts previously raised about the presence of the idea of the ennobling power of love have been resolved. If one assumes that the poems are connected, it becomes clear that the speaker in 184,1 does indeed view his decision to give up his *trûren* within the framework of the uplifting force of love.

Closely related to 184,1 and 61,33 is 62,6 around which Halbach groups a number of more or less loosely connected songs—97,34, 44,11, 73,23, and 63,32, all of which share the theme of the poet's difficulties with people in his environment who are hostile to him. Two of these, 73,23 and 97,34, show no trace of the idea of ennobling love and contain no situations that would lend themselves to its introduction. In 73,23 the poet's relationship with his enemies is treated lightly as he alternates between cursing them humorously and taking back his ill wishes. Halfway through the poem, after stating seriously that, when the *boesen* hate someone with no apparent justification, it is because he is a good person, the speaker turns to the problem of his status with his lady. If she consoled him, he says, he would not care at all about his enemies' hostility. He then swears before the whole world that no one is dearer to him than his beloved; if she has any *triuwe,* he says, she will believe his oath and soothe the pain in his heart. At the end he calls on the knights and his friends in his audience to come to his aid before it is too late, for if he does not prevail in his battle of love, he will never be completely happy again. The deep wound in his heart will remain open forever, he concludes, unless his Hildegunde heals it with her kisses.

At the beginning of 97,34 the speaker complains about the young people of the day who are not interested in attaining joy. But, he goes on, he must be joyful for the sake of his beloved. Even though he is separated from her, his heart is with her; as a result, people often think he is not in possession of his senses. If only his body and both their hearts and minds would come together, then he would hope that those who often rob him of joy might not notice such a union. He follows with a tirade against these watchers who prevent him from seeing his lady. Yet he hopes he will live to see the day when she will be glad to be alone with him. Then he states that many people have asked him who is the woman he has been serving. When he gets tired of their asking, he tells them that he serves three but that his hopes rest with a fourth. Only his beloved—who can heal as well as wound—can understand what this means. At the end of the song he asks Lady Love to attack the woman who has conquered him so that she might realize what it is like to be afflicted by love. If love were to take possession of her, then perhaps she would believe him when he says he loves her with all his heart.

In neither of these songs is the speaker's expectation of being united with his lady in love based on his becoming worthy of her love through self-improvement. In 73,23 he bases his hope on his oath that he loves her more than anyone else; in 97,34 he relies on his ability to dupe the watchers and on his lady's understanding of his predicament after she has been afflicted with the pangs of love. In both songs the predominant effect of love—gaping, incapacitating wounds—is anything but edifying.

Two songs in this set contain passages that tempt one to think in terms of the idea of ennobling love. In 44,11 the speaker says that, even though he is physically separated from his lady, his *sin* is always with her, and he hopes her thoughts go out to him, too. Those responsible for their separation are presumably the liars he now refers to; their successes in doing damage to good people he deplores. Whoever listens to them is bound to come to harm, for what they preach amounts to "unstaete, schande, sünde, unêre" (44,30). Some people still hate him, he continues, because in an earlier poem he said that true love was free of sin and that false love should be called *unminne*. If these people, who are in the service of false love, are able to drive him away, then he hopes the ladies will offer him protection. Finally, he complains that, even though so many people take his advice, he does not know what to do about his own predicament. He concludes by saying that in the future he will be more careful about choosing his friends. Although nothing in this poem points specifically in the direction of the idea of ennobling love, one cannot help feeling that it is not far from the poet's mind. Both the song to which he refers generally (*MF*214,34) and the particular passage he paraphrases here reveal a clear awareness of the morally uplifting force of love.

In 63,32 the speaker says that people have asked him so many times who his lady is that he has finally decided to tell them. She has two names, he says, *genâde* and *ungenâde*. He intimates that whoever prevents him from gaining her favor should be ashamed. If these shameless ones would leave him alone, he would not be bothered by hatred and hostility, but their lack of a sense of decency forces him to go away. When *zuht* still ruled, he laments, a thousand decent people could prevail upon an "ungefüegen man" (64,9) and bring about a change in his thinking. The poet then turns his attention to his lady, affirming that, as long as he continues to sing, he will always find a new song of praise for her. With that he proceeds to extol her, saying that the sight of her delights the eye, just as the sound of people lauding her virtures pleases the ear. In the last stanza he praises the joys of nature and apostrophizes Summer, asking the fair season to help him in his sorrow—what he loves does not love him. This poem, too, reveals no direct evidence of the notion of ennobling love, although it does contain an interesting analogue that is reminiscent of the theme under investigation. When the poet complains about the passing of the good old days, he talks about the edifying influence of the *gefüegen* on those who were not. But because this reference to people with *zuht* does not specifically mention the role of women in bringing about an improvement in others, namely, those in their service, it must be considered too general to be viewed as a clear example of the educative effect of love.

One of the songs in this set, 62,6, presents unambiguous evidence, as well as some variations, of the idea of ennobling love. Here the speaker begins by praising himself for being a courtly man who can put up with insults without taking revenge. Even a hermit, he says, would have lost patience under the kind of provocation he has endured. He is willing to bear it because his lady told him he should try to please people who make him unhappy in the hope that they might then be ashamed of their behavior and become *guot*. Addressing her directly, he tells her she can prove to him that this advice was good. He gives her pleasure, he says, and she makes him sad. She should, therefore, be ashamed and become kind—that would show that she had spoken the truth. Of course, he does not mean to say that she is not *guot*, only that he has never benefited from her goodness. He then reminds her that it would be appropriate for her beauty and her nobility to be accompanied by *genâde*, and he says he cannot help it if his thoughts, dreams, and wishes center around her. But even if she does not pay attention to his singing, he continues, he still is rewarded well, for when his praise makes her known at court, it redounds to his honor. The final stanza is devoted to just such praise of her *lîp*, which he compares to a noble covering in which she has clothed herself. For the gift of such a garment, he concludes, even the emperor would become her minstrel.

In this song Walther once again has more or less turned upside down two of the more traditional aspects of the theory of ennobling love. The idea that the man should look to the lady for guidance is clearly expressed when he says she told him to return good for bad. But, having put her advice into practice, he admonishes her to act in a way that will demonstrate the truth of her teachings. Thus, along with the motif of the lady spurring the man on to self-betterment, one finds here the converse—the man telling the lady how to behave. In addition, the notion that the man's conduct can be rewarded by means other than the lady's love is slightly twisted. Instead of the man's improvement being considered a recompense in itself, here his service in the form of spreading her fame in song brings its own reward even if she ignores him—his activity on her behalf increases his esteem.

The next group consists of three songs Walther presumably composed when he was in his forties: 59,37, 57,23, and 116,33. While the first two are devoid of the idea of ennobling love and offer no opportunities for its introduction, the third contains an example of the theme under investigaton. The first song, 59,37, is an attempt to come to terms with *Frau Welt*. The speaker addresses her directly, complaining that, although he has served her loyally for a long time, he has yet to receive an adequate reward. He also regrets that she seems to prefer foolish youth to wise maturity, and he hopes she will ask "die alten êre" (60,31) to return and instruct her vassals once more. But because the speaker talks only in general terms about the world, and not about love and its role in worldly life, this song need not be discussed in detail.

Although Walther does deal with love in 57,23, *Frau Minne's* behavior is the sole topic of the song. Here the speaker is almost exclusively concerned with the fact that Lady Love, though quite old herself, passes him by in favor of young fools, with whom she cavorts as if she were sixteen. Even though he still has *hôhen muot*, he cannot keep up with those who can jump so high, and he hopes she will not mind if he sits down while they frolic. He concludes by saying that he can devote only the seventh day of the week to her now. Because the song concentrates only on this one problem, it is not surprising that the idea of the educative function of love is completely absent. And if one agrees with von Kraus, who sees here a renunciation of love by the discouraged poet,[31] the poet's lack of concern with the question is fully understandable.

The last of these songs, 116,33, treats not only the same complaints about the world heard in 59,37, but also the problem of love. The poet begins by stating proudly that no one is better able than he to present a happy face to the world while suffering inwardly the pain of love. But, unfortunately, he says, people no longer understand this kind of joy, which is "senender muot mit gerender arebeit" (117,13); such *ungemach* should be praised. Thus some people think he is really experiencing the greatest joy, even though he is not and never will until *tiusche liute* become *guot* again and the lady who causes him so much sorrow consoles him. Although he has served the World a long time, he continues, it has not rewarded him properly, for whenever he asks for something he wants passionately, some fool gets it instead of him. For this reason he no longer knows how to go about his wooing. Although the current fashion is repugnant to him, if he woos in the old manner it might turn out to his disadvantage. Nonetheless, he concludes, he will hope that the wooing of the *ungefüegen* will meet with more approval elsewhere than from his lady.

The treatment of the idea of ennobling love in this song is quite similar to that in 184,1 and 61,33. The poet clearly views his ability to dissemble for the sake of society as praiseworthy when he says, with reference to it, "daz liegen was ab lobelich" (116,39). He also considers his behavior as a sign of his *fuoge*, which he obviously feels should qualify him for some recognition. That he complains so bitterly about his being denied the reward to which he is entitled and about people no longer understanding his style of wooing reveals how old-fashioned the theory of the educative force of love has become. If one is to give credence to the poet, he is just about the last one to believe that striving to maintain *zuht* and *fuoge* in the course of serving a lady makes him worthy of her love.

The last grouping of songs—those presumably composed by Walther in his old age—contain three subgroups, only two of which will be discussed here.[32] The first of these consists of three songs that still deal, either directly or indirectly, with love or love poetry— 64,31, 111,12, and 88,9. Although the first two in this subset show no trace of the idea of ennobling love, the last one presents a variation of it that has been encountered before in Walther's poems. In 64,31 the poet narrows the focus of his previous complaints about the activities of the *ungefüegen*, aiming solely at the "ungefüegen doene" (64,32) that are displacing "hovelîchez singen" (64,31) at the courts. If only someone would put a stop to this new style of singing, he wishes, then *fröide* could be restored. But because he discusses these disturbing forces in only the most general way, without speaking specifically about the treatment of love in either the old or the new poetry, this song need not be examined in any detail. In the second song, the brief ten lines of 111,12, the poet expresses in a rather obtuse manner his preference for natural beauty in a woman over feminine attractiveness that is dependent on artifice. Inasmuch as the relationship between the sexes is not touched upon in any way, this song also need not be of further concern here.

The last song in this subgroup, 88,9, is Walther's only *Tagelied*. Except for a brief narrative introduction and conclusion, it consists entirely of a dialogue between a knight and his beloved lady at the approach of dawn after a night of illicit love. Because the only topics of the conversation are the pain of parting, the necessity of separation, and the desire to be reunited as soon as possible, there is scarcely any opportunity for the traditional version of the ennobling power of love to make an appearance. In the final stanza, however, the narrator, commenting on the knight's having to leave the lady in tears, says: "doch galt er ir mit triuwen / dazs ime vil nâhe lac" (90,7–8). This is another example of Walther's reversal of the standard concept according to which the man's demonstration of his faithfulness might be taken by the lady as a sign that he has become worthy of her love. Here the man's fidelity is considered a reward for the woman's having given herself to him.

The last subgroup of Walther's poems consists of six songs dealing more or less intimately with the theme of the renunciation of the world; with one minor exception, these songs do not concern themselves with the idea of ennobling love. In 41,13 the speaker begins by stating that he keeps his happiness to himself. Although he gladly praises men of excellence, he does not approve of men who boast of their successes. He advises good women to be on their guard against such braggarts, and he forbids boasters and slanderers to make use of his songs. He has observed, he continues, that the joy of love is always accompanied by sorrow. Thus it is perhaps for the best that he has not experienced such love. The only discomfort he knows, he claims, arises when, lost in thought, he becomes oblivious of his surroundings. In the final stanza he says he has never known complete joy, and whatever joys he has known have left him. There is, he concludes, no joy here (on earth) that is not transitory, and for this reason he is not going to strive any longer "nâch valschen fröiden" (42,14). The idea of the ennobling power of love is clearly absent in this song in which the emphasis is so overwhelmingly on the negative, even destructive aspects of love. The poet feels that he is perhaps better off without *herzeliebe* because it will inevitably entail *herzeleit*, and his thoughts of love render him senseless so that he cannot react to those around him.

In 122,24 the only themes are the transitory nature of all earthly life and the necessity of repentance for having devoted oneself to the things of this world. Because the poet does not say what his particular misdeeds were and does not mention earthly love, the poem need not be examined more carefully. The next song, 100,24, consists of a conversation between the poet and *Frau Welt*. Concerned about the salvation of his soul, he takes leave of the world, while she attempts in vain to persuade him to change his mind. Both speakers refer to worldly activities only in the most general terms and do not bring up the topic of love; thus there is also no need to discuss this poem further.

Walther begins 66,21 by telling his audience that it should honor him more than ever for having sung for forty years about love and the proper conduct of life. He also says proudly that he has striven all his life toward *werdekeit*. Then, after addressing the world and expounding on the transitory nature of its rewards, he turns his thoughts to eternity. He hopes his soul will fare well, he says. He brought pleasure to many people in this world, but he wishes that that could have helped him achieve salvation. Now he realizes that praising "des lîbes minne" (67,24) is detrimental to the welfare of the soul; his soul tells him that only true love is perfectly constant and lasts forever. Finally, he admonishes his *lîp* to abandon the love that it has always sought and that will ultimately abandon him and to cleave to a love that is constant. Even though Walther does deal with the question of love here, it is not at all surprising that the idea of ennobling love is not specifically mentioned. It, like all other forms of worldly love, represents the kind of love he is now rejecting in favor of Divine Love, the only love that is real.

The last two of Walther's poems to be reviewed combine the theme of turning away from worldly cares with a more or less directly expressed crusade appeal. In 124,1, his famous elegy, neither the renunciation of the world nor the crusade motif offers anything of interest to this investigaton. This is also true of an additional theme of the song—the decline of courtly culture. Walther's bitter criticism of several features of contemporary society, which he contrasts with the way things used to be, has no bearing on the relationship between the sexes.

Except for one short passage, nothing in 13,5 has to do with love. Hence most of the song need not be scrutinized here. In the first stanza, however, the poet says that whoever is physically and financially able to participate in the crusade but stays home will lose the favor of both the angels and the ladies. This remark touches briefly on one special aspect of the notion of ennobling love that has been observed earlier in several other crusade poems.[33] Even though the idea is not clearly spelled out here, it is obviously implied that a lady would not consider worthy of her love a man who shirked his duty to go on a crusade. In exerting such a pressure on her suitor, the lady could thus be responsible for helping to bring about an improvement in his conduct by inducing him to perform a service to God.

The final section of this study is devoted to the poems generally considered to have been incorrectly ascribed to Walther von der Vogelweide. Of the large number of these, only those concerned with the theme of love will be examined. They will be considered in the groupings indicated by Carl von Kraus.[34]

1. "*Unechtes in Lachmanns Text*."[35] Under this heading ten poems need to be discussed.[36] Three of these show no trace of the idea of ennobling love and offer no opportunities for its introduction. One, 37,24, is not a love song, but a short *Jugendspiegel* containing advice to youth. Only the last line has anything to do with women. In it the poet says: "wilt dû daz allez übergülden, sô sprich wol den wîben" (37,33). Although this wording gives importance to the act of praising women, this activity is not viewed in any larger context of relationships to women and hence has no clear connection with the standard idea of the edifying force of love.

The other two poems in this category, 60,34 and 61,8, are monostrophic songs that, together with 61,20 (to be discussed below in another grouping), have frequently been considered to be more or less closely related.[37] In the first song the poet says he wishes to dispose of his possessions before he departs. To those who cultivate hate and envy he wills his misfortune, and to the slanderers he leaves his sorrow. The confusion of his senses (presumably brought about by love) he bequeathes to those who love "mit velsche" (61,6). Finally, the painful longing for *herzeliebe* he reserves for noble ladies. In the second poem the speaker tells how his lady should behave after he is gone. She should temper the expression of her sorrow, as is appropriate for "senenden frowen" (61,14), and not behave immoderately as so many do in giving vent to their feelings. Both these poems are far removed from the idea of the ennobling power of love. Where love is the subject in 60,34, the only aspects involved are the pain of longing and the debilitating effect of passion on the senses; in 61,8 it is the man who is shown delineating proper behavior for the woman, and not the woman whose conduct is serving as a model for the man.

Another three songs under the heading "Unechtes in Lachmanns Text" contain situations that would have easily lent themselves to the introduction of the idea of ennobling love. The first two are closely related strophes, 27,17 and 27,27, in which the poet lavishly praises *reine frouwen*. In 27,17 he says that none of the joys of nature can compare with the joy experienced when one looks at a beautiful lady.

Such a sight can refresh a "trüeben muot" (27,23) and extinguish all sadness when her sweet red mouth smiles lovingly and she shoots arrows from her sparkling eyes deep into a man's heart. Similarly, the poet says in 27,27 that ladies "mit reiner güete" (27,27) impart a "wünneberndez hôhgemüete" (27,28) and that God has exalted ladies so much that one should speak well of them and serve them at all times. In addition, he claims, "der werlde hort" (27,32) lies with them, and nothing drives away sadness better than looking at "ein schoene frowen wol gemuot" (27,35) when she smiles lovingly at her friend from the depths of her heart. Despite the many opportunities that are presented in these poems, the poet never alludes to the ennobling power of love in describing love's obviously beneficial effects. Over and over again it is the bliss of looking at the ladies and their ability to dispel sorrow by smiling at those they favor that are emphasized. Nowhere is it mentioned that their perfection can act as a model for the man who should improve himself in order to become worthy of the love of such a lofty lady.

The third song in this category, 120,25, is a lament of unrequited love. At the beginning the speaker asks whether his ability to put a happy face to the world, although he is actually suffering, is good or bad. Then he complains that he can help others but not himself. He loves a good and beautiful woman who even lets him talk to her, but he still cannot reach his goal; he would lose heart if it were not for the fact that she smiles a little when she denies him. At least part of the problem, he maintains, is that he is unable to speak properly when he is with her because her presence robs him of his senses. He hopes she is a woman who pays less attention to words than to good intentions. Even though his prospects of happiness are uncertain and his lady questions his faithfulness, he assures her that she is a lasting hope of joy for him. Finally, he says she should see to it that she is inwardly as praiseworthy as she is outwardly beautiful. If this is indeed the case, he concludes, she will not be able to leave his service unrewarded.

Although there are several places where the ennobling power of love might have made an appearance in this song, none of these opportunities is seized by the poet. The notion that the man's success in hiding his true feelings for the sake of society is commendable and helps make him, at least in his own eyes, worthy of the lady's affection, is conspicuously absent here, whereas the poet's uncertainty about the value of his dissembling is immediately evident from his opening question. Another instance arises when the poet discusses his lady's goodness. Instead of regarding her excellent qualities as a source of inspiration for his self-improvement, he considers them as a kind of guarantee that she will not let him suffer too long. In addition, the emphasis on love's destructive effects—expressed in the poet's inability to function either mentally or physically in his lady's presence—tends to leave little room for the idea of the edifying force of love.

One of the songs under the heading "Unechtes in Lachmanns Text" contains a situation that comes close to the notion of ennobling love. In 36,11, a *Fürstenspiegel* that deserves consideration here because it includes some comments about the role of women in the life of the prince being counseled, the poet tells of two happy consequences of the model behavior he recommends—the "reinen süezen frouwen" (36,16) will praise him and he will have a place in heaven. The first of these benefits seems to at least touch upon a variant of the idea of the ennobling power of love, namely, that a lady will bestow her favor if the man leads an exemplary life. Two missing factors, however, make it difficult to view this as a genuine example of the educative effect of love. Although women's praise can be considered a form of favor, there is no clear reference here to women's love as a reward. The poem likewise gives no indication that the prince will be motivated to be good by his desire to please the ladies and win their love. Indeed, the poet seems to be saying the reverse—the approval of the ladies is merely a worthwhile concomitant of princely conduct.

More or less clear cases—or at least variants—of ennobling love are found in three poems under the heading "Unechtes in Lachmanns Text." In 61,20, which is usually associated with 60,34 and 61,8 discussed above in the first category, the speaker has just returned after an absence. Having asserted that he has learned what women want, he claims he will now be able to win many a one for himself. He says he will foreswear "lîp und êre" (61,24) and all his *heil*, and then no woman will be able to resist him. But this he abruptly retracts, stating that God should punish those who swear such oaths as he has just uttered. Although it is not clear precisely what the speaker is referring to in this poem, it is possible to interpret his words as an expression of his bitterness about his apparent lack of success in winning women's favor by behaving in a restrained manner. If this were the case, the poem could be said to illustrate a variation of the theme under investigation—that is, the man tries to act with *fuoge* and feels he should be rewarded for this attempt to improve himself, but he is disappointed to find that belief in such a system is no longer widespread.

The last two poems in this category are the two brief *Sprüche*, 81,31 and 82,3, which both deal with the phenomenon of true love. Although they do not, in their sometimes cryptic formulations and vague generalizations, come to grips with the queston of the ennobling power of love as defined in this study, they do have elements touching upon the problem. In the last line of 81,31 the poet says of love: "si kam in valschez herze nie" (82,2), which certainly would imply that being, or striving to be, free of falsity is a necessary condition of attaining true love. However, the concept of love is in no way treated in the context of love service and self-improvement as a means of becoming worthy of the lady's love. Here, the poet confines his observations on love to statements such as: Love is neither man nor woman; it has neither a soul nor a body; its name is known, but its essence is not; and without it no one can attain God's grace. In 82,3 the poet also sees a connection between true love and salvation. He gives his assurance that anyone who distinguishes false love from the genuine variety and who follows in the latter's train will not be afflicted by *unfuoge*, and he says that love is such a fitting thing in heaven that he asks it to escort him there. What has to do here with the theme under investigation is the idea that a practitioner of true love is safe from *unfuoge*. Even though it is not exactly clear what the poet means by this statement,[38] he does seem to indicate an awareness of an aspect of love's ennobling power that has been encountered relatively infrequently,[39] namely, the view that love is the source of many good qualities and that true lovers are influenced by love to behave in an exemplary way. Perhaps this consideration can also be related to the notion expressed in both these poems that true love is definitely an aid to, if not a condition of, the acquisition of God's favor. Love has an ennobling effect in that it constrains a person to be good, and this in turn makes him worthy of salvation.

2. *"Die Strophen in Lachmanns Anmerkungen."*[40] Of the ten items to be examined in this grouping,[41] eight show no evidence of the idea of ennobling love and present no easy opportunities for its introduction. In 167,1 the poet expresses his longing for winter's departure and the arrival of spring. Although there is no specific reference to a love affair, it can probably be assumed that the joy the speaker so keenly anticipates and that has been promised to him has to do with something more than the pleasure of seeing the grass green again. But even if love's fulfillment will send his depressed spirits soaring, there is no indication here that the ennobling power of love has any role in the relationship alluded to.

The next song, 183,1, is a conversation between a knight and a lady. The man complains that he has no more of his lady than an occasional glimpse. He assures her, however, that he wishes her good fortune and hopes that God will protect her. In addition, he asks her to give him some sign of affection secretly with her eyes. If she does, he will not care if her words are unfriendly. The lady makes it clear in her stanza that she is fond of her suitor, for his departure brings tears to her eyes; if he were not to return, she would be very unhappy. But she is not willing to grant his every desire. If she had done so, she declares, she would never again be "rehte vrô" (183,17). Even if she does not wish to be intimate with him, however, she says she should not regret the time they have spent together talking, and she wants him to know that she wishes him well. In the final strophe the man says that, although he has received nothing from her but her greeting, she has refused him in such a pleasant manner that he will continue to serve her. Moreover, even if he has gotten nothing from her, he derives some satisfaction from the fact that no one else has, either. This song shows not the slightest trace of the idea of the ennobling power of love. The man gives no indication that self-betterment in her service has earned him her love. Similarly, the lady does not reveal that her affection for him is based on his having shown himself deserving in this way, or that her refusal to fulfill his desires is related to any failure on his part to have made himself worthy of her love.

The remaining six entities in this category are additions—all but one monostrophic—to various songs by Walther found in one or more manuscripts. They will be discussed here briefly in the context of the earlier examination of the songs in question. The stanza 176,1 appears in one manuscript as part of 50,19, where Walther tells his beloved to look down at his feet as a sign of her recognition if she does not want to risk revealing her feelings in public by meeting his eyes in greeting. Although an apparent corruption of the text makes it difficult to know precisely what the poet is saying in the first part of the stanza,[42] the gist of it is evidently that others have taken note of the poet's words and that his lady should do so, too, and follow his suggestion of looking in a certain direction. She should not worry about the watchers, he says, for he will see to them. As was the case with 50,19, this related stanza gives no indication of an awareness of the ennobling power of love.

In 181,1, which is contained in one version of the song 57,23, the poet continues Walther's complaints about *Frau Minne's* seeming preference for simpletons.[43] If someone who should really be his fool wins out over him when they are both competing for the same thing, he says, then he is no longer interested in acquiring it. This stanza, like the poem with which it is connected, has nothing to do with the educative function of love.

The two stanzas of 182,1, which are associated with 59,37, expand Walther's railing at *Frau Welt* for not rewarding him adequately for his service.[44] In addition, the poet threatens to deprive her of the joy she gets from his singing if she refuses to make him happy. What applied in the earlier discussion of 59,37 is also valid with regard to these additional strophes. Because nothing specific is said about love and its role in worldly life, they need not be of further concern here.

In 187,1, the monostrophic addition to Walther's 65,33, the author extends the idea of the man's doubts about his ever winning his lady's favor. After praising both her beauty and her *sinne*, he asks despairingly how he could expect to win a woman who is so *saelic* when he himself appears to be marked by misfortune. The only way for him to succeed, he seems to be saying, is by throwing himself on her mercy, as is evident from his concluding words: "ich wil mich rehte an ir genâde lâzen: jâ, / daz ist mîn enderât und ouch mîn endelist" (187,7–8). This basis for hope only tends to reinforce the judgment expressed earlier in connection with 65,33 that there is no evidence of the ennobling power of love.[45] It is quite clear here that the poet's hope is not founded on the belief that he has become worthy of her love by means of self-improvement. Indeed, he seems to have no reason to expect anything from her other than what she will give him based on her sense of pity.

The next of the additional stanzas in this category is 190,1, which is found in several manuscripts between the third and fourth stanzas of 69,1. It amplifies Walther's statement to his lady that no one can praise her better than he. The poet maintains he always wants to sing in such a way that people will say he never sang better. Although his lady does not thank him for it, he points out to her that, because of his songs, others wish her well, just as he does. It is clear that this strophe, like the poem into which it is inserted, has no connection with the ennobling power of love.[46]

In 168,1, the last of the additions to be discussed, the poet complains to *Frowe Minne* about the treatment she has accorded him, just as Walther does in 40,19. He says she should reward him better than others and expresses dismay that she exalts those who cause her dishonor, thereby bringing ruin to those who truly deserve her consideration. Although nothing here specifically reveals a concern with the idea of ennobling love, the poet's complaint, unlike Walther's in 40,19,[47] touches—at least by implication—on the distinction between true and false love and hence brings the theme closer to a sphere where one might expect the educative function of love to be involved.

Aside from the additional strophe just discussed, which barely gives a hint of a missed occasion to introduce the idea of ennobling love, only one song under the heading "Die Strophen in Lachmanns Anmerkungen" belongs in the category of unseized opportunities. In the first stanza of 166,21 the poet waxes eloquent about the wonders of a truly womanly woman who knows how to maintain "wîbes tugent" (166,25) and "wîbes zuht" (166,25). Then he says he is acquainted with such a woman who is indeed an epitome of womanly perfection. She is so good that, if he were to choose one woman in all the world, it would be she. In the second stanza he informs his audience how a lady should conduct herself if she wishes to be praised. She should avoid arrogance, love "zuht und hôhen muot" (166,39), and be "staete an allen dingen" (166,40). In addition, she should be reasonably joyful, kind, and humble, and she should have a pure and merciful heart. In short, he concludes, she should be "nâch wunsche ein wîp" (166,44). Despite the poet's clear interest in the concept of ideal womanly behavior, he does not in any way relate this notion to the educative function of love. Nowhere does he imply that the woman's model behavior should have an influence on the man who is wooing her, even though he openly states that such a woman's goodness attracts him. The second stanza, in particular, where he enumerates the excellent qualities of the ideal noblewoman, would have offered an appropriate occasion to introduce the view that it was the lady's duty to exert an uplifting influence on the man. But apparently this consideration was of no concern to the author.

The one remaining song in this grouping, 177,1, consists of two stanzas that appear in two manuscripts as a substitute for the final strophes of 52,23, but that can be treated independently of the earlier consideration of the latter song.[48] These stanzas contain the only possible example of the idea of ennobling love in the "Strophen in Lachmanns Anmerkungen." The poet complains that his lady keeps putting him off and does not pay attention to his "vil schoene leben" (177,2). Tired of her procrastination, he is inclined to give her an ultimatum. If she shows him *genâde*, he will continue to serve her. But if he turns away from her, he will "dance" elsewhere. In the second stanza he says many men complain that their ladies always say "no." His complaint, however, is that his beloved always says "yes." She always makes him promises, but her failure to fulfill them leads him to believe she is only making fun of him. Thus her "yes" merely causes him pain. Whether or not the idea of ennobling love plays a role in these strophes depends on the interpretation of the poet's rather ambiguous statement that his beloved "versûmet mîn vil schoene leben" (177,2). It is perfectly possible that this indicates she does not adequately consider the fact that he has been leading an exemplary life for her sake. In other words, he expects to be rewarded for having endeavored to conduct himself *schoene* and is disappointed that she has not yet done so. If this were indeed the case, then the notion of the educative effect of love would clearly be in evidence here.

3. *"Die Lieder in Lachmanns Vorrede."*[49] Four of the six songs under this heading are completely untouched by the idea of ennobling love and present no easy opportunities for its introduction. In XIII,11–XIV,24 the speaker pleads with a girl, who is evidently from the lower classes, to make him happy—and through him others, as well—and offers her expensive garments as an inducement. She will be clad so beautifully, he says, that she will grant his desires, and those who envy them will lose heart. Here it is obvious that the reason the girl should fulfill his wishes—his gift of clothing—is as far removed as one could imagine from the view that the man can make himself worthy of the woman's love by means of self-improvement.

The other three songs in this category all have a nature introduction in which the poet laments the onset of winter. The author of XVI,1–42 complains about the ravages of winter, but claims he would not mind them so much if only his beloved would fulfill his desires. After lavishly praising her beauty and her wisdom, he says that the sight of her is enough to make a man lose his senses. Her red mouth and her white chin are the reasons he puts up with so much distress in the hope of winning her favor. In the last stanza he addresses her directly, telling her that being away from her causes him great pain. Her sweet body is so smooth and white, he concludes, that his heart gets very agitated and he does not know how to protect it against such excitement. In XVII,1–30 the poet says that, even though winter ruins so much that gives pleasure in summer, it does have one good thing that he desires—long nights, which can bring joy to lovers who lie in each other's arms. But such delights are, for him, a thing of the past, he complains, giving as the reason his preoccupation with service to others. He concludes by saying it would not be very nice if they did not reward him. In these two songs the strong underscoring of the sensual aspects of love—the physical desire aroused by the lady's beauty, on the one hand, and the remembrance of warm winter nights, on the other—leaves no room for thoughs of the educative function of love.

In XV,1–32, the other song with a nature introduction, the speaker says that winters would be his greatest burden if only his beloved did not delay his reward too long. He complains that he is so far away from her, and he is worried that others have access to her in his absence. If she puts them off as well as she did him, he says, he will be pleased, for then he will be able to get back to her before any damage is done. At the end he confesses that nothing of what he has said is really true—for when asked who his lady is, he answers that he would like to know the answer to that question, too. It is hardly surprising that this song, with its facetious conclusion, has no connection with the idea of ennobling love.

Only one of the songs under the heading "Die Lieder in Lachmanns Vorrede" offers an unseized opportunity to introduce the notion of ennobling love. In XIII,1–10 the poet imagines that he is lying with his beloved. She is so good, he says, that he cannot forget her. Unfortunately, however, she is so well protected that he has no access to her, and he asks his audience to help him lament his plight. Here the poet might have indicated that his lady's virtues were a source of inspiration for him. But he says only that her goodness makes her unforgettable.

The last of the six songs in this grouping, XVII,31–XVIII,21, contains a situation that might tempt one to think in terms of an aspect of the educative function of love. The poet complains that his service remains unrewarded and wonders whether he should perhaps try his luck in another place where his prospects might be better. Even if he were with his beloved for a thousand years, he says, he still could not tell her more than that he speaks the truth and loves "ir lîp und ir êre" (XVIII,4). He is also glad that she has little use for people who are full of idle chatter and is not fooled by smiling flatterers. If only she would reward him, he claims, he would not go to ruin. Finally, in a humorous conclusion, he asks his audience to look at his gray coat and complains that he is getting gray hair and a gray beard like a goat. In this song the poet comes close to saying that his behavior in his lady's presence is better than that of others who are competing for her favor and hence merits recognition, but he does not clearly indicate that he believes his attempt to conduct himself properly might make him worthy of the lady's favor.

4. "*Neue Lieder und Sprüche.*"[50] Only one of the poems under this heading, the fragmentary XXVI,1–12, is a love song and need be discussed here. It is a *Wechsel*-type song, of which only the woman's

first stanza is complete. She speaks of a rendezvous with a knight in a lonely place, and she says she is at this gentleman's disposal. The knight, for his part, seems just as ready to do her bidding, inasmuch as he refers to her as the good woman whom he shall always serve "sunder valschez lôsen" (XXVI,9) and whose cheeks are like lilies and roses. But because this is all one learns of their relationship, it is difficult to make any judgment about the role played by the ennobling power of love. All one can say is that nothing in the surviving part of the poem specifically reveals an awareness of the problem. Of course, the knight's statement that he will serve his beloved "sunder valschez lôsen" could be pointing toward the notion that the knight can become worthy of the lady's love by striving to conduct himself in an exemplary fashion. Without any further information, however, this one clue is insufficient to warrant the conclusion that the educative function of love is in evidence here.

23. Summary and Conclusion

Now that the entire body of lyric poetry from the beginning through the works of Walther von der Vogelweide has been examined for evidence of the idea of the ennobling power of love, it is possible to offer an assessment of the relative importance of this theme. Before such an evaluation is attempted, however, it is well to review briefly the results of this study with regard to the works of the individual poets.

At the beginning of the lyric tradition, when the idea of *Frauendienst* had not yet taken hold, the thirteen poems of Der von Kürenberg—with the possible exception of the *Falkenlied*—are untouched by the notion of the ennobling power of love. Even though they are replete with loving men and women, these poems never even hint that the lady's love was gained by the man's having become worthy through self-improvement. As for the *Falkenlied*, it was observed that, although the image of a woman taming a falcon could be interpreted as an educative influence in a love relationship, the ambiguities of the situation make it impossible to consider the song a clear-cut example of ennobling love.

Of the twenty-five poems under the name of Dietmar von Aist, which range from songs quite similar in tone and theme to those of the Kürenberger to poems in which the ideas of love service and unrequited love predominate, only two clear examples of the educative effect of love were found. In one it is evident that the knight has improved in the lady's service and has already been rewarded with her love, whereas in the other he certainly has hopes of winning her love to the extent that he has become better for her sake. Two other songs of Dietmar contain situations that tempt one to think in terms of ennobling love, but they were shown to be too vague to be considered genuine examples. And of the twenty-one songs revealing no trace of the motif under investigation, eight present easy opportunities for its introduction connected with the idea of service and the theme of praise of the lady's good qualities. It is never suggested, however, that the knight is supposed to become worthy in the course of his service or that the lady's virtues are to be a source of inspiration for the man to emulate.

In the eight anonymous poems included in *MF*, which cover a range of sentiments similar to those in the songs of Dietmar von

Aist, there is no evidence of the edifying power of love, although four of the songs do contain situations where one might be inclined to think in such terms. In two the knight's readiness to do his lady's bidding is emphasized, but there is never any indication that what the lady demands has anything to do with the man's self-improvement. In another the context is too indefinite to allow a connection between the man's willingness to renounce worldly goods in order to attain love and the concept of ennobling love. And in the fourth song the recommendation that *triuwe* be practiced in love relationships cannot be related to the theory of the educative function of love.

The three songs attributed to the Burggraf von Regensburg, which depict women in love, do not indicate that the lady has granted her love because the knight has become worthy by means of self-improvement. A situation in one of the poems comes close to being an example of the ennobling power of love, however, in that it implies a cause-and-effect relationship between the knight's sterling character and the lady's affection for him, although it does not suggest that the man has been ennobled by love. Of the five love songs of the Burggraf von Rietenburg, only one shows evidence of the edifying function of love when the poet uses the simile of the knight in the lady's service being like gold purified in the fire. Another purported example has to be disqualified because it is based on an unjustifiable textual emendation. The other three songs miss the opportunity to connect the idea of service with the notion of the knight's becoming worthy through self-improvement.

Of the dozen songs of Meinloh von Sevelingen, eight show no trace of the idea of ennobling love, although three of these offer unseized opportunities for its introduction in connection with praise of the lady's good qualities and the man's readiness to fulfill the lady's every desire. Two of the other four songs present situations that come close to the idea under investigation—one by stating that the quality of the knight's reward would correspond to that of the service rendered, the other by pointing to a causal connection between the man's virtues and the lady's love, without indicating, however, that he has improved in her service. The remaining two poems contain passages that could be (or have been) regarded as examples of the educative effect of love, but these were shown to allow for other, more plausible interpretations. The three songs ascribed to Kaiser Heinrich all deal with love's positive effects on the man—the feeling of well-being that accompanies love's fulfillment, the giving of meaning and purpose to his life, the adornment of his thoughts.

But none of them provides clear evidence that the effects in question are ennobling, even though one of the poems has been cited by some scholars as an example of the lady's refining influence on the man.

Fourteen of the seventeen poems of Friedrich von Hausen, in which the full range of motifs associated with the theme of unrequited love makes an appearance, reveal no trace of the idea of ennobling love. While five of these concentrate on a particular aspect of the man's troubles and leave no room for thoughts of the problem under investigation, two crusade songs dealing with a conflict between the knight's duty to his lady and his obligation to God show love having results that are the opposite of ennobling in that love conspires to keep the knight from serving God as a crusader. Seven of these poems offer many passages that seem ideally suited to the introduction of aspects of ennobling love. Yet the poet consistently fails to take advantage of such opportunities. Thus it is not indicated that the man's willingness to bear pain and suffering will make him a better person, nor is it revealed that the lady as a model of perfection has inspired the man to become like her and hence worthy of love. As a result, love is portrayed as having thoroughly debilitating effects rather than edifying ones. Examples of ennobling love appear in three songs, however, two of which reveal a connection between the man's having become steadfast and his lady's goodness. The third poem in this category is a crusade song offering a variation of the idea of the educative effect of love when the speaker states that a truly good and noble lady would not love a man who refused to fulfill his duty to God as a crusader. In addition, the one poem listed as *unecht* under Friedrich von Hausen's name presents a situation that comes close to the notion of ennobling love, inasmuch as it depicts a lady who is about to reward a knight because of his good qualities. There is, however, no indication that he has become a better person as a result of his love for her.

In four of his seven laments Rudolf von Fenis devotes considerable attention to the concept of service, but the idea that the knight can improve in the lady's service and thereby become worthy of her love is conspicuously absent. On the contrary, the basic premise of the feudal relationship is opposed to the notion of self-improvement. The knight being of lower station and humbly given over into her hand, the lady would reward him—if at all—because it is incumbent upon her to exercise *genâde*. Rudolf von Fenis also touches upon the theme of the lady's good qualities. Instead of being a source of inspiration, however, her goodness has a destructive effect in that it devastates the knight like the flame that attracts a moth and then consumes it. Only one song comes close to an awareness of ennobling love by stating the belief that behaving in a certain exemplary way should lead to the reward of love, even though it does not imply that such conduct would represent an improvement in the knight's deportment. In the one poem listed as *unecht* under the name of Rudolf von Fenis, it is indicated that anything worth having is worth striving and suffering for; however, this is not connected clearly with the notion that betterment will result from the struggle.

All of the six songs of unrequited love by Bernger von Horheim contain passages that would have easily lent themselves to the introduction of the idea of the ennobling power of love. Yet none of his themes—his awareness of his lady's goodness, his inability to learn how he could please her, his duty to fulfill his military obligations, his fantasies about his lady's having rewarded him, his emphasis on his service, and his knowledge of the importance of women in courtly society—lead to the "right" conclusion, namely, that he will win love's reward through self-improvement.

Of the seven songs of Heinrich von Rugge dealing with love, none reveals a trace of the idea of the ennobling force of love, even though three of them offer some occasion for possible comment on the theme in connection with praise of the lady's goodness and emphasis on the importance of a woman's inner qualities. One song even underscores the opposite of an edifying effect of love, in that love has paralyzed the knight's ability to control himself. Only in his *leich*, which is basically a crusade appeal, does the idea of the educative effect of love appear in the words of a lady who states that a knight has to fulfill his obligations to God as a crusader in order to be worthy of love.

In six of the fourteen poems listed as unauthentic under Heinrich von Rugge's name the notion of the ennobling power of love plays no role. Three of these, however, do present easy opportunities for its introduction in connection with the lady's goodness, which was seen neither as an inspiration for the knight to emulate her, nor as a force that would encourage him to perform his feudal duties, but rather merely as the basis of his hope that the lady will take pity on him as a suffering vassal. In another poem the man's readiness to do whatever his lady desires tempts one to think in terms of ennobling love, but there is never any indication that the fulfillment of her wishes has anything to do with his self-improvement. Three other songs present a situation that comes close to the idea of ennobling love, namely, the man's recognition of the need to conform to a high standard of behavior if he wants to win the lady's favor. Finally, four poems contain clear examples of the notion of ennobling love. Whereas two of these songs show evidence of the man's having improved in the course of his service, the other two depict the lady as being conscious of her responsibility to pressure the knight to display exemplary conduct and of her obligation to reward him.

Of the four songs by Hartwic von Rute, two reveal no trace of the uplifting power of love. Another contains a passage that inclined one to think at first in terms of ennobling love by referring to the knight's ability to restrain himself; however, this was shown ultimately to be an unlikely indication of an educative effect of his love service. In the fourth poem a knight is clearly attempting to exhibit exemplary behavior. This song at least implies that such deportment represents an improvement on his part, although it does not take advantage of an opportunity to introduce a variation of the idea under investigation, that is, the notion that a man can become worthy of love by fulfilling his obligations as a knight. One of Bligger von Steinach's two love poems fails to make use of an occasion to present the idea of ennobling love in relation to the theme of faithfulness; instead, the lady is making the knight suffer to discourage him from his suit rather than to have him improve in her service. The other gives evidence of at least one aspect of the educative effect of love when the suitor claims he has renounced all other women and therefore expects to be rewarded for this improvement in his conduct.

In the one love song of Ulrich von Gutenberg the lady's taming of the knight was found to be too ambiguous to be considered an example of the woman's educative influence on the man; however, it becomes clear the poet is conscious of the theory that a man who strives to behave in an exemplary manner deserves his lady's love. This same idea is also found occasionally in Ulrich's extensive *leich*, where the notion that the lady serves as a model for the man's self-improvement is at least hinted at in one passage. But the poet does not use all the numerous other opportunities to make a connection between the lady's goodness and the educative function of love, and for the most part the *leich* conveys the feeling that the effects of love are overwhelmingly negative and debilitating.

In one of the two poems of Engelhart von Adelnburg almost everything points away from the idea of the ennobling force of love, although it is possible to interpret the man's faithfulness as having been inspired by the lady's goodness. His second song, which defends love service against the charge of sinfulness, comes close to the notion of the edifying power of love in that it states that only a worthy man can woo a woman properly. What is missing is the idea that the man becomes a better person in the process.

Of the twenty songs of Heinrich von Veldeke showing no trace of the motif of ennobling love, three emphasize love's destructive results by focusing on death as the ultimate end of the knight's unrequited passion. Five dealing with the theme of requited love never offer any evidence that the lady's love was won by the man's having become worthy through self-improvement. Another four in this group present unseized opportunities to introduce the idea under investigation in connection with the theme of the decline of true love or the notion of the extreme length of the knight's courtship. Five poems either contain passages that tempt one to think in terms of ennobling love or depict situations approaching it. In two of these the reward of love is related to lengthy and even painful service; however, because it is never explained why the knight has to serve and suffer so long, it is not possible to view these situations as examples of ennobling love. In another song the image of the knight being afraid of his lady just as a child fears the switch might incline one to think of the educative function of love, but nothing else in the poem justifies the assumption that the lady has played an active role in encouraging the knight to improve his behavior. The two songs making up the extended *Wechsel* create the proper environment for introducing the idea of ennobling love. But although the situation depicted initially comes close to the notion of the educative force of love, this concept is actually reversed when a deterioration in the knight's conduct incurs the lady's wrath. Furthermore, there is no indication that what little favor the knight previously enjoyed was gained by means of self-improvement. Only in the two songs in praise of love is the idea of the edifying power of love clearly discernible. Whereas one of them implies that all good things come from love and that the lover becomes a better person from having loved, the second one seems to indicate that the man's ennoblement is directly related to his looking to the lady as a model for his own behavior. Finally, of the five songs dealing with love and listed as unauthentic under Heinrich von Veldeke's name, three songs of requited love never intimate what has induced the lady to grant her affection. Another poem misses the opportunity to introduce the idea of ennobling love when it speaks of the advantages men can derive from women. Only one unauthentic song reveals an awareness of the ennobling power of love by stressing conscious self-improvement to make oneself worthy of love.

Two of the fourteen songs of Albrecht von Johansdorf dealing with love contain clear evidence of the motif under investigation. One states that a love free of falseness not only has an ennobling effect, but also keeps a person free of sin; the other presents the first instance of the idea that the knight's improvement in the lady's service is considered to be a goal in itself. Of the twelve songs untouched by the concept of the elevating power of love, four reveal ideas that are directly opposed to the notion of ennobling love in that the woman is anything but a source of inspiration for the man's exemplary behavior. In another four poems in this group the poet fails to take advantage of easy opportunities to introduce the idea of ennobling love— once in connection with praise of the lady's good qualities, once in reference to the lady's views on true love, and twice in a crusade context with regard to the conflict between the knight's responsibilities to God and his lady. In addition, neither of the two poems listed as *unecht* under Albrecht von Johansdorf's name, which both touch upon the theme of the lady's goodness, indicates in any way that the woman's virtues spurred the man on to improve himself to become worthy of her love.

Five of the fourteen songs of Hartmann von Aue treating the theme of love have nothing to do with the idea of ennobling love, and only one of these presents an easy opportunity for its introduction when it emphasizes that steadfastness is the cause of the lover's distress. Another four songs contain situations that either tempt one to think in terms of ennobling love or come very close to the concept. One of these approaches the idea of women as models of exemplary behavior to be emulated by men (without linking this notion, however, with that of love service); another shows a causal connection between a lady's readiness to reward her lover and his sterling character, but gives no indication that he has changed in any way to merit her love; a third makes one think at first of the educative effect of love as it pertains to the crusades, although on balance it appears that the woman's sending the man to fight the heathens has more to do with her reaping a religious benefit for herself than with inspiring him to become worthy of her love by participating in a crusade; and the fourth, though not a love song, transfers the idea of love constraining a knight to improve his behavior from the worldly realm to the sphere of divine love. Finally, the motif of the ennobling power of love plays a definite role in five of Hartmann's songs. These poems present the clearest statement yet of the view that the man should consciously try to improve himself for his lady's sake and that his hopes of being compensated are directly connected with this endeavor. Closely linked with this idea is the knight's assertion that, if his lady has not rewarded him, it is his own fault for not having lived up to the standard she expected of him. Of the three poems listed as unauthentic under Hartmann's name, two having in common the motif of the loving woman do not contain the slightest trace of the theme under investigation. The third song, the so-called widow's lament, hints at the topic of ennobling love when the lady praises the departed man's good qualities, but there is no evidence that his virtues were instrumental in winning her love. It was also noted that it is plausible to interpret the poem as the lament of a lady whose lover has gone on a crusade, in which case one could speak of an unseized opportunity to introduce the idea of ennobling love as it has been seen in relation to the crusades.

Only one of the thirty-three songs of Heinrich von Morungen presents a clear example of an aspect of the notion of ennobling love when the knight states that he has renounced inconstancy for his lady's sake. Another poem tempts one to think in terms of ennobling love by emphasizing the knight's faithfulness and his belief that he deserves to be rewarded, but nothing in the song points clearly to the man's having improved in the lady's service. The remaining poems show no trace of the edifying effect of love, although there are seventeen instances of unseized opportunities. Most of these are connected with the motif of praise of the lady's virtues, which are never regarded as a source of inspiration for the man's self-improvement, but mainly as a reason to hope that the lady will some day show him mercy. In four cases the woman's goodness has even had disastrous consequences for the man. Indeed, in approximately half the songs love has had anything but an uplifting result, having robbed the knight of his senses and made him sick or wounded him to the point of death. And in a few poems the lady herself is the opposite of a model of good behavior; rather, she is a hardhearted and cruel woman, desirous of the man's destruction.

In eighteen of the twenty-four songs of Reinmar von Hagenau untouched by the notion of ennobling love the poet does not take advantage of easy opportunities to introduce this idea. In three of these, which depict a lady who is interested only in a platonic relationship, there is never any mention of the concept of self-improvement as a goal in itself. Five songs contain the idea that, despite the woman's reluctance to bestow her love, the man does receive some good from his service; but it is never even hinted that this benefit consists in the man's becoming a better person. Another four poems emphasize the man's willingness to do whatever the lady desires, without, however, indicating that what she demands has anything to do with the man's improvement. Unseized opportunities were also noted in connection with the man's readiness to endure pain and his ability to control himself in public, as well as with the notion that the goal the man has set for himself is too lofty. In addition, although the motif of the lady's goodness appears a half-dozen times, nowhere is it intimated that her good qualities are supposed to have an exemplary effect on the knight. Instead, they are represented as a reason for the man to hope that she will be touched by his suffering and reward him. Two of Reinmar's songs tempt one to think in terms of ennobling love, one by mentioning the man's concern with his behavior and the woman's desire for him to do her will, the other by stating that the woman could make the man esteemed if she wanted to. But it was shown that none of these features have anything to do with the man's becoming worthy of love by means of self-improvement. In five of the six poems containing situations that come close to the concept of the educative function of love, the virtues of constancy and patient waiting play a role; in the remaining song the man's ability to endure distress stoically is underscored. Although the man's awareness of the need to conform to a high standard of behavior does approach the idea under investigation in all six poems, there is never any indication that an improvement in the man's character is involved. More or less clear examples of ennobling love were discovered in only three of Reinmar's songs. Whereas one poem contains a veiled reference to the elevating effect of a man's association with women, another implies that the knight's conscious efforts to act in an exemplary fashion make him worthy of love. In the third song in question it is evident that the man's behavior has improved, inasmuch as he has turned from inconstancy to steadfastness as a result of his love.

Seven of the thirty-six poems listed as unauthentic under Reinmar's name contain more or less clear examples of ennobling love. One is a crusade song touching on the concept of the edifying force of love by ascribing to good women the attitude that knights who shirk their duty as crusaders are not worthy of their love. In another song the man's efforts to behave in the best possible way are not specifically related to the courting of a lady, but the echoes of love service are so strong that it seems likely that ennobling love is involved. Two of the poems deal with the theme of the elevating power of love only in connection with the man's having become steadfast in the lady's service, whereas another two offer evidence of the general principle that the man can become worthy of love by striving to improve himself. One of these even presents the view that the endeavor itself is of some value, even if the quest for love is unsuccessful. In the seventh song in this group the lady plays an active role in encouraging the knight to behave in an exemplary fashion, and the man in question has improved his conduct in the hope of receiving the reward of love. A group of five songs contain situations that either come close to, or tempt one to think in terms of, the idea of ennobling love. In two of these the lady indicates that her lover is worthy of her love because he is virtuous, and in another the man conducts himself impeccably toward the lady in public. Nowhere, however, is there any evidence that the man's deportment has improved. Another song makes it appear as if the lady's good qualities have inspired the man to do good, but it is more likely that he merely wants to be nice to her because she has been kind to him. And in the final song in the group the joy of love has an edifying effect on the singer by enabling him to make other people happy. But this uplifting force is the result of love's fulfillment and not the consequence of a conscious effort to become worthy of love. The remaining twenty-one poems contain no trace of the idea of ennobling love, although ten of them do present easy opportunities for its introduction. In three of these the benefits a man derives from love are emphasized, but the notion of self-improvement as one of them is conspicuously absent. On four occasions the woman's good qualities are praised, yet it is never implied that they are supposed to inspire the man to emulate the lady. In two songs the man is ready to do what the woman demands; what she wants, however, is in no way related to the man's self-improvement. In another two songs the feudal nature of the man's relationship to the lady is underscored, but the poet fails to connect this relationship with the notion that the knight can expect to be rewarded by becoming worthy in the course of his service. And in the final song in the group the man states clearly that he deserves a reward without indicating that such compensation has anything to do with his having become better and hence worthy of the lady's affection.

Three of the nine poems by Walther von der Vogelweide categorized as his earliest songs contain unseized opportunities to introduce the idea of ennobling love in connection with the speaker's emphasis on the lady's good qualities. An additional occasion is missed in one of these songs when a knight pleads with his lady to let him earn a greeting appropriate for lovers without explaining what he intends to do to deserve his reward. Another three of the earliest songs depict loving women whose love was won because of the knights' good qualities; however, because there is never any indication that the men *became* worthy of the ladies' affection, these situations come close to but cannot be considered genuine examples of the edifying power of love. Unambiguous evidence of ennobling love is provided in four of these earliest songs. In two *Botenlieder* the knights are fully conscious of the need to strive to behave in the best possible manner if they hope to win love's reward. Whereas the ladies in these two poems seem completely unaware of any role they are supposed to play in this process, another song offers one of the relatively rare examples of a woman who takes an active part in guiding a man to become worthy of at least one of the rewards of love. Finally, the idea that love is a treasure trove of good things and an inspiration for good behavior appears in two of these songs.

Two of the next set of seven of Walther's early songs present easy opportunities to introduce the concept of ennobling love when love is praised as the source of life's true joy. But in neither case is there any mention of the acquisition of worthiness in the course of the man's service to a lady as a possible benefit to be derived from love. The remaining five poems in this set contain generalizations about true love that reveal an awareness of one or more aspects of the concept of the uplifting power of love. Two of these offer very clear statements not only of the proposition that a man should strive to improve himself to become worthy of love, but also of the notion that the man's ennoblement is of value even if he is not rewarded with a particular lady's affection. Nonetheless, the knight's ennoblement is still regarded as something that will make him appealing to other women, one of whom is certain to reward him with her love. In addition, one of these two songs presents a rare variation of the theme of love's edifying effect—instead of the man being inspired to excellence by the hope of winning love, it is the possession of love that moves a man to behave impeccably. In another two of this group prominence is given to the woman's role in the process of ennoblement. One emphasizes the point that a woman of noble qualities should serve as a guiding light for the man who endeavors to lead an exemplary life; the other reveals the lady as an active participant in the procedure by having her discriminate between proper and improper behavior and hence having her exert an educative effect on her suitor, who will consciously strive to meet her demanding standards. In the last of the five poems the theme of the elevating power of love is restricted to the man's cultivation of the specific virtue of constancy in his effort to become worthy.

In ten of Walther's next twelve songs (written between 1198 and

1203) the idea of the ennobling power of love seems conspicuously absent. Although six of them offer opportunities to introduce it in the context of high praise of the lady, the other four concentrate on the speaker's dissatisfaction with his lady's shabby treatment of him. Instead of love having an uplifting result in these songs, only its destructive and debilitating consequences are emphasized when the man speaks of the devastating impact of the lady's glances and the wound love has inflicted on his heart, on the one hand, and of his inability to function properly because of love's effect on his senses, on the other. Of the two remaining songs in this group, one, though emphasizing love's destructive results, approaches the idea of ennobling love when it implies that the man's loyalty merits a reward; the other, a plea for mutual love, contains a possible reference to love's edifying power. The ambiguity of the language in the passage in question, however, does not permit it to be identified as a clear example of the phenomenon under investigation.

Two of the next set of six songs by Walther (written at the height of his powers) concentrate on the visual impression made by women and thus offer no occasion to think in terms of ennobling love. Another, the *Preislied*, which does not deal seriously with the relationship between the sexes, also reveals no concern with the theme of this study. In the other poems, however, the motif of the edifying power of love does play a prominent role. One of the two songs consisting of conversations between a man and a woman presents not only the notion of the lady as a source of inspiration for the man to improve himself, but also the idea of the lady taking an active part in the process by rendering advice. What the nature of the man's reward is to be, however, is not clear, because the ambiguous conclusion of the song allows for different interpretations. In the other conversation the man openly offers to improve himself, but only if he is certain he will be rewarded with the lady's love. Indeed, the man's proposition comes very close to being a reversal of the standard conception of the uplifting force of love in that the promise of the man's improved behavior could be considered an inducement for the woman to compensate him, instead of the lady's favor being the reward for exemplary conduct. The remaining song in this set clearly associates the ennobling power of love with *hôhe minne* when the poet claims that the latter incites the man to strive for goals that will increase his worth.

Only one of the next set of four songs (closely associated with the *Preislied*) reveals any consciousness of the educative power of love by presenting a clear example of the reversal of the usual idea—the man is not willing to improve his behavior until after he has been granted the lady's favor. The other three have in common the speaker's extreme dissatisfaction with the lady's behavior toward him; however, his displeasure never has anything to do with the idea of the ennobling power of love, even though there are a number of places where it might have made an appearance in connection with the lady's goodness and the knight's emphasis on the feudal concept of service and reward. In addition, one song contains a passage that tempts one to think in terms of ennobling love when the knight talks of his good intentions, but it is doubtful that his words indicate a conscious effort on his part to do good.

The next group of Walther's poems is divided into two subsets, the first of which contains two songs. In one the poet laments the decline of courtly values and blames women generally for the way men are behaving; in the other he bitterly criticizes his own lady's failure to treat him as he deserves. Both songs reveal evidence of the topic under discussion: the former, explicitly, by complaining about the breakdown of the concept of the uplifting force of love, inasmuch as women are no longer taking the proper initiative to insist on exemplary behavior from men; the latter, implicitly, by portraying his lady as the type of woman he is complaining about. The three songs of the second subgroup all deal at least in part with the pitiful state of society. In one, where women's reluctance to allow distinctions among themselves is seen as damaging to the social fabric, the issue of the ennobling power of love is neglected. In the other two, however, it does play a role. One, containing Walther's renunciation of love service to noble ladies, again points to women's failure to differentiate between good and bad behavior in men as the primary cause of the decay of courtly society. By not caring about their suitors' conduct, the ladies have rendered the educative function of love inoperative. The other song expresses the speaker's bitterness about his lack of success despite his clinging to the belief that the man should strive to conform to a high standard of behavior if he wishes to win the love of a good woman.

In the group of three songs labeled *Ebene Minne: I,* only one clearly touches on the theme of the ennobling power of love when the speaker speculates about what might attract his beloved and hopes it is the quality of his behavior rather than his appearance. The other two, which are evidently directed at women of lower social standing, do not reveal an awareness of the educative function of love. Even though they both emphasize the women's good qualities, neither poem indicates that these qualities are supposed to have an edifying effect on the man.

The two songs comprising the nucleus of the set of six called *Ebene Minne: II* offer in their depiction of scenes of love's physical fulfillment no trace of familiarity with the concept of the ennobling power of love. Two of the remaining four poems in the group, which share the theme of the poet's doubts about his ever obtaining the lady's favor, likewise are untouched by the idea under investigation, even though one of them clearly places the speaker's hopes within the framework of the notion of reward for service rendered. In the last two songs, however, the educative force of love is clearly evident when the man speaks of making a conscious effort to improve his conduct—referring specifically to developing the ability to compose or restrain himself in public—so that he will become worthy of love's reward.

In the next group of five songs, all dealing more or less with the speaker's relationship with his enemies, only one touches on the theme under discussion when the man looks to the lady for guidance. But another example of Walther's turning the notion of ennobling love upside down is found in the same poem when the man proceeds to tell the lady how she should behave. Although two of the other four poems are untouched by the elevating force of love, the other two do make one think in such terms—one by referring back to an earlier poem where the motif in question was clearly in evidence, the other by presenting an analogue in which good people have an edifying influence on those who are not. The next group of three songs, which presumably were composed when Walther was in his forties, attempts to come to terms with Lady World and Lady Love. But only one of these songs furnishes evidence of the ennobling power of love when the poet expresses his bitterness about the fact that he seems to be the only person left in the world who still believes that striving to maintain *fuoge* and *zuht* qualify him for the reward of love.

The songs Walther wrote in his old age contain two subgroups, the first of which treats the topic of love or love poetry. None of this group of three shows any familiarity with the standard notion of the edifying force of love, although one, a *Tagelied*, offers another example of the reversal of the usual concept in that the man's fidelity is considered a reward for the woman's having given herself to him. In the last six of Walther's songs, all dealing with renunciation of the world, the turning away from earthly love necessarily results in the neglect of the idea of ennobling love. The only exception appears in one of the poems that combines the notion of renunciation with a crusade appeal when the speaker touches on one aspect of the problem observed in several other crusade poems, namely, whoever stays home will lose the favor of both the angels and the ladies.

The first group of ten poems incorrectly ascribed to Walther von der Vogelweide, "Unechtes in Lachmanns Text," contains three more or less clear examples or variants of ennobling love. In one song the speaker expresses his bitterness about the apparent lack of faith in the efficacy of striving to maintain *fuoge* as a means of achieving love's reward. Two *Sprüche*, which deal in the most general terms with the theme of true love, touch on certain aspects of ennobling love by referring to love as a source of virtue and as something that constrains a person to be good and thus qualifies him for salvation. Another song, a *Fürstenspiegel*, comes close to the educative function of love when women's praise is mentioned as a consequence of a prince's striving to behave in an exemplary manner. The remaining six songs are devoid of the notion of ennobling love, although three of them do present occasions that would have easily lent themselves to its introduction. Yet the poets consistently fail to take advantage of such opportunities, even when describing women's beneficial effects on men or when praising women's good qualities.

Of the ten items in the next group, "Die Strophen in Lachmanns Anmerkungen," six consist of additions to various poems by Walther and, like the songs they are supplementing, have no connection with the idea of the edifying force of love, although one does hint at a missed occasion when it touches on the distinction between true and false love. The three complete songs in this grouping likewise show no evidence of the theme under investigation. One of these, however, is concerned primarily with the ideal of womanly perfection and hence could easily have pointed to the concept of the woman's virtues as a model for the man to emulate. The only possible example of ennobling love is found in the two stanzas appearing as a substitute for the final strophe of one of Walther's songs when the knight expects a reward for attempting to lead an exemplary life for the sake of his lady.

Five of the six songs in the group designated "Die Lieder in Lachmanns Vorrede" are untouched by the idea of ennobling love. One of them, however, does present an unseized opportunity to introduce the motif under discussion in connection with the knight's emphasis on his lady's goodness. The remaining poem contains a situation that approximates the notion of the educative function of love, but it is never made clear that the knight believes his striving to conduct himself properly might make him worthy of the lady's love. Finally, the one fragmentary song discussed under the heading "Neue Lieder und Sprüche" does not reveal enough about the relationship between the knight and his loving lady to determine whether the educative effect of love plays a role.

Although numerous examples of an awareness of the ennobling power of love can be found throughout the period in question, it is obvious that this motif was a primary concern for only a small number of minnesingers. Of the major figures, only Hartmann von Aue and Walther von der Vogelweide deal with the question extensively. Aside from the works of minor poets for whom only one or two songs have been preserved, such as Bligger von Steinach and Ulrich von Gutenberg, the only other place where the theme appears in a third or more of the poems examined is in the fourteen songs listed as *unecht* under the name of Heinrich von Rugge. For the rest, the notion of the ennobling power of love is encountered only sporadically, and in a majority of these instances only a very narrow aspect of the problem is involved, namely, that the knight's constancy represents an improvement in his behavior and thus makes him worthy of a reward.

In considering the different variations or aspects of the theme of the ennobling power of love separately, one is struck by how few examples there are of certain ideas that have been commonly promulgated as being prevalent or important. Most conspicuous by its relative absence is the view that self-improvement, instead of being the means toward achieving the goal of attaining the lady's love, is in itself a worthwhile end or its own reward. This idea, or variations of it, is expressed only six times in the more than three hundred poems examined, although its introduction would have been highly appropriate in numerous places, such as in Reinmar's three woman's songs where the lady, who clearly cares for her suitor, insists on keeping the relationship on a platonic level.

Another facet of the "traditional" notion of the elevating power of love that is noticeably missing in the lyric poems under investigation is the motif of the lady's virtues as a model for the knight to follow in an attempt to improve his behavior and hence become worthy of her love. Poet after poet, in poem after poem, sings his lady's praises and speaks specifically of her good qualities. Yet, despite the many passages that would have been appropriate for the introduction of this aspect of the idea of the edifying power of love, almost nowhere is the lady's goodness held up as a source of inspiration for the suitor.

Instead, time and again, the knight derives from the contemplation of his lady's virtues the hope that anyone as good as she could not possibly let him suffer indefinitely and fail to reward him for his service. In addition, in several instances the lady's goodness even has a debilitating effect on her suitor. Similarly, where the idea is expressed that the knight has chosen as his lady a woman who represents a particularly lofty goal, it is never intimated that great effort on his part to emulate her could raise him to her level and thus make him worthier of her love, even though such passages seem to beg for the introduction of such a notion. On the contrary, any such references to the loftiness of the object of the wooer's affection give rise only to despair at the hopelessness of ever reaching his goal.

Closely related to the concept of the lady's virtues as a source of inspiration is the motif of the woman playing an active role in encouraging the man to improve himself or at least to conform to a certain standard of behavior. This idea, too, was found relatively rarely in the poems examined, and primarily in the works of the two poets for whom the ennobling power of love is an important theme, Hartmann von Aue and Walther von der Vogelweide. For the most part, however, the ladies appearing or referred to in the songs studied seem to be completely unaware that it might be incumbent on them to exert pressure on their suitors to improve themselves as a means of achieving their aims. Similarly, in the woman's monologues or woman's stanzas in *Wechsel*-type poems in which loving women express their views and feelings, there is almost no evidence that the ladies' love was earned by means of the men's self-improvement.

In addition to the above-mentioned aspects of the idea of the ennobling power of love that are conspicuously absent or encountered only rarely, a number of prevalent themes in the body of poetry reviewed contribute to the impression that the importance of the concept of the edifying force of love has been overstated in the past. Most noticeable of these is the pervasiveness of the general mood of despair and hopelessness dominating the major category of songs, the laments of unrequited love. The overwhelming sadness expressed in these poems clearly seems to outweigh any feeling of optimism necessarily connected with the idea of the ennobling effect of love. Moreover, besides the general domination of the mood of gloom, the specific theme of the destructive or debilitating power of love was found in almost as many poems as the motif of love's elevating force. When poet after poet, in poem after poem, sings of the effects of love as being the direct opposite of edifying, the theme of the ennobling power of love cannot help pale in significance.

Finally, another widespread motif that tends to diminish the importance of the idea of the ennobling power of love is that of the most commonly encountered basis for the man's expectation that he will be—or should be—rewarded with the lady's love. Again and again, throughout the entire period under investigation, it was seen that the knight courting the lady was not counting on the fact that he had become worthy of her love through self-improvement, but rather either on the basic feudal principle that service deserves a reward or on the lady's kindness, which ultimately must compel her to take pity on his suffering. Indeed, this premise was found to be intrinsically hostile to the notion of the ennobling power of love, inasmuch as the assumption that the vassal is fundamentally inferior to the lord precludes the possibility that the knight can rise to the level of the lady and hence be deemed to have become worthy of her. In such a situation the lady would have to reward the knight because it was her duty to be gracious to an inferior who had rendered service, and not because he had improved himself.

Although the idea of the ennobling power of love clearly played a role in the minnesong up to and including Walther von der Vogelweide, it has been seen that a number of considerations have minimized the significance of this motif. First it became clear that only a very few poets deal with the theme extensively, and that it appears only sporadically throughout the remainder of the period. Then it was shown that a number of the aspects of the theme generally held to be important appear only very rarely in the poems examined, even though there are numerous places where the introduction of these ideas seems not only appropriate, but also called for. Finally, it was observed that several widespread motifs tend to counterbalance the idea of love's elevating force by emphasizing its opposite effects. It thus seems only reasonable to conclude that the importance of the idea of the ennobling power of love has been considerably exaggerated in most previous references to the subject.

Notes

1. Introduction

1. Helmut de Boor, *Die höfische Literatur: Vorbereitung, Blüte, Ausklang (1170–1250)*, vol. 2 of *Geschichte der deutschen Literatur von den Anfängen bis zur Gegenwart*, by Helmut de Boor and Richard Newald (Munich: Beck, 1953), p. 255: "Die tragende Grundlage ist das unerwiderte und ungelohnte Dienen, . . . dessen letzter Sinn, die veredelnde Vollendung des Mannes, aber eben an die Unerfülltheit geknüpft ist."

2. William T. H. Jackson, *The Literature of the Middle Ages* (New York: Columbia University Press, 1960), p. 219.

3. Friedrich Ranke, "Die höfisch-ritterliche Dichtung (1160 bis 1250)," in *Deutsche Literaturgeschichte in Grundzügen*, 3rd ed., ed. Bruno Boesch (Bern: Francke, 1967), p. 59.

4. Hans Eggers, "Deutsche Dichtung der Stauferzeit," in *Die Zeit der Staufen*, vol. 3, Catalog of an Exhibit at the Württemberg State Museum, 26 March–5 June 1977 (Stuttgart: n.p., 1977), p. 197.

5. Gustav Ehrismann, *Geschichte der deutschen Literatur bis zum Ausgang des Mittelalters*, part II, section II, second half (Munich: Beck, 1935), p. 188.

6. Hennig Brinkmann, ed., *Liebeslyrik der deutschen Frühe in zeitlicher Folge* (Düsseldorf: Schwann, 1952), p. 23.

7. Maurice O'Connel Walshe, *Medieval German Literature: A Survey* (Cambridge: Harvard University Press, 1962), p. 98.

8. See, for example, August Closs, "Minnesang and Its Spiritual Background," in *Medusa's Mirror: Studies in German Literature* (London: The Cresset Press, 1957), p. 45; Bert Nagel, *Staufische Klassik: Deutsche Dichtung um 1200* (Heidelberg: Stiehm, 1977), pp. 36, 47, 81; Friedrich Neumann, *Geschichte der altdeutschen Literatur (800–1600): Grundriß und Aufriß* (Berlin: de Gruyter, 1966), p. 167; Hermann Schneider, *Heldendichtung, Geistlichendichtung, Ritterdichtung*, rev. ed. (Heidelberg: Winter, 1943), p. 413; David P. Sudermann, ed., *The Minnelieder of Albrecht von Johansdorf: Edition, Commentary, Interpretation*, Göppinger Arbeiten zur Germanistik, 201 (Göppingen: Kümmerle, 1976), p. 48; Franz Taiana, *Amor purus und die Minne*, Germanistica Friburgensia, 1 (Freiburg: Universitätsverlag Freiburg Schweiz, 1977), pp. 32, 48, 74–75, 106; Herbert Walz, *Die deutsche Literatur im Mittelalter: Geschichte und Dokumentation* (Munich: Kindler, 1976), p. 58; Peter Wapnewski, *Deutsche Literatur des Mittelalters: Ein Abriß* (Göttingen: Vandenhoeck & Ruprecht, 1960), pp. 77–79.

9. The only scholarly voice I have been able to discover suggesting that the ennobling power of love has been overemphasized is that of Julius Schwietering, "Der Liederzyklus Heinrichs von Morungen," *Zeitschrift für*

deutsches Altertum, 82 (1948), 80, who stated that "die von der Forschung oft betonte, vielvach überbetonte erzieherische Tendenz tritt bei Morungen zurück."

10. Carl von Kraus, ed., *Des Minnesangs Frühling*, 34th ed. (Stuttgart: Hirzel, 1967). Unless otherwise indicated, all citations of poems (except for those of Walther von der Vogelweide) will be made from this edition (hereafter *MF*), instead of from the 36th revised edition by Hugo Moser and Helmut Tervooren (Stuttgart: Hirzel, 1977), because the latter has abandoned the system of labeling by which the poems traditionally have been identified and referred to in most of the scholarly writings dealt with in this study.

11. Because in many cases the authorship of the poems relegated to the status of *unecht* by Carl von Kraus and his predecessors is still disputed and because the problem of authenticity is not really relevant in this study, which attempts to review the entire body of lyric poetry through Walther von der Vogelweide, I have chosen to retain the ascriptions of von Kraus without discussing the justifiability of his or anyone else's position.

2. Der von Kürenberg

1. Roswitha Wisniewski, *"werdekeit* und Hierarchie. Zur soziologischen Interpretation des Minnesangs," in *Strukturen und Interpretationen: Studien zur deutschen Philologie* (Festschrift Horacek), ed. A. Ebenbauer, F. Knapp, and P. Krämer (Vienna: Braumüller, 1974), p. 349, claims that the *Frauenstrophe* 7,1 shows "Belehrung des Mannes durch die *vrouwe*," but there is no need to interpret this admonition by the lady to her lover to be faithful in the framework of the concept of the ennobling power of love. Simply because the stanza opens with a sententious statement about the desirability of maintaining friendships is not a sufficient reason to view it as an example of the woman attempting to have an uplifting effect on the man.

2. Bert Nagel, *Staufische Klassik: Deutsche Dichtung um 1200* (Heidelberg: Stiehm, 1977), p. 294, has stated not only that the falcon is tamed and ennobled, but also that the very image of the falcon being tamed by a woman is a "Realsymbol" of the idea of the educative function of love. He does not, however, justify this position in any way. That the falcon-knight has been ennobled has also been maintained by Peter Wapnewski, "Des Kürenbergers Falkenlied," *Euphorion*, 53 (1959), 18, and by Franz H. Bäuml, *Medieval Civilization in Germany: 800–1273* (New York: Praeger, 1969), p. 126. Without going into any detail, both Wapnewski (implicitly) and Bäuml (explicitly) interpret the gold decorations of the falcon as a symbol of the knight's ennoblement. Although such an interpretation is possible, there is neither anything in the poem itself nor any parallel use elsewhere to support such a view. It seems more reasonable to regard the lady's precious gifts merely as a token of her favor. Similarly, Wisniewski, p. 349, considers the gold "als Metapher für *werdekeit* durch den Partner," although she must admit that, because of the

metaphorical treatment of the problem, the song cannot provide "eindeutige Aussagen."

3. For details of this approach, see Stephen J. Kaplowitt, "A Note on the 'Falcon Song' of Der von Kürenberg," *German Quarterly*, 44 (1971), 519–24.

4. Joachim Bumke, *Die romanisch-deutschen Literaturbeziehungen im Mittelalter: Ein Überblick* (Heidelberg: Winter, 1967), p. 42, states outright that there is no trace of the notion of love as a means to moral improvement in the poems of the Kürenberger.

3. Dietmar von Aist

1. In the *Frauenstrophen* of the *Wechsel*, 32,13, Roswitha Wisniewski, "*werdekeit* und Hierarchie: Zur soziologischen Interpretation des Minnesangs," in *Strukturen und Interpretationen: Studien zur deutschen Philologie* (Festschrift Horacek), ed. A. Ebenbauer, F. Knapp, and P. Krämer (Vienna: Braumüller, 1974), p. 349, sees another example of "Belehrung des Mannes durch die *vrouwe*" when the lady tells the man she loves not to be so sad because they are parted. As was the case with 7,1 of the Kürenberger, this, too, should not be interpreted as an example of the lady attempting to have an elevating effect on the knight in order to make him worthy of love, but rather as a piece of advice to help him get through the pain of separation.

2. See Friedrich Vogt, ed., *Des Minnesangs Frühling*, 23rd ed. (Leipzig: Hirzel, 1920), pp. 310–11.

3. See Vogt, p. 311.

4. Günther Schweikle, *Die frühe Minnelyrik*, vol. 1 of *Die Mittelhochdeutsche Minnelyrik* (Darmstadt: Wissenschaftliche Buchgesellschaft, 1977), p. 403, notes that *Des Minnesangs Frühling* changed the plural verb form of the manuscript, *benement*, to the singular, *benimt*, but that the manuscript version is also quite plausible: "Die Ausweitung des Schlußgedankens der handschriftlichen Fassung in eine allgemeine Sentenz ist aber auch möglich, bezogen auf die läuternde Gesellschaft aller Damen." Leaving the manuscript as it is would thus add some depth to the idea of the educative force of love by expanding the situation to include not only the influence of the individual lady of the poem, but also that of noble ladies in general.

5. Carl von Kraus, *Des Minnesangs Frühling: Untersuchungen* (Leipzig: Hirzel, 1939), p. 79, states that the word *bezzer* is not used here "in eigentlich moralischem Sinn, . . . sondern ist soviel wie *tiurer*." That this view has not been universally accepted is clear from several recent studies. Cf., for example, Wisniewski, p. 350 ("In der Mannesstrophe 33,24 bekennt der Mann ausdrücklich den versittlichenden Einfluß der *vrouwe*"), and Schweikle's translation of the verse, p. 141 ("Du hast meinen Sinn veredelt"). But whatever might be the actual nature of the improvement that has taken place, there should be no difficulty in viewing this poem as an example of the ennobling power of love.

6. Wisniewski, p. 347, turns the function of the physical fulfillment upside down by claiming that it is a means of achieving ennoblement: "Die Mannesstrophe 33,24 erhofft die Vollendung der Steigerung durch die Hingabe der Frau." Although variations of this idea are found later in three poems (see the discussion below of *MF*11,1 on pp. 21–22, of *MF*184,31 on p. 116, and of Walther von der Vogelweide's 92,9 on pp. 126–27), I cannot see that Dietmar's song indicates anything but the hope of physical union as a reward for the man's improvement. Strangely enough, Alois Kircher, *Dichter und Konvention: Zum gesellschaftlichen Realitätsproblem der deutschen Lyrik um 1200 bei Walther von der Vogelweide und seinen Zeitgenossen*, Literatur in der Gesellschaft, 18 (Düsseldorf: Bertelsmann, 1973), p. 20, quotes the first three lines of this stanza to support his contention that, "bei Versagen der Liebeserfüllung in Form der Vereinigung der Partner," the only meaning that *Minnewerben* can have is "in einer angenommenen Sittigung und Läuterung des Werbenden." Citing this poem as an example of the idea of the man's ennoblement as an end in itself, when the fourth line of the stanza points so clearly to the notion of physical fulfillment, seems completely unjustifiable.

4. Anonymous Songs

1. For a summary of the problems involved see von Kraus, *Untersuchungen*, pp. 1–2, as well as the recent edition by Jürgen Kühnel, *Dû bist mîn. ih bin dîn: Die lateinischen Liebes- (und Freundschafts-) Briefe des clm 19411: Abbildungen, Text und Übersetzung*, Litterae, 52 (Göppingen: Kümmerle, 1977). It should also be noted that nothing in the poem itself points to the fact that the speaker is a woman—the words could just as easily be spoken by a man.

2. For a discussion of the various interpretations see von Kraus, pp. 3–9, which has recently been updated in the 36th edition of *Des Minnesangs Frühling* (Stuttgart: Hirzel, 1977) by Moser and Tervooren, vol. 2, p. 65.

3. In a discussion of this poem Bert Nagel, *Staufische Klassik: Deutsche Dichtung um 1200* (Heidelberg: Stiehm, 1977), p. 293, contends—with reference to the term *hôher muot*—that love is to be viewed as "eine moralische Kraft" because it is a "Spenderin jener Hochstimmung der Seele, die nicht nur individuelle Beglückung ist, sondern zugleich eine allgemeingültige Wertsteigerung des Menschen, ein moralisches Plus im Blick auf die Mitwelt bedeutet. Denn der *hôhe muot*, den die Minne spendet, wird als die höchste Tugend des mitmenschlichen Daseins, als sittliche Pflicht im Zusammenleben der Menschen gewertet. Indem die Minne den Menschen zur Freude beschwingt, erzieht sie ihn zu den wünschenswerten Formen kultivierter Geselligkeit." There is, to be sure, some truth in this contention. To the extent that love results in the lover's happiness, which may then have the consequence that he appears joyful in society, it can be said that love has both a private and a public effect. That this effect is beneficial, there can be no doubt. It is not at all clear, however, that it is also educative, for the state-

ment that love, by making people happy, educates them in the desirable forms of cultivated social behavior, is simply not valid. All that love does—from a social point of view—by providing *hôher muot* is make it possible for people to fulfill without effort the requirement to appear happy in public. It would therefore be very misleading to imply that every instance of *hôher muot* should be considered as an example of the educative force of love. A similar, but not clearly expressed point of view concerning *hôher muot* is offered by Eleonore Manson, "Motivationen der Minne in der höfischen Liebeslyrik," *Acta Germanica*, 9 (1974), 26. She merely states that even in the early *Minnesang* love is something "die den Wert des Mannes erhöht—sie verleiht *hôhen muot*." How *hôher muot* increases a man's worth, or what is meant by *Wert*, is not explained.

7. Meinloh von Sevelingen

1. Karl-Heinz Schirmer, "Die höfische Minnetheorie und Meinloh von Sevelingen," in *Zeiten und Formen in Sprache und Dichtung: Festschrift für Fritz Tschirch zum 70. Geburtstag*, ed. Karl-Heinz Schirmer and Bernhard Sowinski (Cologne: Böhlau, 1972), pp. 64–65, claims that the situation in 13,27 presupposes an educative function in the relationship between the lady speaking and the man she has chosen: "Die Wahl eines jungen Mannes zum Geliebten . . . weist auf das Verständnis der Liebe als Bildungsverhältnis." Although it is not possible to prove that this view is incorrect, there is also no reason to assume that the lady's choice of a *young* man points in this direction, for the poem is perfectly intelligible in its own right without any such presupposition. Schirmer also asserts that the lady's claim that she deserves to be the one most loved by her knight becomes understandable if one supposes that she has had an educative function, for then it can be assumed that what she has done to be so deserving has increased the man's worth. This assertion is just as far-fetched as the previous one, inasmuch as there is no need whatever to explain what her being deserving means in this way. It is certainly sufficient to read these lines in a general sense to mean that the lady, without specifying how, says she has behaved toward the man in a manner that has won his love. (One can imagine any number of things she could have done to gain his affection, the least likely of which would be to have had an educative effect on him.) Nothing in the poem points to the idea of the educative function of the lady. All of Schirmer's contentions are read into the poem based on his knowledge of the existence of this idea in other texts.

2. Horst Wenzel, *Frauendienst und Gottesdienst: Studien zur Minne-Ideologie*, Philologische Studien und Quellen, 74 (Berlin: Schmidt, 1974), p. 134, apparently assumes that the man's eagerness to serve such a paragon of virtue implies a desire to be ennobled, for he cites the last three verses of 15,1 ("durch daz wil ich mich flîzen, / swaz sie gebiutet, daz daz allez sî getan")

as evidence that the lady "veredelt das Wesen des Mannes." But because nothing is said in the poem itself either about what is expected of the knight or about the possible effect of the lady's goodness on him, such an assumption is not warranted. Simply because a knight decides to serve a good and beautiful lady is no reason to automatically suppose that the purpose of such service is the self-improvement of the knight.

3. Cf. the discussion of a similar situation in 16,1 by the Burggraf von Regensburg on p. 17.

4. See, for example, Günther Schweikle, *Die frühe Minnelyrik*, vol. 1 of *Die Mittelhochdeutsche Minnelyrik* (Darmstadt: Wissenschaftliche Buchgesellschaft, 1977), p. 383, who states that an important motif found in the poem is "die läuternde Kraft der Minne"; and Wenzel, p. 134, who contends, with reference to this poem, that the lady "veredelt das Wesen des Mannes."

5. Schweikle, p. 382, states that *getiuret* really means "im menschlichen und sozialen Wert gesteigert," thus suggesting that both values could be implied here at the same time. Olive Sayce, ed., *Poets of the Minnesang* (Oxford: Clarendon, 1967), p. 210, clearly refers to the social value when she interprets the line to mean the "bestowal of her love would confer a unique distinction." Both Wenzel, p. 134, and Anna Lüderitz, *Die Liebestheorie der Provençalen bei den Minnesingern der Stauferzeit*, Literarhistorische Forschungen, 29 (Berlin: Emil Felber, 1904), p. 75, interpret the passage as an example of the ennobling power of love. Elisabeth Lea, "Die Sprache lyrischer Grundgefüge: MF11,1 bis 15,17," *Beiträge zur Geschichte der deutschen Sprache und Literatur*, 90 (Halle, 1968), 328–30, speaks of "Erhöhung" und "Wertsteigerung" without making it clear whether she means moral betterment or increase of esteem or both.

8. Kaiser Heinrich

1. Roswitha Wisniewski, "*werdekeit* und Hierarchie: Zur soziologischen Interpretation des Minnesangs," in *Strukturen und Interpretationen: Studien zur deutschen Philologie* (Festschrift Horacek), ed. A. Ebenbauer, F. Knapp, and P. Krämer (Vienna: Braumüller, 1974), p. 348, claims that the *Frauenstrophe* of 4,17 culminates in a *laudatio* of the lady's beloved, "dessen *werdekeit* die Konsequenz leiblicher Zustimmung verlangt." But because all she says about the knight in the last line (4,34–35) is that no one ever pleased her more ("mir geviel in al der welte nie nieman baz"), it hardly seems appropriate to say that the knight's *werdekeit* merited her love. For clear examples of this motif elsewhere, however, see above, pp. 17 and 21.

2. Helmut de Boor, *Die höfische Literatur: Vorbereitung, Blüte, Ausklang (1170–1250)*, vol. 2 of *Geschichte der deutschen Literatur von den Anfängen bis zur Gegenwart*, by Helmut de Boor and Richard Newald (Munich: Beck, 1953), p. 8.

3. For a discussion of *hôher muot*, see Anonymous Songs, n. 3, pp. 188–89.

4. For a discussion of the arguments concerning the persona of the speaker, see von Kraus, pp. 111–12; Olive Sayce, ed., *Poets of the Minnesang* (Oxford: Clarendon, 1967), p. 212; and Hubert Heinen, "Observations on the Role in *Minnesang," Journal of English and Germanic Philology*, 75 (1976), 204–6.

5. Sayce, p. 212.

6. Cf. the translations of "du zierest mîne sinne" by Günther Schweikle, *Die frühe Minnelyrik*, vol. 1 of *Die Mittlehochdeutsche Minnelyrik* (Darmstadt: Wissenschaftliche Buchgesellschaft, 1977), p. 265 ("Du verschönst meine Gedanken"), and Karl Bertau, *Deutsche Literatur im europäischen Mittelalter*, vol. 1 (Munich: Beck, 1972), p. 582 ("Schön machst du mir meine Gedanken"). Theodor Frings, "Edelstein und Gold," in *Studien zur deutschen Philologie des Mittelalters* (Festschrift Panzer), ed. Richard Kienast (Heidelberg: Winter, 1950), p. 46, also does not see a refining influence of the lady on the man, for he believes that the stanza remains "im Sinnlichen" and does not refer to anything in the moral realm, even though he claims that the woman is "wie ein Edelstein, der den Mann schmückt." This interpretation seems to ignore the line "du zierest mîne sinne," which makes it clear that the woman—if it is a woman speaking—embellishes the man's *sinne*, not the man.

7. That this is so is supported by the fact that so many scholars have taken the stanza in question for a *Frauenstrophe* and hence have completely ignored the possibility that the lines under discussion could refer to a refining influence of the lady on the man.

9. Friedrich von Hausen

1. Horst Wenzel, *Frauendienst und Gottesdienst: Studien zur Minne-Ideologie*, Philologische Studien und Quellen, 74 (Berlin: Schmidt, 1974), p. 138, implies that 50,19 shows the educative power of love in that the poet begins by praising God for having given him the *sinne* to take the lady into his *gemüete*, for she is worthy of love. This insight on his part "ist bereits Indiz einer gewissen Gottnähe auch auf seiten des Mannes, die ihn weiterführt zur Ausbildung seiner Tugend." Similarly, Hans Schottmann, "Mittelhochdeutsche Literatur: Lyrik," in *Kurzer Grundriß der germanischen Philologie*, vol. 2, ed. L. E. Schmitt (Berlin: de Gruyter, 1971), p. 474, refers to this poem as evidence when he states: "Schon früh legitimierte der Dichter die Minne als erzieherische Macht von Gott her." It is difficult to see how the poet's thanking God for having given him the insight to love a lady who is worthy of love can be used as the basis for an assumption about the educative power of love. Just because the lady's goodness is praised is no reason to assume that the man means to use her example as a model for improving himself. See the discussion of 52,37 below, p. 28.

2. I have chosen to retain Lachmann's emendation of lines 46,21–25 (also accepted by von Kraus) for the sake of clarity, even though D. G. Mowatt, ed., *Friderich von Hûsen: Introduction, Text, Commentary and Glossary* (Cam-

bridge: University Press, 1971), pp. 28–30, has expressed the view that the sense of this emendation "is not noticeably different from that of BC" (p. 29).

3. The only extant text has "wunde," which von Kraus changed to "sunde."

4. Although a few scholars have argued that the six stanzas in question comprise one song, the majority of researchers considers them to be two separate entities. For a recent treatment of the arguments pro and con, see Hugo Bekker, *Friederich von Hausen: Inquiries into His Poetry*, University of North Carolina Studies in the Germanic Languages and Literatures, 87 (Chapel Hill: University of North Carolina Press, 1977), pp. 18–19.

5. This paraphrase of lines 42,19–22 is based on Mowatt's reading (pp. 145–47), which reinstated the manuscripts' preterit form *muosen* (in line 21), in contrast to the emended present *müezen*, which had been universally accepted until that time. The more common reading based on the present tense could be paraphrased as follows: "My heart must be her shrine as long as I live; therefore all women must always be unjostled there," which was generally taken to mean that there was room in his heart only for his lady, not for any other women. For a summary of the various interpretations see Bekker, pp. 10–11.

6. Hennig Brinkmann, *Friedrich von Hausen* (Minden-Westfalen: August Lutzeyer, 1948), p. 112, merely says the poet's steadfastness "ist von der güete der Frau geweckt," which does not elucidate the poet's words in any way. Bekker's interpretation will be discussed below.

7. Bekker, p. 13.

8. Ibid.

9. Ibid., p. 14.

10. Cf. similar situations in 16,1 by the Burggraf von Regensburg, p. 17, and in 14,26 by Meinloh von Sevelingen, p. 21.

12. Heinrich von Rugge

1. See above, p. 19.

2. Elisabeth Lea, "Erziehen—Im Wert erhöhen—Gemeinschaft in Liebe," *Beiträge zur Geschichte der deutschen Sprache und Literatur*, 89 (Halle, 1967), 269, claims that the words *guot gewin* (103,32) refer to a "gegenseitige Erhöhung im Wert," but there is no need to view the mutual advantages that accrue to both partners in the relationship in such a narrow and specific sense.

3. Lea, "Erziehen," p. 266, interprets the lady's insistence that the man be *staete* as a demand that he be *gebildet* and that this insistence on having "den 'gebildeten' Geliebten" makes her into an *Erzieherin*. Although it is true that the lady in this poem clearly does function as an *Erzieherin*, it is simply not justifiable to state—without any demonstration of the validity of the statement—that *staete* always means *gebildet* or courtly.

13. Hartwic von Rute

1. See above, p. 39.

15. Ulrich von Gutenberg

1. Günther Schweikle, *Die frühe Minnelyrik*, vol. 1 of *Die Mittlehochdeutsche Minnelyrik* (Darmstadt: Wissenschaftliche Buchgesellschaft, 1977), p. 536, states, without going into detail, that this passage indicates "Läuterung durch die Minne."

16. Heinrich von Veldeke

1. See Theodor Frings and Gabriele Schieb, "Heinrich von Veldeke, die Entwicklung eines Lyrikers," in *Festschrift für Paul Kluckhohn und Hermann Schneider* (Tübingen: Mohr, 1948), pp. 101–21; Helmut Thomas, "Zu den Liedern und Sprüchen Heinrichs von Veldeke," *Beiträge zur Geschichte der deutschen Sprache und Literatur*, 78 (Halle, 1956), 173–76; Werner Schröder, "Dido und Lavine," *Zeitschrift für deutsches Altertum*, 88 (1957/1958), 164–66; and Elisabeth Lea, "Erziehen—Im Wert erhöhen—Gemeinschaft in Liebe," *Beiträge zur Geschichte der deutschen Sprache und Literatur*, 89 (Halle, 1967), pp. 269–74.

2. Stephen J. Kaplowitt, "Heinrich von Veldeke's Song Cycle of 'Hohe Minne,'" *Seminar*, 11 (1975), 125–40.

3. Two songs, 59,11 and 66,1, have nothing to do with love and hence need not be discussed here.

4. Only if this poem can be connected with the set of poems, 56,1 and 57,10, as was attempted by Frings and Schieb, p. 114, can such a progression or development be assumed. For detailed arguments against making such an assumption, see Kaplowitt, "Heinrich von Veldeke," p. 132.

5. Von Kraus, *Untersuchungen*, p. 168.

6. Frings and Schieb, p. 113.

17. Engelhart von Adelnburg

1. This is the manuscript reading, rather than von Kraus's emendation. For an explanation of the sense of the manuscript version see Günther Schweikle, *Die frühe Minnelyrik*, vol. 1 of *Die Mittlehochdeutsche Minnelyrik* (Darmstadt: Wissenschaftliche Buchgesellschaft, 1977), p. 545.

18. Albrecht von Johansdorf

1. For a justification of the emendation see von Kraus, *Untersuchungen*, p. 225.

2. Anna Lüderitz, *Die Liebestheorie der Provençalen bei den Minnesingern der Stauferzeit*, Literarhistorische Forschungen, 29 (Berlin: Emil Felber, 1904), p. 81, claims that in 88,33 the poet is supporting the notion that "Enthaltsamkeit, Unterdrückung der Sinnlichkeit" is a "notwendige Voraussetzung einer reinen Minne." This view is based on the interpretation of the lines "man sol mîden boesen kranc" (88,37) and "kunden sie ze rehte beidiu sich bewarn"(89,3) as meaning that the lovers must control their sensual desires. This is patently false; 88,37 merely says that one should avoid evil or "unedle Schwäche" (Günther Schweikle, *Die frühe Minnelyrik*, vol. 1 of *Die Mittelhochdeutsche Minnelyrik* [Darmstadt: Wissenschaftliche Buchgesellschaft, 1977], p. 331), and 89,3 means "if the two of them can behave correctly" ("Konnten sie beide geziemend sich bewahren," Schweikle, p. 331). Nowhere in the poem is it implied that *boesen kranc* refers to sexual desires or that behaving correctly means refraining from fulfilling sensual urges. There is no need to assume, as Lüderitz does, that 88,33 must represent the same viewpoint clearly expressed in the dialogue, 93,12, namely, that the man's reward consists only in his ennoblement.

3. It might be well to remember, as has been pointed out by Hubert Heinen, "Lofty and Base Love in Walther von der Vogelweide's 'sô die bluomen' and 'aller werdekeit,' " *German Quarterly*, 51 (1978), 473, that the context of this poem is "ironic and playful" and that hence its significance as a classic example of the idea of the ennobling power of love has perhaps been exaggerated.

4. Elisabeth Lea, "Erziehen—Im Wert erhöhen—Gemeinschaft in Liebe," *Beiträge zur Geschichte der deutschen Sprache und Literatur*, 89 (Halle, 1967), p. 280, offers the opening lines of this poem—"Diu Saelde hât gekroenet mich / gein der vil süezen minne" (92,35–36)—as an example of "männlicher Läuterung." This interpretation would seem to be based on a misreading of the verses in question. Cf. Schweikle's translation, p. 343: "Das Glück hat mich auserwählt / für die so süße Minne." There appears to be no justification for equating *kroenen* here with *tiuren* or *hoehen*, as Lea obviously does.

19. Hartmann von Aue

1. Contrary to the prevailing consensus, Hubert Heinen, "*Mit gemache lân*: A Crux in Hartmann's 'Maniger grüezet mich alsô' (MF216,29)," *Studies in Medieval Culture*, 12 (1978), 85–90, maintains that this song does not represent a rejection of the idea of courtly love service, but rather a "rejection of the failure, engendered by a desire for an easy conquest, of a singer/knight to undertake an arduous love service" (p. 88) and a "reminder and affirma-

tion of the complexities and delicious pains of courtliness." But because this radical departure from the "standard" view does not shed any light on the problem under investigation—even if this reading were accepted, the song would still be included in the category of songs showing no trace of the idea of ennobling love—it shall not be discussed here in detail.

2. Cf. the discussion of 16,1 by the Burggraf von Regensburg, p. 17; 14,26, by Meinloh von Sevelingen, p. 21; and 54,1, under the name of Friedrich von Hausen, p. 32. It is also interesting to note that Hubert Heinen, "The Woman's Songs of Hartmann von Aue," in *Vox Feminae: Studies in Medieval Woman's Songs*, ed. John F. Plummer, *Studies in Medieval Culture*, 15 (1981), 101, views the woman's "assertion of her lover's personal worthiness" as her means of achieving honor: "His value is placed so high that it sheds honor on her (a situation which more commonly obtains in the suitor's praise of his lady)." But this should not be viewed as a reversal of the idea of the woman having an ennobling effect on the man, because the woman's behavior or character here is not improved; rather, only her honor is enhanced.

3. For a discussion of the arguments for considering this a crusade song— despite the fact that nothing in the text specifically mentions a crusade, but only a journey overseas—see Hugo Kuhn, "*Minnesang* and the Form of Performance," in *Formal Aspects of Medieval German Poetry*, ed. Stanley N. Werbow (Austin: University of Texas Press, 1969), pp. 27–41.

4. See below, pp. 123–24.

5. For a fairly recent summary of the scholarship concerning this song see Ekkehard Blattmann, *Die Lieder Hartmanns von Aue*, Philologische Studien und Quellen, 44 (Berlin: Schmidt, 1968), pp. 13–55.

6. Cf. Heinz Stolte, "Hartmanns sogenannte Witwenklage und sein drittes Kreuzlied," *Deutsche Vierteljahrsschrift für Literaturwissenschaft und Geistesgeschichte*, 25 (1951), 184–98; Richard Kienast, *Das Hartmann-Liederbuch C²*, Sitzungsberichte der deutschen Akademie der Wissenschaften zu Berlin, Klasse für Sprachen, Literatur und Kunst, 1 (Berlin: Akademie, 1963), pp. 47–61; and Blattmann, pp. 13–55.

20. Heinrich von Morungen

1. The text forming the basis of the following paraphrase of 131,25 is that presented by Helmut Tervooren as poem #XIb in his edition of *Heinrich von Morungen: Lieder*, Universal-Bibliothek, 9797 (Stuttgart: Reclam, 1975), pp. 68–72.

2. It should be noted that in manuscript A the word *liebe* (instead of *diu guote*) is given as the subject of the verb *gît* (cf. Tervooren, p. 66). According to this reading, the lover's exultation and joy would be direct benefits of love. But in this case, too, what would be missing as an effect of love is any mention of ennoblement in the sense of this investigation.

3. Frederick Goldin, in his chapter on Heinrich von Morungen in *The Mirror of Narcissus in the Courtly Love Lyric* (Ithaca: Cornell University Press, 1967), pp. 107–66, sees in Morungen's introduction of the quotation about the parrot and the starling an example of ennobling love. He maintains that the poet is now criticizing his earlier plea to the lady "in which he asked her to say the word that would end his grief. He realizes that he has inadvertently asked her to be like those whom he now rebukes; any mindless creature can say a word, but the lady is his judge, far wiser and more virtuous than he. Therefore in referring to the earlier song he . . . also makes a partial retraction, he corrects the fault he has committed and the imperfect understanding that caused it. Here is the visible sign of his ennoblement; he has become more wise and more patient" (p. 114). This view is based primarily on Carl von Kraus's emendation and interpretation of line 132,10, which immediately follows the quotation from the earlier song and which reads in the two manuscripts where it appears: "wol, sprich daz unde habe des iemer danc"; this in turn is translated by Tervooren as: "Nun denn, sprich es und sei versichert, ich bin dir dafür immerfort dankbar" (p. 69). Von Kraus's version of the verse reads: "wol sprechent siz and habent des niemer danc," which he translates as: "Gut sprechen sie's und denken dabei nichts" (*Heinrich von Morungen*, ed. Carl von Kraus [Munich: Verlag der Bremer Presse, 1925], p. 71). Because von Kraus's textual manipulation goes far beyond what is considered acceptable today and his reading of the expression "er hât es danc" as "he doesn't think about it"—although technically possible—is certainly farfetched under the circumstances, it is extremely difficult to accept Goldin's view that the quotation from the earlier poem is being used to criticize the poet's previous attitude and that he has hence changed for the better and given evidence of the ennobling power of love. For the most prevalent meaning of "er hât es danc" see G. F. Benecke, W. Müller, F. Zarncke, Mittelhochdeutsches Wörterbuch, vol. 1 (Leipzig, 1854; repr., Hildesheim: Olms, 1963), p. 353.

4. The fact that so much of Heinrich von Morungen's imagery is derived from, or dependent on, language used in poetry and prose venerating the Virgin Mary, and that his portrayal of his lady is often remarkably similar to that of Mary in such literature, might make one wonder why the ennobling force of love is not more evident in Morungen's songs than it is. If one examines the passages that might have served as the poet's models, however, one sees little that is reminiscent of the basic premises of ennobling love. Mary's perfection and goodness are no more looked upon as a source of inspiration to self-improvement by those venerating her than are the lady's good qualities in Morungen's songs. Mary, like the lady in the poems, is viewed primarily as the ultimate source of grace or mercy. For references to, and discussions of, the influence of the veneration of the Virgin on Heinrich von Morungen see, for example, Theodor Frings, "Erforschung des Minnesangs," *Beiträge zur Geschichte der deutschen Sprache und Literatur*, 87 (Halle, 1965), 15–19 (originally published in *Forschungen und Fortschritte*, 26 [1950]);

E. J. Morrall, "Light Imagery in Heinrich von Morungen," *London Medieval Studies*, 2 (1951), 116–24; Peter Dronke, *Medieval Latin and the Rise of European Love-Lyric*, vol. 1 (Oxford: Clarendon, 1965), pp. 125–36; and especially Peter Kesting, *Maria-Frouwe: Über den Einfluß der Marienverehrung auf den Minnesang bis Walther von der Vogelweide*, Medium Aevum, 5 (Munich: Fink, 1965), pp. 93–113.

5. Goldin, p. 136, correctly assumes that, when the knight first saw the lady, he perceived her as "the smiling image of virtue and nobility" and "as a portrait of the ideal." But when he says that "in that moment the quality within him found the image of its fulfillment, and he knew immediately what he ought to resemble and how he might be judged," he is going beyond what is permissible based on the evidence in the text. Throughout his essay Goldin assumes that *Minne* is a priori ennobling; hence he believes that, whenever a knight praises a lady's goodness, the knight knows he should emulate her virtues, even when nothing in the text points in this direction, as is the case here.

6. The general lack of importance of the motif of the ennobling power of love in the poems of Heinrich von Morungen was pointed out by Julius Schwietering, "Der Liederzyklus Heinrichs von Morungen," *Zeitschrift für deutsches Altertum*, 82 (1948), p. 80. Ulrich Pretzel, "Drei Lieder Heinrichs von Morungen," in *Interpretationen mittelhochdeutscher Lyrik*, ed. Günther Jungbluth (Bad Homburg: Gehlen, 1969), p. 119, agreed with this assessment and summarized his view with the statement: "Weniger die bildende Wirkung der entsagenden Liebe als die Unendlichkeit der Liebe an sich, unabhängig von der Erfüllung, ist das Thema seiner Kunst" (p. 120). Bert Nagel, *Staufische Klassik: Deutsche Dichtung um 1200* (Heidelberg: Stiehm, 1977), p. 294, citing Pretzel, gives a misleading picture of the situation when he says: "Morungen greift jedoch über den Erziehungsgedanken hinaus." This would make it appear as if the idea of the educative function of love does play at least a somewhat important role in Morungen's work, which, as has been seen, is clearly not the case.

21. Reinmar von Hagenau

1. The absence of any awareness of the educative power of love in these three *Frauenlieder* was underscored by William E. Jackson, "Reinmar der Alte in Literary History: A Critique and a Proposal," *Colloquia Germanica*, 9 (1975), 195, when he criticized Helmut de Boor, who had said in his literary history (*Die höfische Literatur: Vorbereitung, Blüte, Ausklang (1170–1250)*, vol. 2 of *Geschichte der deutschen Literatur von den Anfängen bis zur Gegenwart*, by Helmut de Boor and Richard Newald [Munich: Beck, 1953], p. 291): "Nun ist die Frau schon aus der Reinheit ihrer Natur jener Vollkommenheit näher, die der Mann erst erstrebt und durch den Minnedienst erreichen kann." Jackson correctly calls this statement "a baseless fiction" that could "hardly be

more irrelevant for Reinmar's 'Frauenlieder.' " A similar "baseless fiction" is found in Bert Nagel, *Staufische Klassik: Deutsche Dichtung um 1200* (Heidelberg: Stiehm, 1977), p. 168, where it is stated, with reference to 178,1: "Wenn die *frouwe* sagt: *des er gert daz ist der tôt*, so heißt das, daß das *gern* des Minners nicht erfüllt werden darf, da Liebeserfüllung die erzieherische Wirkung der Herrin beenden und damit seelischen Tod bedeuten würde." As has been seen in the above discussion, the lady's refusal to fulfill the man's desires has nothing to with the educative effect of love.

2. *Staete* has been seen in this poem as a prerequisite for obtaining a woman's love by Xenja von Ertzdorff, "Reinmar von Hagenau: wiest ime ze muote, wundert mich (MF153,14)," in *Interpretationen mittelhochdeutscher Lyrik*, ed. Günther Jungbluth (Bad Homburg: Gehlen, 1969), pp. 140–42. Her interpretation is based on a reading of the verbs *taete* and *pflaege* as referring to past time. Thus she understands the speaker's question in 153,18–19 to mean: "Auch wüßte ich gerne, wie er sich verhalten hat, / war er in bewundernswerter Weise beständig?" (p. 140). Although it is perfectly possible for the MHG subjunctive forms in question to be used to express past ideas in dependent clauses (cf. Hermann Paul, *Mittelhochdeutsche Grammatik*, 18th ed. rev., Walther Mitzka [Tübingen: Niemeyer, 1960], pp. 227–28), in the context it seems more likely that the speaker wishes to know how the person who has been successful in love *behaves*, not how he *behaved*. The poem begins with the question in the present: "Wiest ime ze muote . . . dem herzeclîchen liep geschiht?" and all other references to this hypothetical person are in the present, including the speaker's statement immediately following the word *staete* and referring to it: "diu sol im wesen von rehte bî" (153,20). In addition, this view is supported by the parallel use of *staete* in the last stanza as a quality necessary in a relationship of mutual love. The fact that Reinmar is aware of *staete* as a precondition for the lady's granting her love in other poems—which von Ertzdorff uses to support her view (p. 142, n. 26)—does not mean that in this poem he is merely repeating ideas he has stated elsewhere. Carl von Kraus, *Die Lieder Reinmars des Alten*, part 1, Abhandlungen der Bayerischen Akademie der Wissenschaften, Philosophisch-Philologische und Historische Klasse, 30, no. 4 (Munich: Bayerische Akademie der Wissenschaften, 1919), p. 58, also interprets the verbs in question as referring to present time.

3. Roswitha Wisniewski, "*werdekeit* und Hierarchie: Zur soziologischen Interpretationen des Minnesangs," in *Strukturen und Interpretationen: Studien zur deutschen Philologie* (Festschrift Horacek), ed. A. Ebenbauer, F. Knapp, and P. Krämer (Vienna: Braumüller, 1974), p. 359, presumably with reference to 165,33-34 ("swes du mit triuwen phligest, wol im, derst ein saelic man / und mac vil gerne leben"), speaks of "veredelnder Beglückung." It should be clear from the following discussion, however, that nothing in these verses points to the idea of ennoblement.

4. Cf. below, pp. 103–5.

5. Cf. below, pp. 102–3 and 104–6.

6. Von Kraus, *Die Lieder Reinmars*, p. 7.

7. Nagel, p. 178.

8. Three short gnomic poems (H.S.308,V.S.430 and two stanzas listed as H.S.214,V.S.436) need not be examined here because they do not deal with relationships between the sexes.

9. Whether the last stanza (169,33) belongs to this poem or should be considered separately is debatable. For a summary of the different proposals that have been made, see the notes in Hugo Moser and Helmut Tervooren, ed., *Des Minnesangs Frühling*, 36th ed. (Stuttgart; Hirzel, 1977), vol. 1, p. 328, and vol. 2, p. 109. If this stanza were treated independently, it would have no clear connection with the theme of love and would not need to be discussed in this study.

10. Generalizations about the role played by the ennobling or educative power of love in Reinmar's poems abound. See, for example, Ulrich Pretzel, "Drei Lieder Heinrichs von Morungen," in *Interpretationen mittelhochdeutscher Lyrik*, ed. Günther Jungbluth (Bad Homburg: Gehlen, 1969), p. 119, who talks about "jenes Motiv *daz ich dîn bezzer worden sî* oder *dû hast getiuret mir den lîp*, das bei Reinmar immer als Trost lebendig ist"; Nagel, p. 168, who states: "Vor allem aber geht es um den Vorgang der Erziehung durch die höfische Minne"; and Hermann Schneider, "Die Lieder Reinmars des Alten: Ein Versuch," in *Kleinere Schriften* (Berlin: de Gruyter, 1962), p. 251 (originally published in *Deutsche Vierteljahrsschrift für Literaturwissenschaft und Geistesgeschichte*, 17 [1939], 312–42), who says: "Minne, das ist Reinmars Ansicht, erzieht und erhöht auf alle Fälle." On the other side of the scale, Anna Lüderitz, *Die Liebestheorie der Provençalen bei den Minnesingern der Stauferzeit*, Literarhistorische Forschungen, 29 (Berlin: Emil Felber, 1904), p. 85, maintains that Reinmar did not say anything about "der läuternden und erziehenden Wirkung der Liebe," that he never celebrated "seine Herrin als Lehrmeisterin." None of these generalizations is based on a detailed analysis of Reinmar's songs. The examination given above, however, has shown that the importance of the role of the motif in question in the poems under Reinmar's name in *MF* lies somewhere between the two extremes represented by Nagel and Lüderitz.

22. Walther von der Vogelweide

1. Kurt Herbert Halbach, *Walther von der Vogelweide*, 3rd ed., Sammlung Metzler, 40, (Stuttgart: Metzler, 1973). All citations of poems by Walther are from *Die Gedichte Walthers von der Vogelweide*, 13th ed., ed. Karl Lachmann and Carl von Kraus, rev. Hugo Kuhn (Berlin: de Gruyter, 1965).

2. The poem consists of the stanzas from *MF*, 214,34–215,13, which in manuscripts A and C are attributed to Hartmann von Aue, and three stanzas from Lachmann's edition of Walther, L.217,1–9, L.120,16–24, and L.217,10–18.

3. Hubert Heinen, "The Woman's Songs of Hartmann von Aue," in *Vox Feminae: Studies in Medieval Woman's Songs*, ed. John F. Plummer, *Studies in Medieval Culture*, 15 (1981), who treats the first three stanzas of *MF*214,34 as a poem of Hartmann von Aue, states that the poet is affirming here "a positive power in accepting the rigors of love service" (p. 98), but he does not specify that that power is ennoblement.

4. No further references are made in this study to this feud, inasmuch as it is not otherwise involved with the investigation of the motif of ennobling love. For a survey of the Reinmar-Walther feud see Peter Wapnewski, ed. and trans., *Walther von der Vogelweide: Gedichte*, 7th ed. (Frankfurt: Fischer, 1970), pp. 227–37.

5. This paraphrase of line 111,29 follows the interpretation summarized by Wapnewski, *Walther*, p. 231.

6. Precisely what this means is not clear. Does it indicate moral self-improvement? Or does it mean that the man derives benefit from associating with a lady of such good character in the sense that his *Ansehen*, his esteem, is increased? Cf. W. Wilmanns, ed., *Walther von der Vogelweide*, 4th ed., rev. Victor Michels (Halle: Buchhandlung des Waisenhauses, 1924), p. 331, note on 92,29: "Die Tugenden der Frau gereichen dem Mann zur Ehre."

7. Martha Mayo Hinman, "*Minne* in a New Mode: Walther and the Literary Tradition," *Deutsche Vierteljahrsschrift für Literaturwissenschaft und Geistesgeschichte*, 48 (1974), 252–53, claims that in the last stanza of this poem Walther provides us with a reason why "the mere wooing of a lady, even when unrequited, increases the personal worth of the lover," namely, "the increase in worth follows naturally from the wooing, since a man who tries to please one lady will be pleasing to others as well" (p. 253). This statement seems to misrepresent the situation, inasmuch as what Hinman sees as a reason is in reality the consequence. The man is pleasing to other women because he has acted in such a way that his personal worth has been increased.

8. See the discussion of *MF*11,1 on pp. 21–22 and of *MF*184,31 on p. 116. Hinman, p. 253, views the final lines of the poem ("swer guotes wîbes minne hât / der schamt sich aller missetât") as a slipping "back into the convention," in contrast to the preceding verses, where Walther is testing "the boundaries of the fiction" or the tradition according to which the wooing of a lady increases the worth of the suitor. Because this study has shown that the entire body of lyric production in *MF* contains only one possible and one clear-cut example of this variation of the idea of the ennobling power of love (*MF*11,1 and *MF*184,31), it is difficult to see how Walther's use of the motif in question is a return to the conventional. On the contrary, the idea that requited love has an ennobling effect is found several times in Walther's poems (see below, pp. 140–41 and 155) and could be looked upon just as much as a testing of the boundaries of tradition as the idea that the man's ennoblement makes him attractive to other women.

9. George F. Jones, *Walther von der Vogelweide*, Twayne's World Authors Se-

ries, 46 (New York: Twayne, 1968), pp. 56–57, in speaking of Walther's beginnings under the influence of other minnesingers, says that "he soon followed suit in declaring his devotion and dedication to a superior and inaccessible lady, whom he loved without hope of reward and only for the elevating effect of the service itself." Our examination of 91,17 and 92,9—the only two poems in which the idea of ennoblement being its own reward appears—has shown that even here it is not possible to state that the speaker is advocating that a knight serve a lady "only for the elevating effect of the service itself," for in both cases it is quite clear that the knight's ennoblement, even though it has value in itself, is still regarded as something that will make him appealing to other women, one of whom is bound to reward him with her love.

10. As usual, it is not clear whether *wirde* means inner worth or only esteem. If only the latter is involved, then one cannot cite this as an example of the ennobling power of love. There is, however, other evidence of ennoblement in the poem, as further discussion will show.

11. Cf. Wilmanns, p. 339, note to 96,4.

12. Two additional songs included by Halbach in this group, 55,35 and 102,29, are not concerned with love and are not considered here.

13. Cf. Wilmanns, p. 187, note to 42,25.

14. Cf., for example, Wilmanns, p. 250, note to 63,23: "Sie Geliebte nennen zu dürfen tut wohl, sie zur Herrin zu haben erhebt."

15. Cf. the translation by Hans Böhm, ed. and trans., *Die Gedichte Walthers von der Vogelweide*, 2nd ed. (Berlin: de Gruyter, 1955), p. 208: "Geliebte ist ein holder Name, aber Herrin ehrt über alles." The verse is similarly translated as " 'Geliebte' ist ein liebes Wort, doch 'Herrin' ehrt über alles" by Joerg Schaefer, ed. and trans., *Walther von der Vogelweide: Werke* (Darmstadt: Wissenschaftliche Buchgesellschaft, 1972), p. 135.

16. Cf. the translation by Wapnewski, *Walther*, p. 95: " 'Geliebte' ist ein Wort, das im Herzen beglückt, / 'Herrin' anderseits ehrt und erhebt."

17. Halbach, pp. 64–65.

18. A summary of the views that have been suggested can be found in Carl von Kraus, *Walther von der Vogelweide: Untersuchungen* (Berlin: de Gruyter, 1935), pp. 144–46. For more recent opinions see Theodor Frings, "Walthers Gespräche," in *Festschrift für Dietrich Kralik* (Horn: Ferdinand Berger, 1954), repr. in *Walther von der Vogelweide*, ed. Siegfried Beischlag, Wege der Forschung, no. 112 (Darmstadt: Wissenschaftliche Buchgesellschaft, 1971), pp. 428–30; and Schaefer, p. 458.

19. It should be clear from the above discussion that the view expressed by Wilmanns (p. 316, note to 86,1) that the poem presents "die gewöhnliche Anschauung von der veredelnden Macht der Minne" is not wholly tenable.

20. A summary of the problems involved can be found in Halbach, pp. 61–64. For more recent interpretations cf. Karl Heinz Borck, "Walthers Lied *aller werdekeit ein füegerinne* (Lachmann 46,32)," in *Festschrift für Jost Trier*, ed. William Foerste and Karl Heinz Borck (Cologne: Böhlau, 1964), pp. 313–34;

Wolfgang Bachofer, "Walther von der Vogelweide: *aller werdekeit ein füegerinne* (46,32)," in *Interpretationen mittelhochdeutscher Lyrik*, pp. 185–203; Gerhard Meissburger, " 'Wes brot ich esse, des liet ich singe'? Zu Walther 46,32ff (= M.80)," *Amsterdamer Beiträge zur älteren Germanistik*, 10 (1976), 15–41; and Hubert Heinen, "Lofty and Base Love in Walther von der Vogelweide's 'sô die bluomen' and 'aller werdekeit,' " *German Quarterly*, 51 (1978), 465–75.

21. Halbach, p. 68.

22. One of these five—96,29—was also included by Halbach in an earlier group and was discussed above, pp. 128–29.

23. Wolfgang Bachofer, "Zur Wandlung des Minne-Begriffs bei Walther," in *Festgabe für Ulrich Pretzel*, ed. Werner Simon, Wolfgang Bachofer, and Wolfgang Dittmann (Berlin: Schmidt, 1963), p. 146, claims the fact that the poet regrets the time he has spent in the lady's service, but not the *nôt* and *arebeit* involved, indicates that Walther subscribed to the view that the overcoming of such distress and effort represents a "bildende Kraft." But the poet's emphasis on the point that the *only* thing he has gotten for his endeavors has been his *kumber* makes this seem unlikely.

24. Cf. Wilmanns's comment on 59,11 (p. 238): "Nur der Tugendhafte wird zum Dienst zugelassen." This would make it appear that the idea of *becoming* worthy is not applicable here—one must already be worthy before one can even begin to serve a lady. There is, however, no reason to assume that Walther meant to be so restrictive here.

25. For a recent enlightening analysis of this poem see Hugo Kuhn, "Herzeliebez vrowelîn (Walther 49,25)," in *Medium Aevum deutsch: Festschrift für Kurt Ruh zum 65. Geburtstag*, ed. Dietrich Huschenbett, Klaus Matzel, and Georg Steer (Tübingen: Niemeyer, 1979), pp. 199–214.

26. Only three of the related songs—65,33, 110,27, and 184,1—will be discussed. The rest—39,1, 94,11, and 75,25—have nothing to do with love and need not be treated in this study.

27. Jones, p. 57, states that "what was new in Walther's song was that he was the first to discover that, to be ennobling, the lady did not have to be of noble birth. For him, the simple girl of the *Mädchenlieder* could inspire good behavior and high ideals in her lover just as well as a grand lady could." It has become clear from the above examination of the songs referred to by some scholars as *Mädchenlieder* (39,11; 74,20; 49,25; 50,19; 65,33; and possibly 51,13; 110,13; and 53,25) that there is no evidence of the ennobling power of love in any of them.

28. Cf. von Kraus, *Walther von der Vogelweide: Untersuchungen*, pp. 247–55, and Halbach, p. 76.

29. The manuscripts have *êre; zuht* is von Kraus's emendation (*Walther von der Vogelweide: Untersuchungen*, p. 254).

30. Von Kraus, *Walther*, pp. 247–55.

31. Ibid., p. 228.

32. The third consists of crusade songs; purely religious in character, they need not be considered here.

33. Cf. Friedrich von Hausen, *MF*48,13; Heinrich von Rugge's *Kreuzleich* (*MF*98,28ff.); and *MF*180,28 under the name of Reinmar von Hagenau.

34. Cf. von Kraus, *Walther*, pp. 473–87.

35. Ibid., p. 473.

36. Four additional poems listed in this category have already been treated elsewhere: 71,19–34 plus *MF*152,25 (see above, p. 88); 91,17–92,8 (see above, p. 126); 111,12–21 (see above, p. 154); and 122,24–123,40 (see above, p. 155).

37. Cf. Wilmanns, pp. 241–44, and von Kraus, *Walther*, pp. 244–47.

38. For a discussion of the ambiguities involved see von Kraus, *Walther*, p. 321.

39. Cf. the discussion of Albrecht von Johansdorf, *MF*88,33, p. 68; Heinrich von Veldeke, *MF*61,33, pp. 60–61; Walther von der Vogelweide, *MF*214,34, pp. 123–24, 13,33, pp. 124–25, and 92,9, pp. 126–27.

40. Von Kraus, *Walther*, pp. 473–75.

41. Three additional poems listed under this category have already been discussed: 171,1–24 (see above, p. 151); 184,1–40 (see above, pp. 148–50); and 217,1–24 (see above, pp. 123–24).

42. For a discussion of the problems involved see von Kraus, *Walther*, pp. 177–78.

43. See above, p. 153.

44. See above, p. 153.

45. See above, pp. 147–48.

46. See above, pp. 129–30.

47. See above, p. 129.

48. See above, pp. 138–39.

49. Von Kraus, *Walther*, pp. 477–80. Von Kraus's third category, "Lieder in Minnesangs Frühling" (pp. 475–77), is not included in the above discussion; the poems in question have all been considered elsewhere in this study. For *MF*84,37, *MF*203,24 and *MF*214,34, see above, pp. 36–37, 109–10, and 123–24, respectively.

50. Von Kraus, *Walther*, pp. 480–87.

Bibliography

Bachofer, Wolfgang. "Walther von der Vogelweide: *aller werdekeit ein füege-rinne* (46,32)." In *Interpretationen mittelhochdeutscher Lyrik*, edited by Günther Jungbluth, pp. 185–203. Bad Homburg: Gehlen, 1969.

―――. "Zur Wandlung des Minne-Begriffs bei Walther." In *Festgabe für Ulrich Pretzel*, edited by Werner Simon, Wolfgang Bachofer, and Wolfgang Dittmann, pp. 139–49. Berlin: Schmidt, 1963.

Bäuml, Franz H. *Medieval Civilization in Germany: 800–1273*. New York: Praeger, 1969.

Bekker, Hugo. *Friedrich von Hausen: Inquiries into His Poetry*. University of North Carolina Studies in the Germanic Languages and Literatures, 87. Chapel Hill: University of North Carolina Press, 1977.

Benecke, G. F., W. Müller, and F. Zarncke. *Mittelhochdeutsches Wörterbuch*. Leipzig, 1854. Reprint. Hildesheim: Olms, 1963.

Bertau, Karl. *Deutsche Literatur im europäischen Mittelalter*. Vol. 1. Munich: Beck, 1972.

Blattmann, Ekkehard. *Die Lieder Hartmanns von Aue*. Philologische Studien und Quellen, 44. Berlin: Schmidt, 1968.

Böhm, Hans, ed. and trans. *Die Gedichte Walthers von der Vogelweide*. 2nd ed. Berlin: de Gruyter, 1955.

Boor, Helmut de. *Die höfische Literatur: Vorbereitung, Blüte, Ausklang (1170–1250)*. Vol. 2 of *Geschichte der deutschen Literatur von den Anfängen bis zur Gegenwart*, by Helmut de Boor and Richard Newald. Munich: Beck, 1953.

Borck, Karl Heinz. "Walthers Lied *aller werdekeit ein füegerinne* (Lachmann 46,32)." In *Festschrift für Jost Trier*, edited by William Foerste and Karl Heinz Borck, pp. 313–34. Cologne: Böhlau, 1964.

Brinkmann, Hennig. *Friedrich von Hausen*. Minden-Westfalen: August Lutzeyer, 1948.

―――, ed. *Liebeslyrik der deutschen Frühe in zeitlicher Folge*. Düsseldorf: Schwann, 1952.

Bumke, Joachim. *Die romanisch-deutschen Literaturbeziehungen im Mittelalter: Ein Überblick*. Heidelberg: Winter, 1967.

Closs, August. "Minnesang and Its Spiritual Background." In *Medusa's Mirror: Studies in German Literature*, pp. 43–56. London: The Cresset Press, 1957.

Dronke, Peter. *Medieval Latin and the Rise of European Love-Lyric*. Vol. 1. Oxford: Clarendon, 1965.

Eggers, Hans. "Deutsche Dichtung der Stauferzeit." In *Die Zeit der Staufen*, vol. 3, pp. 187–204. Catalog of an Exhibit at the Württemberg State Museum, 26 March–5 June 1977. Stuttgart: n.p., 1977.

Ehrismann, Gustav. *Geschichte der deutschen Literatur bis zum Ausgang des Mittelalters.* Part II, section II, second half. Munich: Beck, 1935.

Ertzdorff, Xenja von. "Reinmar von Hagenau: wiest ime ze muote, wundert mich (MF153,14)." In *Interpretationen mittelhochdeutscher Lyrik,* edited by Günther Jungbluth, pp. 137–52. Bad Homburg: Gehlen, 1969.

Frings, Theodor. "Edelstein und Gold." In *Studien zur deutschen Philologie des Mittelalters* (Festschrift Panzer), edited by Richard Kienast, pp. 45–47. Heidelberg: Winter, 1950.

———. "Erforschung des Minnesangs." *Forschungen und Fortschritte,* 26 (1950), 9–16 and 39–43. Reprinted in *Beiträge zur Geschichte der deutschen Sprache und Literatur,* 87 (Halle, 1965), 1–39.

———. "Walthers Gespräche." In *Festschrift für Dietrich Kralik,* pp. 154–62. Horn: Ferdinand Berger, 1954. Reprinted in *Walther von der Vogelweide,* edited by Siegfried Beischlag, pp. 420–30. Wege der Forschung, 112. Darmstadt: Wissenschaftliche Buchgesellschaft, 1971.

———, and Gabriele Schieb. "Heinrich von Veldeke, die Entwicklung eines Lyrikers." In *Festschrift für Paul Kluckhohn und Hermann Schneider,* pp. 101–21. Tübingen: Mohr, 1948.

Goldin, Frederick. *The Mirror of Narcissus in the Courtly Love Lyric.* Ithaca: Cornell University Press, 1967.

Halbach, Kurt Herbert. *Walther von der Vogelweide.* 3rd ed. Sammlung Metzler, 40. Stuttgart: Metzler, 1973.

Heinen, Hubert. "Lofty and Base Love in Walther von der Vogelweide's 'sô die bluomen' and 'aller werdekeit.'" *German Quarterly,* 51 (1978), 465–75.

———. "'Mit gemache lân: A Crux in Hartmann's 'Maniger grüezet mich alsô' (MF216,29)." *Studies in Medieval Culture,* 12 (1978), 85–90.

———. "Observations on the Role in *Minnesang.*" *Journal of English and Germanic Philology,* 75 (1976), 198–208.

———. "The Woman's Songs of Hartmann von Aue." In *Vox Feminae: Studies in Medieval Woman's Songs,* edited by John F. Plummer. *Studies in Medieval Culture,* 15 (1981), 95–110.

Hinman, Martha Mayo. "*Minne* in a New Mode: Walther and the Literary Tradition." *Deutsche Vierteljahrsschrift für Literaturwissenschaft und Geistesgeschichte,* 48 (1974), 249–63.

Jackson, William E. "Reinmar der Alte in Literary History: A Critique and a Proposal." *Colloquia Germanica,* 9 (1975), 177–204.

Jackson, William T. H. *The Literature of the Middle Ages.* New York: Columbia University Press, 1960.

Jones, George F. *Walther von der Vogelweide.* Twayne's World Authors Series, 46. New York: Twayne, 1968.

Kaplowitt, Stephen J. "Heinrich von Veldeke's Song Cycle of 'Hohe Minne.'" *Seminar,* 11 (1975), 125–40.

———. "A Note on the 'Falcon Song' of Der von Kürenberg." *German Quarterly,* 44 (1971), 519–24.

Kesting, Peter. *Maria-Frouwe: Über den Einfluß der Marienverehrung auf den*

Minnesang bis Walther von der Vogelweide. Medium Aevum, 5. Munich: Fink, 1965.

Kienast, Richard. *Das Hartmann-Liederbuch* C^2. Sitzungsberichte der deutschen Akademie der Wissenschaften zu Berlin, Klasse für Sprachen, Literatur und Kunst, I. Berlin: Akademie, 1963.

Kircher, Alois. *Dichter und Konvention: Zum gesellschaftlichen Realitätsproblem der deutschen Lyrik um 1200 bei Walther von der Vogelweide und seinen Zeitgenossen*. Literatur in der Gesellschaft, 18. Düsseldorf: Bertelsmann, 1973.

Kraus, Carl von, ed. and trans. *Heinrich von Morungen*. Munich: Verlag der Bremer Presse, 1925.

————. *Die Lieder Reinmars des Alten*. Part I. Abhandlungen der Bayerischen Akademie der Wissenschaften, Philosophisch-Philologische und Historische Klasse, 30, no. 4. Munich: Bayerische Akademie der Wissenschaften, 1919.

————, ed. *Des Minnesangs Frühling: Untersuchungen*. Leipzig: Hirzel, 1939.

————. *Walther von der Vogelweide: Untersuchungen*. Berlin: de Gruyter, 1935.

————, ed. *Des Minnesangs Frühling*. 34th ed. Stuttgart: Hirzel, 1967.

Kuhn, Hugo. "Herzeliebez vrowelîn (Walther 49,25)." In *Medium Aevum deutsch: Festschrift für Kurt Ruh zum 65. Geburtstag*, edited by Dietrich Huschenbett, Klaus Matzel, and Georg Steer, pp. 199–214. Tübingen: Niemeyer, 1979.

————. "Minnesang and the Form of Performance." In *Formal Aspects of Medieval German Poetry*, edited by Stanley N. Werbow, pp. 27–41. Austin: University of Texas Press, 1969.

Kühnel, Jürgen, ed. *Dû bist mîn. ih bin dîn: Die lateinischen Liebes- (und Freundschafts-) Briefe des clm 19411: Abbildungen, Text und Übersetzung*. Litterae, 52. Göppingen: Kümmerle, 1977.

Lea, Elisabeth. "Erziehen—Im Wert erhöhen—Gemeinschaft in Liebe." *Beiträge zur Geschichte der deutschen Sprache und Literatur*, 89 (Halle, 1967), 254–81.

————. "Die Sprache lyrischer Grundgefüge: MF11,1 bis 15,17." *Beiträge zur Geschichte der deutschen Sprache und Literatur*, 90 (Halle, 1968), 305–79.

Lüderitz, Anna. *Die Liebestheorie der Provençalen bei den Minnesingern der Stauferzeit*. Literarhistorische Forschungen, 29. Berlin: Emil Felber, 1904.

Manson, Eleonore. "Motivationen der Minne in der höfischen Liebeslyrik." *Acta Germanica*, 9 (1974), 25–46.

Meissburger, Gerhard. " 'Wes brot ich esse, des lied ich singe'? Zu Walther 46,32ff (= M.80)." *Amsterdamer Beiträge zur älteren Germanistik*, 10 (1976), 15–41.

Morrall, E. J. "Light Imagery in Heinrich von Morungen." *London Medieval Studies*, 2 (1951), 116–24.

Moser, Hugo, and Helmut Tervooren, ed. *Des Minnesangs Frühling*. 36th ed. Vols. 1 and 2. Stuttgart: Hirzel, 1977.

Mowatt, D. G., ed. *Friderich von Hûsen: Introduction, Text, Commentary and Glossary*. Cambridge: University Press, 1971.

Nagel, Bert. *Staufische Klassik: Deutsche Dichtung um 1200.* Heidelberg: Stiehm, 1977.

Neumann, Friedrich. *Geschichte der altdeutschen Literatur (800–1600): Grundriß und Aufriß.* Berlin: de Gruyter, 1966.

Paul, Hermann. *Mittelhochdeutsche Grammatik.* 18th ed., rev. Walther Mitzka. Tübingen: Niemeyer, 1960.

Pretzel, Ulrich. "Drei Lieder Heinrichs von Morungen." In *Interpretationen mittelhochdeutscher Lyrik,* edited by Günther Jungbluth, pp. 109–20. Bad Homburg: Gehlen, 1969.

Ranke, Friedrich. "Die höfische-ritterliche Dichtung (1160 bis 1250)." In *Deutsche Literaturgeschichte in Grundzügen,* 3d ed., edited by Bruno Boesch, pp. 58–87. Bern: Francke, 1967.

Sayce, Olive, ed. *Poets of the Minnesang.* Oxford: Clarendon, 1967.

Schaefer, Joerg, ed. and trans. *Walther von der Vogelweide: Werke.* Darmstadt: Wissenschaftliche Buchgesellschaft, 1972.

Schirmer, Karl-Heinz. "Die höfische Minnetheorie und Meinloh von Seve-lingen." In *Zeiten und Formen in Sprache und Dichtung: Festschrift für Fritz Tschirch zum 70. Geburtstag,* edited by Karl-Heinz Schirmer and Bernhard Sowinski, pp. 52–73. Cologne: Böhlau, 1972.

Schneider, Hermann. *Heldendichtung, Geistlichendichtung, Ritterdichtung.* Rev. ed. Heidelberg: Winter, 1943.

————. "Die Lieder Reinmars des Alten: Ein Versuch." *Deutsche Viertel-jahrsschrift für Literaturwissenschaft und Geistesgeschichte,* 17 (1939), 312–42. Reprinted in *Kleinere Schriften,* pp. 233–58. Berlin: de Gruyter, 1962.

Schottmann, Hans. "Mittelhochdeutsche Literatur: Lyrik." In *Kurzer Grund-riß der germanischen Philologie,* vol. 2, edited by L. E. Schmitt, pp. 464–527. Berlin: de Gruyter, 1971.

Schröder, Werner. "Dido und Lavine." *Zeitschrift für deutsches Altertum,* 88 (1957/1958), 161–95.

Schweikle, Günther. *Die frühe Minnelyrik.* Vol. 1 of *Die mittelhochdeutsche Minnelyrik.* Darmstadt: Wissenschaftliche Buchgesellschaft, 1977.

Schwietering, Julius. "Der Liederzyklus Heinrichs von Morungen." *Zeit-schrift für deutsches Altertum,* 82 (1948), 77–104.

Stolte, Heinz. "Hartmanns sogenannte Witwenklage und sein drittes Kreuz-lied." *Deutsche Vierteljahrsschrift für Literaturwissenschaft und Geistesge-schichte,* 25 (1951), 184–98.

Sudermann, David P., ed. *The Minnelieder of Albrecht von Johansdorf: Edition, Commentary, Interpretation.* Göppinger Arbeiten zur Germanistik, 201. Göppingen: Kümmerle, 1976.

Taiana, Franz. *Amor purus und die Minne.* Germanistica Friburgensia, 1. Frei-burg: Universitätsverlag Freiburg Schweiz, 1977.

Tervooren, Helmut, ed. and trans. *Heinrich von Morungen: Lieder.* Universal-Bibliothek, 9797. Stuttgart: Reclam, 1975.

Thomas, Helmut. "Zu den Liedern und Sprüchen Heinrichs von Veldeke." *Beiträge zur Geschichte der deutschen Sprache und Literatur,* 78 (Halle, 1956), 158–264.

Vogt, Friedrich, ed. *Des Minnesangs Frühling.* 23rd ed. Leipzig: Hirzel, 1920.

Walshe, Maurice O'Connel. *Medieval German Literature: A Survey.* Cambridge: Harvard University Press, 1962.

Walther von der Vogelweide. *Die Gedichte Walthers von der Vogelweide.* 13th ed. Edited by Karl Lachmann and Carl von Kraus. Revised by Hugo Kuhn. Berlin: de Gruyter, 1965.

Walz, Herbert. *Die deutsche Literatur im Mittelalter: Geschichte und Dokumentation.* Munich: Kindler, 1976.

Wapnewski, Peter. *Deutsche Literatur des Mittelalters: Ein Abriß.* Göttingen: Vandenhoeck & Ruprecht, 1960.

————. "Des Kürenbergers Falkenlied." *Euphorion,* 53 (1959), 1–19.

————, ed. and trans. *Walther von der Vogelweide: Gedichte.* 7th ed. Frankfurt: Fischer, 1970.

Wenzel, Horst. *Frauendienst und Gottesdienst: Studien zur Minne-Ideologie.* Philologische Studien und Quellen, 74. Berlin: Schmidt, 1974.

Wilmanns, W., ed. *Walther von der Vogelweide.* 4th ed. Revised by Victor Michels. Halle: Buchhandlung des Waisenhauses, 1924.

Wisniewski, Roswitha. *"werdekeit* und Hierarchie: Zur soziologischen Interpretation des Minnesangs." In *Strukturen und Interpretationen: Studien zur deutschen Philologie* (Festschrift Horacek), edited by A. Ebenbauer, F. Knapp, and P. Krämer, pp. 340–79. Vienna: Braumüller, 1974.

Index of Personal Names

211

University of North Carolina
Studies in the Germanic Languages
and Literatures

45 PHILLIP H. RHEIN. *The Urge to Live. A Comparative Study of Franz Kafka's "Der Prozeß" and Albert Camus' "L'Etranger."* 2nd printing. 1966. Pp. xii, 124.

50 RANDOLPH J. KLAWITER. *Stefan Zweig. A Bibliography.* 1965. Pp. xxxviii, 191.

52 MARIANA SCOTT. *The Heliand. Translated from the Old Saxon.* 1966. Pp. x, 206.

56 RICHARD H. ALLEN. *An Annotated Arthur Schnitzler Bibliography.* 1966. Pp. xiv, 151.

58 WALTER W. ARNDT ET AL., EDS. *Studies in Historical Linguistics in Honor of George S. Lane.* 1967. Pp. xx, 241.

60 J. W. THOMAS. *Medieval German Lyric Verse.* In English Translation. 1968. Pp. x, 252.

67 SIEGFRIED MEWS, ED. *Studies in German Literature of the Nineteenth and Twentieth Centuries. Festschrift for Frederic E. Coenen.* 1970. 2nd ed. 1972. Pp. xx, 251.

68 JOHN NEUBAUER. *Bifocal Vision. Novalis' Philosophy of Nature and Disease.* 1971. Pp. x, 196.

70 DONALD F. NELSON. *Portrait of the Artist as Hermes. A Study of Myth and Psychology in Thomas Mann's "Felix Krull."* 1971. Pp. xii, 146.

72 CHRISTINE OERTEL SJÖGREN. *The Marble Statue as Idea: Collected Essays on Adalbert Stifter's "Der Nachsommer."* 1972. Pp. xiv, 121.

73 DONALD G. DAVIAU AND JORUN B. JOHNS, EDS. *The Correspondence of Arthur Schnitzler and Raoul Auernheimer, with Raoul Auernheimer's Aphorisms.* 1972. Pp. xii, 161.

74 A. MARGARET ARENT MADELUNG. *"The Laxdoela Saga": Its Structural Patterns.* 1972. Pp. xiv, 261.

75 JEFFREY L. SAMMONS. *Six Essays on the Young German Novel.* 2nd ed. 1975. Pp. xiv, 187.

76 DONALD H. CROSBY AND GEORGE C. SCHOOLFIELD, EDS. *Studies in the German Drama. A Festschrift in Honor of Walter Silz.* 1974. Pp. xxvi, 255.

77 J. W. THOMAS. *Tannhäuser: Poet and Legend.* With Texts and Translation of His Works. 1974. Pp. x, 202.

78 OLGA MARX AND ERNST MORWITZ, TRANS. *The Works of Stefan George.* 2nd, rev. and enl. ed. 1974. Pp. xxviii, 431.

79 SIEGFRIED MEWS AND HERBERT KNUST, EDS. *Essays on Brecht: Theater and Politics.* 1974. Pp. xiv, 241.

80 DONALD G. DAVIAU AND GEORGE J. BUELOW. *The "Ariadne auf Naxos" of Hugo von Hofmannsthal and Richard Strauß.* 1975. Pp. x, 274.

81 ELAINE E. BONEY. *Rainer Maria Rilke: "Duinesian Elegies."* German Text with English Translation and Commentary. 2nd ed. 1977. Pp. xii, 153.

82 JANE K. BROWN. *Goethe's Cyclical Narratives: "Die Unterhaltungen deutscher Ausgewanderten" and "Wilhelm Meisters Wanderjahre."* 1975. Pp. x, 144.

83 FLORA KIMMICH. *Sonnets of Catharina von Greiffenberg: Methods of Composition.* 1975. Pp. x, 132.

84 HERBERT W. REICHERT. *Friedrich Nietzsche's Impact on Modern German Literature.* 1975. Pp. xxii, 129.

85 JAMES C. O'FLAHERTY, TIMOTHY F. SELLNER, ROBERT M. HELMS, EDS. *Studies in Nietzsche and the Classical Tradition.* 2nd ed. 1979. Pp. xviii, 278.

86 ALAN P. COTTRELL. *Goethe's "Faust." Seven Essays.* 1976. Pp. xvi, 143.

87 HUGO BEKKER. *Friedrich von Hausen: Inquiries into His Poetry.* 1977. Pp. x, 159.

88 H. G. HUETTICH. *Theater in the Planned Society: Contemporary Drama in the German Democratic Republic in Its Historical, Political, and Cultural Context.* 1978. Pp. xvi, 174.

89 DONALD G. DAVIAU, ED. *The Letters of Arthur Schnitzler to Hermann Bahr.* 1978. Pp. xii, 183.

For other volumes in the "Studies" see preceding page and p. ii.

Send orders to:
The University of North Carolina Press, P.O. Box 2288
Chapel Hill, N.C. 27514

Volumes 1–44 and 46–49 of the "Studies" have been reprinted.
They may be ordered from:
AMS Press, Inc., 56 E. 13th Street, New York, N.Y. 10003
For a complete list of reprinted titles write to:
Editor, UNCSGL&L, 441 Dey Hall 014A, UNC, Chapel Hill, N.C. 27514